D1707057

India, China and Globalization

*Also by Piya Mahtaney*

THE ECONOMIC CON GAME: Development Fact or Fiction?

GLOBALIZATION: Con Game or Reality?

THE CONTEMPORARY RELEVANCE OF KANTILYA'S ARTHASHASTRA (*co-author*)

**This book is dedicated to my mother Kunti for her unstinted support**

# India, China and Globalization

## The Emerging Superpowers and the Future of Economic Development

Piya Mahtaney

HC
435.3
.M346
2007
#134993240
112906244

© Piya Mahtaney 2007

All rights reserved. No reproduction, copy or transmission of this
publication may be made without written permission.

No paragraph of this publication may be reproduced, copied or transmitted
save with written permission or in accordance with the provisions of the
Copyright, Designs and Patents Act 1988, or under the terms of any licence
permitting limited copying issued by the Copyright Licensing Agency,
90 Tottenham Court Road, London W1T 4LP.

Any person who does any unauthorized act in relation to this publication
may be liable to criminal prosecution and civil claims for damages.

The author has asserted her right to be identified
as the author of this work in accordance with the Copyright,
Designs and Patents Act 1988.

First published 2007 by
PALGRAVE MACMILLAN
Houndmills, Basingstoke, Hampshire RG21 6XS and
175 Fifth Avenue, New York, N.Y. 10010
Companies and representatives throughout the world

PALGRAVE MACMILLAN is the global academic imprint of the Palgrave
Macmillan division of St. Martin's Press, LLC and of Palgrave Macmillan Ltd.
Macmillan® is a registered trademark in the United States, United Kingdom
and other countries. Palgrave is a registered trademark in the European
Union and other countries.

ISBN-13: 978–0–230–50051–8
ISBN-10: 0–230–50051–X

This book is printed on paper suitable for recycling and made from fully
managed and sustained forest sources. Logging, pulping and manufacturing
processes are expected to conform to the environmental regulations of the
country of origin.

A catalogue record for this book is available from the British Library.

Library of Congress Cataloging-in-Publication Data
Mahtaney, Piya.
   India, China and globalization : the emerging superpowers
   and the future of economic development / by Piya Mahtaney.
      p.   cm.
   Includes bibliographical references.
   ISBN 0–230–50051–X (alk. paper)
   1. India—Economic policy.   2. India—Foreign economic relations.
   3. China—Economic policy.   4. China—Foreign economic relations.
   5. Globalisation—Economic aspects.   I. Title.
HC435.3.M346 2007
338.951—dc22                                              2007021655

10   9   8   7   6   5   4   3   2   1
16   15   14   13   12   11   10   09   08   07

Printed and bound in Great Britain by
Antony Rowe Ltd, Chippenham and Eastbourne

# Contents

# List of Tables, Figures and Boxes

**Tables**

## Figures

## Boxes

# 1
# The New Age Paradox

*Development eludes many countries. This is not the outcome of not knowing what do but not doing what is known.*

*For all the growth 'booms' that the world has witnessed, how many development 'booms' have there been? Hardly any.*

Economic thought has evolved over time, technology is becoming increasingly sophisticated and affluence continues to scale dizzying heights. This sequence of events would have been wonderfully flawless were it not for the alarming proportion of deprivation and poverty that relentlessly persists and does so in most parts of the world. I could say that underdevelopment is perhaps the most globalized phenomenon of contemporary times.

If the panacea for underdevelopment were merely economic growth the challenge would probably have been a simpler one to surmount. A striking manifestation of this fact is a widening disconnect between growth strategies and human development and it is the emergence of this gap between two inextricably linked objectives that may be illustratively termed as the new age paradox. The alarming possibility that an increase in national income growth rates may not result in a commensurate or significant reduction of underdevelopment is not a far-fetched one. As a matter of fact, this feature has gathered momentum in recent times.

In this context it would be useful to present an overview that will demonstrate that the antecedents of the new age paradox were sown over the preceding two decades during which period economic agendas pursued scuttled the priorities and considerations to weed out underdevelopment.

## The new age paradox: inevitability and implications

It is not enough to say that the preceding 50 years (from 1950–2000) heralds the end of an era; perhaps even more significant is that this period has an expanse of empirical evidence that has brought with it, among other lessons, an extremely vital one, which is that growth is one instrumentality and not the only one required to step up the pace of development. By no means is this realization a recent one. This is evidenced by a UN report released in 1949, which stated that:

> If economic development is to achieve its purpose of increasing the security and welfare of the great mass of mankind and enabling them to enjoy a fuller and more fruitful life its benefits must be widely distributed.

Understandably, one would have anticipated that cognizance of this fact would have translated into strategies and consequently policies that are overtly pro-development. It is obvious that this has not happened and the imperatives that confront the present era are fairly similar to what existed a few decades ago, and this despite the tumultuous changes and tremendous economic progress that has occurred during this period (see Box 1.1).

---

## Box 1.1   Scorecard on development: some facts

In 1951, the UN released a book titled *Measures for the Economic Development of Underdeveloped Countries* in which it stated that, 'the widening gap between developed and developing countries is the central problem of our times'.

The UN launched the first development decade in 1961. The objective was to create conditions in which developing countries would have their national incomes increasing at a rate of 5 per cent annually by 1970 and thereafter. This is a goal that continues to elude us.

UNICEF's study, titled *Adjustment with a Human Face* (1987), was about the impact of structural adjustment policies pursued during the 1980s and indicated that these had resulted in declining investment in health, falling school enrolments and rising malnutrition. According to the *Human Development Report* (UN, 2003), more than 1.2 billion people, one in every five on earth, survive in less than $1 a day. During the 1990s, the share of people suffering from extreme poverty fell from 30 per cent to 23 per cent. But with a growing world population the number fell by just 123 million, a small fraction of the progress needed to eliminate poverty.

An overview presented by UNCTAD (in 1999) about the situation of least developed countries United Nations elucidates that, at the end of the 1990s, the number of less developed countries had grown from 25 in 1971 to 48 at that time, and their combined population of over 600 million people had failed to derive appropriate benefits from the ongoing processes of liberalization and globalization. The organization describes the 1990s as a decade of increasing marginalization, inequality, poverty and social exclusion for the least developed countries.

The systematic and continuous subordination of developmental imperatives to tactical considerations that were either political, militaristic, or any other has been the highlight of the preceding two decades. In retrospect, thus, it is not sufficient to say that the initiatives to combat underdevelopment were inadequate because measures in this direction that had been undertaken by most developing countries at the inception of the post-colonization period (early 1950s) were sidelined or ran out of steam by the late 1970s.

The pronounced emphasis on the attainment of developmental objectives was the predominant concern of economic thinking until structural adjustment ushered in its wake a cataclysmic shift from the priorities and policies that existed earlier. 'Macroeconomic stabilization' mattered over all else, including the exigent need to mitigate underdevelopment. This message rang loud and clear during the early 1980s as a consequence of the advent of the debt crisis that a number of Latin American countries found themselves reeling under. The precipitous instability that these nations encountered during the crisis compelled the enforcement of structural adjustment programmes.

The ensuing phase in Latin America and Sub-Saharan Africa was a period that was devoid of any growth because fiscal discipline Bretton Woods style led to a cutback in public expenditures. The axe fell on physical and human investment and inevitably poverty and income distribution worsened. Moreover, Latin America transferred US$100 billion (between 1982 and 1984) to the banks of advanced countries in the Northern Hemisphere. Sadly, this fall-out cannot even be described as the price for growth. (The transfers were made towards debt servicing and direct savings.)

One of the far-reaching implications of the crisis was that the policy changes which ensued therein fettered and, in many instances, severely curtailed the scope of the leadership in many countries of Latin America and Sub-Saharan Africa to determine the economic or, more precisely, the development agendas of their respective nations. So far, there has been no discernible reversal of this trend in most countries of the regions specified.

The apparent objective of the structural adjustment programme was the restoration of the current account deficit (in the regions confronted by the debt crisis) to sustainable levels and this may have been the immediate pretext for the restructuring of the economy in a manner that would facilitate liberalization and minimize the role of the state. However, the main theme underlying the policy changes was: Set the stage for the global application of neo-liberalism.

The means to this end encompassed structural adjustment and was provided an impetus by Reaganomics and Thatcherism. The cumulative outcome of policies pursued therein was the roll-out of the Washington Consensus. This consisted of ten prescriptions or guiding principles that would underpin priorities specified and agendas formulated.

Economic strategies worldwide were supposed to adhere to parameters that would facilitate the process of deregulation, privatization, financial and trade liberalization. The corollary of this was that the imperative to respond expeditiously to the pressing concerns of underdevelopment was relegated to the background, a fact that was vividly exemplified when the role of the Bretton Woods institutions superseded that of the UN.

Nothing vindicates or contradicts belief more than reality. A backdrop of falling real wages, repeated occurrence of financial crises, de-escalation of growth, acute income and non-income disparities certainly does not prop up the assumptions and propositions that steered the structural adjustment programmes, the Washington Consensus or the liberalization prescriptions that have been implemented so far.

After two decades of buying into the rationale underlying the premise of the structural adjustment programmes and the Washington Consensus, the countries of Latin America and Sub-Saharan Africa had levels of GDP (per capita) in 1998 that were below the levels that they had achieved many years earlier. As indicated in Table 1.1 the countries of Eastern Europe and Russia registered a sharp downturn in economic performance at the beginning of the transition to a market economy over a decade ago and most of these nations have yet to recover the levels of prosperity that prevailed prior to the transition. In the context of these countries, ascribing the decline on

*Table 1.1*   Growth in GDP (%)

| Region | 1970–80 | 1980–90 | 1990–98 |
| --- | --- | --- | --- |
| World | 3.6 | 3.2 | 2.5 |
| High-income countries | 3.2 | 3.1 | 2.3 |
| Middle-income countries | 5.5 | 2.6 | 2.2 |
| Low-income countries* | 4.4 | 4.1 | 3.7 |
| Sub-Saharan Africa | 3.8 | 1.6 | 2.3 |
| Eastern Europe and Central Asia | 5.4 | 2.4 | −2.9 |
| East Asia and Pacific | 6.9 | 8.0 | 7.9 |
| Latin America and Caribbean | 5.2 | 1.7 | 3.6 |
| Middle East and North Africa | – | 2.0 | 3.0 |
| South Asia | 3.5 | 5.8 | 6.1 |

*Excluding India and China.
*Source*: UN History Project (2001) *Ahead of the Curve*.

practically every socio-economic indicator to the 'transitional losses' does not constitute a sound explanation.

Liberalism could be have become a development initiative; however, the instances where this has been achieved are few and far between. In this context, studying the impact of liberalization brings forth a fundamental revelation. Empirical evidence over the last two decades reveals unmistakably that a set of erroneous assumptions stilted projections about the impact that liberalization would have on development. In essence, the basis underlying the fundamental proposition was a highly flawed one and, thus, it was inevitable that the process of implementation would not deliver the designated outcomes.

The facts that will be enumerated should not be interpreted as a scathing criticism about economic liberalism: the attempt is to provide an objective evaluation of the performance of a strategy that has been propagated for at least two decades as the most dynamic and practical route for a country to pursue.

At this point it would be useful to elucidate the flawed assumptions that 'guided' and structured vital aspects of economic thinking globally for about two decades. These are as follows:

1. Assuming that a higher degree of openness will invariably result in higher economic growth.
2. Presuming that liberalization would result in the restoration of market forces that function competitively and efficiently.
3. Assuming that the outcome of higher economic growth would be poverty reduction.
4. Assuming that countries would do better by minimizing the role of government and its adjuncts, such as the state-owned or public-sector enterprises.

Fundamental facts challenged the credibility and validity of what stood at the core of neo-liberalism. For further substantiation of this point, these facts are presented as follows.

i) Dramatic strides in economic progress were made in countries where these were not expected to occur. A notable exception to this was India, which, despite all the disadvantages it found itself beset with at the time of independence, was viewed as among the most promising nations of the developing world. The trail-blazing performance of East Asia, South-East Asia and China that has been one the highlights of the global economy over the last three decades was not anticipated even in the remotest sense during the early 1950s.

As indicated in Table 1.2, East Asia and South Asia (which include China and India respectively) have notched up the most pronounced improvements in the direction of poverty reduction and this is in stark contrast

*Table 1.2*  Population living below the poverty line*

| Region | Millions of people | | Share of population (%) | |
|---|---|---|---|---|
| | 1990 | 2001 | 1990 | 2001 |
| East Asia | 472 | 271 | 30 | 15 |
| Eastern Europe and Central Asia | 2 | 17 | 1 | 4 |
| Latin America and Caribbean | 49 | 50 | 11 | 10 |
| Middle East North Africa | 6 | 7 | 2 | 2 |
| South Asia | 462 | 431 | 41 | 31 |
| Sub-Saharan Africa | 227 | 313 | 45 | 46 |

* Poverty line is $1.08 a day.
*Source*: Report to the UN Secretary General (2005) *Investing in Development: A Practical Plan to Achieve the Millennium Development Goals.*

to the scenario in Africa, Latin America and Eastern Europe. As has been mentioned above, in the latter three regions a rather ardent adherence to the principles of neo-liberalism predominated over policy prescriptions for a considerable period of time. Fervent advocacy of neo-liberalism, as though there was no practical alternative to it, should have been preceded by a scrutiny of the preconditions and circumstances that were likely to corroborate these assumptions. Instead, populist presumptions generalized that these assumptions are truisms that apply irrespective of other prevalent contexts and conditions in any country. This was a serious and some would even say fatal misjudgement.

The policy practice of neo-classical economics or second generation growth economics during recent times is itself an incomplete variant of the earlier prescriptions of the neo-classicalists. Interestingly its emphasis to supplant the role of government intervention was plausibly even more fervent than the advocacy by the arbiters of first generation development economics to assign to government a more important, and, in the instance of communist and socialist countries, a preponderant function in economic systems.

Second generation growth economics did not do much for growth and development, its impact was in terms of an improvements in human development indicators which across most developing countries was discernibly quite unlike the positive outcomes (muted as it may have seemed) that precedent first generation development economics had.

In the light of recent empirical evidence, particularly the findings that emanate from the economic experience of the most successful globalizers-East Asia, China and India, it is remarkably obvious that it is the combination of first generation development strategies with neo-classical economics that has worked effectively albeit relatively efficiently in East Asia and with lesser efficiency in India and China. This is among the most important tenets that third generation development strategies have to embody because the demarcations between governments, markets, liberalization and protectionism are a blur in the contemporary global economy. Perhaps this is what is meant by the New World Order.

(i) Interestingly as originally presented by John Williamson in 1990 the Washington Consensus did favour some withdrawal of the state in the economic sphere but he did not advocate a complete exit of the government from the same. As a matter of fact Williamson stated that he had not mentioned the term capital account liberalization even though this was an operational objective that the International Monetary Fund has propagated from the late eighties.

(ii) It would be difficult to reconcile the current state of affairs regarding underdevelopment with the desirability of dispensing with or minimizing the role of government. Take, for instance, the 'East Asian miracle', a title used to describe the record-breaking growth performance of the region. This was not the outcome of passive governments that functioned on the periphery of commercial activity. On the contrary, it was the interventionist policies of the government that guided decision-making by business and entrepreneurs. Furthermore, trade liberalization, which has been a crucial facilitator of the progress in the region, was 'managed' by the policy makers in a manner that would serve the larger nationalist imperatives.

The inception of initial strategies of development also described was based on the fundamental proposition that an undue reliance of the market economy would not tackle the causes and perpetrators of underdevelopment. The laissez-faire principle did not have an inherent mechanism of self correction that would remedy the multivariate shortages and inconsistencies that resulted in underdevelopment and this was the basis for first generation development economics to advocate that the visible hand of the government supplement the working of the invisible hand.

This line of thinking was purported as non pragmatic and inefficient by the early eighties because of the rather disappointing growth outcomes that it was believed to have resulted in. Spiraling economic growth rates in East Asia a phenomenon that was illustratively described as the East Asian miracle was compared by multi-country studies undertaken during the seventies and eighties to the deceleration of most Latin American economies that was occurring at the time.

Some of the conclusions drawn from these findings were half-truths in so far as these concluded that the difference between the performance of East Asian countries and the LAC was attributable to the export-promotion trade regime that existed in the former compared to the import-substitution trade regime that prevailed in the latter. It was this fact along with some others (as will be enumerated in the Chapter: Revisiting the East Asian Miracle) including the distinct and well defined role that that the government had in putting into place an 'outward orientated economic structure that was closely coordinated with an entire range of meticulously planned goals and a sequenced economic agenda.

(iii) Thus if trade and financial liberalization resulted primarily from the existence of free-market forces, economic history would undoubtedly have been different. The reality is that policies pertinent to both have been structured in a manner that is weighted against the intrinsic interests of developing nations. Once again, the presumption that the reciprocity of economic liberalism would exist proved to be a major miscalculation. So far the story as it has emerged is one where most developed nations have the approach that 'we will sell in your markets' but 'you cannot, with the same ease, sell in ours'. Thus, the reduction of trade barriers and subsidies by developing nations on those goods in which most advanced nations have a comparative advantage has not been matched by reciprocal measures in the developed world. Although this may not be the only contributory cause, it certainly has played a major role in perpetuating the persistently adverse terms of trade encountered by the exports from LDCs.

(iv) Misconceptions about the role of the market vis-à-vis the functions of the state are rather primordial and have dogged economics and every discipline of it. Until about a decade and half ago, sharply defined ideological demarcations were rooted in contrasting approaches about the functions of these two agents. Political systems were defined in terms of which ideologue they supported. As the excesses of centralized state control began to take a heavy toll on the efficiency and prosperity of communist and socialist countries, they paved the way for the end of the Cold War and the only 'ism' that prevailed and triumphed thereafter was capitalism.

In the context of strategy formulation, the resonant implication was to make the market the decision-maker and the problem-solver, the underlying assumption being that it would be a mechanism that would grapple with an entire gamut of ills that arise essentially from economic stagnation and poverty. This rationale could have provided the solution that we require if markets were free, fair and perfect; the first two attributes are difficult to come by and the third exists only within the realm of theory. Thus, there exists a vast terrain of opportunities and demand that lies outside the purview and inherent functions of the imperfect and fragmented market structures. Furthermore, empirical evidence is replete with instances that demonstrate that gross inefficiencies and uncompetitive practices are not exclusive characteristics of government enterprises. They characterize a wide spectrum of corporations, regardless of their ownership status.

## The way ahead

Taking further the cognizance about the extremely fallible approach underlying populist perceptions about the neo-liberal policies pursued evokes an imminent question: do we have the structures and circumstances that will compel developing countries to adopt a set of policies that may spur growth but do so by having a regressive impact on socio-economic indicators? Alternatively expressed, do we run the risk of repeating the oversights and mistakes of the past?

Finding the answer to this is one of objectives of this book. At this point, I would say that the status quo is one where prevalent circumstances and policies that characterize the present global context perpetuate, if anything, the problems of debt, crisis and adverse terms of trade that many developing nations find themselves mired in.

The emergence of powerful forces on the horizon of the global economy could, equally, countervail the trends that have culminated in the emergence of the new age paradox.

A concise description of these trends is as follows:

1. In the current global economy it is not altruism or idealism but unbridled pragmatism that defines the need for a development paradigm. Suffice it to say that, in the absence of this, the doyens of commerce will find it extremely difficult to sustain viability. The reason is a simple one, the task an exigent and challenging one. Besides India and China, the new growth centres of the world also include Brazil and Russia and it is the pace and extent of opportunity creation in these nations that will have a profound impact on determining the prospects and outlook of the global economy. Given that the nations mentioned are at different stages of the development process, the priority would be to create 'enabling structures' that will not just step up the growth rates of their respective national incomes but will also catalyze the momentum at which development proceeds.

2. In the year 2000, the United Nations Millennium Declaration defined the Millennium Development Goals. These are the world's time-bound and quantified targets for addressing extreme poverty in its many dimensions – income, poverty, hunger, lack of disease, lack of adequate shelter and exclusion – while promoting gender equality, education and environmental sustainability. The deadline is 2015 and attaining the MDG by the year specified may not be tenable for all countries. However, of foremost significance is the fact that these goals reflect concurrence by the world community on the pervasive nature of underdevelopment and the compelling need to tackle it in a global context. Furthermore, the deadline underscores the fact that procrastinating over a concerted solution to the rather rampant problems economic ills of our times is not an option that any nation really has.

   Whether the targets are achieved by 2015 or a few years later, there is unanimity this achievement is crucial and it is likely that the MDG could be a beginning towards prioritizing development.

3. The ascendancy of India and China as economic superpowers will usher in phenomenal changes that will span not just the economic realm but also the political, social and cultural. This is a widely acknowledged fact and it brings with it a distinct dimension to development thinking and strategy.

Box 1.2 presents some of the findings of the Goldman Sachs report (2004) about the ascendancy of Brazil, Russia, India and China (collectively referred to as the BRIC economies). It predicts that they could become a much larger force in the world economy over the next 50 years. The report provides a further endorsement of the resonating importance of China and India in the global economy over ensuing decades.

---

## Box 1.2   Emerging economic powers

If things go right, in less than 40 years the BRIC economies together could be larger than the G6 (EU, USA, Australia, Brazil, India, Japan) in US dollar terms. By 2025, they could account for over half the size of the G6. Only the US and Japan may be among the six largest economies in US dollar terms in 2050. It should be noted that currently the BRIC countries account for less than 15 per cent of the G6 in US dollar terms.

In US dollar terms, China could overtake Germany in the next four years, Japan by 2015 and the US by 2039. India's economy could be larger than all but the US and China in 30 years. Russia would overtake Germany, France, Italy and the UK. India has the potential to have the fastest growth over the next 30 years and close to 5 per cent as late as 2050, if development proceeds.

The overall growth for the BRIC economies is likely to slow significantly over this time frame. By 2050, only India, on our projections, would be recording growth rates significantly above 3 per cent.

---

In an environment where developing countries, including Brazil and Russia, will assume a significant role in shaping trends of economic progress worldwide, globalization will need to change from an instrument of cost-cutting and increasing levels of efficiency to a facilitator of development. The key to unlocking sizable potential for economic expansion in China, India, Brazil and Russia lies in stepping up the pace of poverty reduction so that the millions who find themselves marginalized and without adequate means of sustenance will be able to afford a decent standard of living. This is not a utopian aspiration; it is eminently practical because it would provide a massive impetus to demand and it is a prerequisite for sustainable development.

A snapshot of the present economic era indicates, as mentioned in Box 1.2, that China, India, Brazil and Russia are the frontrunners among the emerging markets. These nations along with others in the developing world account for over 40 per cent of the world exports which is a discernible increase from the 20 per cent of global exports that these accounted for in 1970. Furthermore these consume half of the world's energy and have contributed to four-fifths, of the growth in demand for oil over the last year.

Global geo-politics is unfolding a scenario of the new economic equations and engagements wherein it does appear that the scales are tilting in favor of the developing world. Although this represents an important feature of the emerging global order, it is still a small aspect of a story that continues to have a larger context where the beneficiaries of globalization be they in the developed or the developing world have been few. Thus the sustainability of a process of globalization that has been overtly and singularly capital-intensive does seem questionable.

The ubiquitous influence of the corporate elite and politically powerful needs to be accompanied by a decisive endeavor to strengthen the impact of globalization on employment and opportunity creation. In the absence of this if globalization were to proceed on the current course it would be nothing more than a 'new-found old hat'. The genesis of the new wave of globalization and for that matter how widespread and long- lasting it would be will be determined by its ability to become more inclusive at a pace that is faster and an extent that is much more expansive.

Despite much faster growth, individuals in BRIC are likely to be poorer, on average, than individuals in the G6 economies by 2050. Russia is the exception, essentially catching up with the poorer of the G6 in terms of income per capita by 2050. China's per capita income would be similar to where the developed economies are now (about US$30,000 per capita). By 2030 China's income per capita would be roughly what South Korea's is today. In the US, per capita income could reach about $80,000. Demographics play an important role in the way the world will change. The decline in the working-age population will take place later in the BRIC economies; it will be steeper in China and Russia than in India and Brazil.

The key assumption underlying the projections of the BRIC report is that the countries concerned maintain policies and develop institutions that are supportive of growth. Each of the BRICs do have challenges in keeping development on track.

Numerically, the projections made by the Goldman Sachs report might may viewed as too optimistic by some analysts; however, the empirical findings that it cites and the inferences that it arrives at are corroborated by most studies about foreseeable trends in the world economy during the subsequent decades.

In the context of development strategy, one of the most interesting points that it makes is that, despite the higher growth rates that BRIC will have, the per capita incomes will not be as high as those prevalent in the currently advanced nations. Be this is as it may, it is essential that these countries also experience an extent of development that will enable the elimination of abject poverty.

The multifaceted aspects of India and China's growth experience will be analyzed in detail in subsequent chapters. At this point suffice it to say that viewing the growth empirics of both countries provides us with a wide range of insights that will help significantly in the evolution of the development paradigm. For instance, one such insight stems from a resonant similarity between both nations. Despite their divergent economic and political systems, both countries opted for a prescription of liberalization that may be described as a model of 'selective liberalism'.

Furthermore, in the cases of India and China the prelude to reaping the gains from liberalization encompassed the build-up of certain institutions and the formulation of a wide gamut of sector-specific policies. The precedent to liberalization in India was a mature and fairly well-stratified industrial economy and in China it was the critical role of provincial and central planning that charted out its trade and investment strategy. Despite being wrought with a host of inefficiencies and imperfections, these constituents played a decisive role in the economic progress of both nations. Had the prevalent contexts of India and China been more rudimentary it is extremely unlikely that the outcome of liberalization would have been positive.

# Part I

# The Rising Superpowers: Issues, Implications and the Future

# Introduction to Part I

When two developing nations, one an economic powerhouse and the other potentially a superpower, are among the fastest-growing nations it is inevitable that this fact will become a matter of avid discussion. Perhaps a few nations in the contemporary world are perceived to be as exciting and promising as India and China:

> China and India will shake the world. Together they are home to 40 per cent of the world's population. Both are among the world's fastest growing economies: China 8–10 per cent, India 6–7 per cent. China is the factory of the world. India the outsourcing service centre first in call centres and now moving into more sophisticated business process operations and clinical research activities of global corporations. The Chinese and Indians are learning not just from Japan and the Asian NIEs but from the advanced countries (An excerpt of the keynote speech by Lee Kuan Yew, Minister Mentor, former Prime Minister of Singapore, at the inauguration of the Lee Kuan Yew School of Public Policy, April 2005)

In a world that has been unipolar for almost a decade and a half, since the fall of the Berlin wall, the rapid ascent of India and China heralds an era of profound change in geopolitics, as it gives a new facet to existent power equations. The India – China story is epoch-making. First, it is about of two of the world's most populous countries, which have notched up the highest growth rates. Second, it embodies, for the developing world, the possibility of consistent economic advancement by countries that found themselves enmeshed in a host of constraints, challenges and even periods of adversity.

The Boston Consulting Group's recent study (2006) stated:

> A revolution in global business is underway. Companies based in rapidly developing economies such as Brazil, Russia, China and India armed with ambitious leaders, low costs, appealing products or services, modern facilities and systems are expanding overseas and will radically transform industries and markets around the world.

The developing world is headed towards a cataclysmic transition and an integral constituent of this is the ascendancy of India and China on the front line of the global economy. As both these economic powerhouses make their strides on the somewhat tortuous path to becoming the superpowers that they are expected to become, a treasure trove of strategic insights will become apparent, giving a distinct dimension to development economics.

Having traversed a path strewn with obstacles, dogged by upheaval, trauma and deprivation, laced with uncertainty and enmeshed by rampant poverty, China and India have attained remarkable levels of economic progress. Theirs is a story of achievement against all odds, including the vast numbers that lived below the poverty line. GDP growth in both countries was not financed by international financial assistance; the success, insofar as economic liberalization was concerned, is one but not the only reason for the present levels of economic progress and buoyant prospects envisioned for both nations.

Most interestingly, both India and China had rather disparate ideological underpinnings; India is a democracy and China has managed a rather intriguing combination of authoritarianism and economic liberalism. Expanding markets, increasing incomes in these countries will play an increasingly important part in fuelling economic progress in the world economy. Having emerged as among the most important growth centres, both India and China are witnessing discernible shifts in consumption patterns that have unleashed tremendous potential for opportunity creation, although this can be considered to be in its initial phase.

The objective of presenting the analysis in this way is to highlight factors of relevance to other developing and less developed nations. It is important that we take note of this. It would be wonderfully convenient if developing countries had before them, at this point in time, a universally applicable development model. This is not the case but we could be close to the evolution of a paradigm that could provide practical and effective solutions for the ills confronting contemporary developing countries.

Studying the causes underlying economic progress in countries that have a context and a set of challenges that are comparable to those confronting other developing nations (even if the latter comprise the poorer nations) produces observably different results from evaluating the applicability of growth models underlying development in the US and the countries of Europe. India and China embody a demonstrably unique and interesting instance of progress; they are both among the most important nations of the world, in more ways than one a position that they have managed to attain despite being developing countries. Straddled between two realms – one of technological sophistication and advancement and the other of poverty, underdevelopment and inequalities of income and opportunity – the lessons emanating from these two nations are amazing. Their economic experiences offer lessons in affirmative action as well as inconsistencies that should be avoided.

The next section, Chapters 2–13, presents an analysis of different aspects of the economic experiences of both India and China.

*Table I.1*   Rising significance of China and India in the global economy

| | Share in GDP of world (%) | | Share in GDP of developing Asia (16 economies) | | Growth rate of GDP (%) | |
|---|---|---|---|---|---|---|
| | **1989–95** | **1995–2003** | **1989–95** | **1995–2003** | **1989–95** | **1995–2003** |
| China | 7.64 | 10.91 | 36.37 | 41.68 | 9.94 | 7.13 |
| India | 4.95 | 5.97 | 24.10 | 22.89 | 5.03 | 6.15 |
| China and India | 12.59 | 16.88 | 50.47 | 64.57 | – | – |

*Source*: *Economic and Political Weekly*, 3 September 2005, 'China, India and the World Economy'.

# 2
# India's Story: As it Rolls On

From the larger perspective of the developing world, India's resonance on the global economy is a milestone. This, coupled with the ascendancy of China, will herald a pre-eminent shift in geopolitics.

I have heard many express the view in academic and business fora that India does not offer a model of development. Given the tacit sense of the term, India does not exemplify a single specific model of development. India's journey towards economic progress has been a chequered one, which has met with its share of pitfalls, and an analysis of this provides us with insights that can guide the evolution of a multifaceted and pluralistic model of development.

India combines the achievements of a developed country with the challenges of a developing one and, in this sense, it is literally a nation of contrasts (indicating the country's track record of an impressive performance in certain sectors and persistent underachievement in some others).

It has the attained the highest standards of technical excellence and research standards on the one hand and, on the other, it is characterized by the prevalence of considerable socio-economic backwardness and deprivation in certain regions. India is among the most industrialized nations and yet this hasn't changed the fact that agriculture continues to be an important sector. India provides us with an illustrative instance of a dualistic economy, and attaining development will not mean an elimination of dualism. Instead, it would, in all likelihood, result in a transition from a situation where development coexists with underdevelopment to one where high levels of development coexist with modest levels of the same. Developed India has the challenge of sustaining and even increasing present levels of economic progress and developing India has to unleash the process of consistent economic advancement.

Chapters 2–6 present an analysis of the empirics of India's economic experience and, in doing so, will delve into important issues and challenges that confront the Indian economy.

# 3
# India: Her Tryst with Globalization

*On the eve of India's independence in August 1947, Jawaharlal Nehru, post-independence India's first prime minister, spoke of the country's tryst with destiny ... Over five decades later, India has a tryst with globalization. This country is a superpower waiting to happen. The odds are stacked in her favour, the challenge is to ensure that this is the case for a long time to come.*

## The turning point

1991 was the beginning of a new phase for India, a profound one from the standpoint of changing prevalent attitudes towards, and in the realm of, the commercial establishment. In no uncertain terms, economic imperatives could not be shackled by the confines of a mildly socialist framework and regimented government control. India's partially closed markets had to be opened to the external economy. This meant that competitiveness would be at the centre-stage of business and economic priorities and it was the ability, or the lack of it, that would determine the survival of most enterprises in the ambit of manufacturing and services.

Equally true and vital is the fact that the upswing in India's growth performance began a decade prior to the liberalizing of her markets and trade. In a sense, liberalization was a broader and a more overt manifestation of a process that commenced in the early 1980s. Substantiation of this point entails looking at the subtle and almost inscrutable shift in policy stance that heralded improvements in the country's growth performance. For India, the 1970s was a phase of economic stagnation and development inertia, and it was during this period that the rumble and tumble of politics overshadowed much else. The seeds of a reorientation in the country's policy stance were sown by the early 1980s, and the initial signs of this were an increase in the levels of both public and private investment (including corporate investment).

In effect, there appears to have been a shift at the time from the statist, socialist-conditioned model of development to what can be termed as a growth-first strategy. Undeniably, this was a change that was not easily discerned or even visible in the economic mainstream because it was ensconced within the confines of overarching government control. However, the government–business alliance began to change in that the veritably antithetical approach of the state towards private-sector business houses was beginning to wane. One cannot describe the changes that ensued during the 1980s as liberalization because it did not involve a blatantly unhindered freeing of the market forces; however, it was significant because it assigned a greater role to capitalism or capitalist forces and, given the country's economic circumstances and predominant political ideology, this was perhaps India's first turning point after 1950.

Evidently, by 1982 the point of emphasis had moved away from redistributive socialism, which had been an avowed priority of the country's economic agenda until the early 1970s. This had, in any case, not made much of dent in the extent of poverty during that time. *The lesson learnt from this was not ambiguous – anti-poverty policies would not have much success if growth rates were not increasing and the impediments to growth were rather obvious.*

Inefficiency of the public-sector investments, coupled with a decline of the same in agriculture, and the widespread lack of a business-friendly macroeconomic environment were some of the obstacles to stepping up growth rates. It is not that the deterrents were eliminated during the 1980s, as a matter of fact some of these persisted; however, there were unmistakable indicators that the policy framework was becoming more growth-oriented. Thus, the implementation of certain measures that were conducive to the business environment, such as the dilution of the Monopolies Restrictive Trade Practices Act (MRTP), the removal of licensing restrictions so that private sector companies would enter core industries (including chemicals, drugs, ceramics and cement) and the selective reduction on restrictions on capital goods imports did represent a stride in the direction of internal economic liberalization for India.

Increasing levels of public investments related to modernizing defence and sustaining infrastructure-related expenditures, a rising import bill as a result of the increasing imports of machinery and technology and a rise in the price of oil led inevitably to a foreign exchange squeeze. In response to this, in 1981 India finalized a loan agreement with the IMF for an amount of US$5 billion. Notably, in a departure from the norm, structural adjustment wasn't one of the conditionalities that accompanied the extension of this loan. In consonance with this fact, the IMF did not insist on a cutback in public expenditure as it usually did in the instance of other developing countries.

It was not exactly a bolt from the blue when the 1983–4 budget reimposed import restrictions and India terminated its agreement with the IMF even before it could avail itself of the entire amount of the loan sanctioned. In a sense, in the context of the external economy, India's liberalization had not taken wing, its cautious attempt at partial import liberalization was not exactly an occurrence of importance, certainly not insofar as lowering trade and foreign investment barriers were concerned. Having said this, one can describe this phase as the prelude to a higher degree of openness in the subsequent years.

Importantly, over the entire time span following Indian independence in 1947, there had been two rather crucial points in its trajectory of growth; one was 1950 and the other as has been elucidated was the early 1980s or, more precisely, 1980. In the 50 years that ensued after 1950 India made considerable progress on the developmental front and this was consistent with the priorities that were earmarked by the leaders of the nation at the outset of post- independence India. At some point the momentum of progress slowed down and by the 1970s it had petered out. Thereafter, by the late 1970s the country changed course in a gentle and subtle manner.

When viewed in historical perspective, 1950 also marked the beginning of a new era for India and for more reasons than one. The end of colonization, accompanied by the inception of a stolid endeavour towards modernization and industrialization of the country, would obviously be a momentous time in the history of post-independence India. It heralded a structural transformation that would make the nation among the most industrialized in the developing world within three decades. This fact is reflected in an increase in growth rates, which was by far the first uptrend that the Indian economy witnessed in the 20th century.

As indicated in Tables 3.1 and 3.2, in terms of growth performance, there was a step-up in economic growth rates after 1980. Over the period 1950–1 to 1979–80 the average annual growth rate of GDP was 3.5 per cent. Per capita GDP was 1.4 per cent. During 1980–1 to 1990–91 GDP grew at a rate of 5.6 per cent per annum. Per capita GDP increased by 3.6 per cent per annum (*Economic and Political Weekly*, 15 April 2006, National Accounts Statistics of India).

According to Angus Maddison's estimates over the period 1900–47 growth in GDP was about 0.8 per cent per annum. Econometric analysis reveals that the most important structural break insofar as the growth rate of national

*Table 3.1*   Basic trends in growth rates (%)

|                      | 1950–64 | 1965–79 | 1980–90 | 1991–2004 | 1980–2004 |
|----------------------|---------|---------|---------|-----------|-----------|
| GDP growth           | 3.7     | 2.9     | 5.8     | 5.6       | 5.7       |
| Industrial growth    | 7.4     | 3.8     | 6.5     | 5.8       | 6.1       |
| Agricultural growth  | 3.1     | 2.3     | 3.9     | 3.0       | 3.4       |
| Gross investment/GDP | 13.0    | 18.0    | 22.8    | 22.3      | 22.5      |

*Source*: Atul Kohli, 'Politics of Economic Growth in India, 1980–2005, Part 1', *Economic and Political Weekly*, 1 April 2006.

*Table 3.2* Sectoral real GDP growth rates (%) at factor cost (at 1999–2000 prices)

|  | 2003–4 | 2004–5 | 2005–6 |
|---|---|---|---|
| 1. Agriculture and Allied | 10.0 | 0.0 | 6.0 |
| II. Industry, | 7.4 | 9.8 | 9.6 |
| Mining and Quarrying | 3.1 | 7.5 | 3.6 |
| Manufacturing | 6.6 | 8.7 | 9.1 |
| Electricity, Gas and Water Supply | 4.8 | 7.5 | 15.3 |
| Construction | 12.0 | 14.1 | 14.2 |
| III. Services | 8.5 | 9.6 | 9.8 |
| Trade, Hotels and Transport and Communication | 12.1 | 10.9 | 10.4 |
| Financial Services | 5.6 | 8.7 | 10.9 |
| Community, Social and Personal Services | 5.4 | 7.9 | 7.7 |
| Total GDP at Factor Cost | 8.5 | 7.5 | 9.0 |

*Source*: Central Statistical Organization, Government of India.

income in India was 1950–1. Thereafter, growth rates in GDP increased on an average of 4 per cent; illustratively speaking this was the commencement of the Hindu rate of growth that sets the pace of the country's average GDP annual increase for the next 30 years.

Evidently the strides towards having a more liberal macroeconomic environment became visible after 1987 under the premiership of the late Rajiv Gandhi. Some of the changes included:

- Easing the restrictions of the entry of the private sector into certain spheres that had been exclusively dominated by the presence of public-sector units up to that time;
- Reducing import barriers: this consisted of increasing the number of imports not subject to licensing from 5 per cent in 1980–1 to about 30 per cent in 1987–8. Duty-free imports of capital goods were permitted in selected industries;
- 90 out of 180 industries were freed from Monopoly Restrictive Trade Practices Act (MRTP) regulation;
- The provision of export incentives, among the most important of these was making 50 per cent of profits from exports tax deductible in 1985. In 1988 these profits from exports were accorded exemption from income tax;
- By 1990, 31 industries, including coal, motor vehicles, sugar and steel, were delicensed;
- The abolition of price and distribution controls on cement and aluminum;
- There were significant concessions on corporate and personal income taxes.

Partial though the process of internal economic liberalization may have seemed, its impact was decisively positive on Indian industry. Industrial growth accelerated from 4.5 per cent in 1985–6 to 10.5 per cent in 1989–90. This expansion in Indian industry was also accompanied by a rise in productivity. Furthermore, tax concessions resulted in an increase in the inflow of private investments, particularly into certain spheres such as the consumer goods industry. Notably during this period, the government also encouraged the expansion of information technology (IT) and electronics sectors, which were provided with supply-side support. Furthermore, a minimization of protection accorded to these spheres also ensured that these would remain competitive.

A noteworthy observation that can be made about industrial policy at the time was that incentives granted to encourage the expansion of certain sectors did not exclude the role of competition. This aspect was almost divergent from industrial policy that prevailed in the precedent era, where the implicit and plausibly most important incentive that would encourage expansion in both the public and private sector was to shut out or stifle the competition. The subsequent emergence of the IT sector as one of the foremost core competences of the country can be attributed partly to initiatives taken during this period.

Attributing the encouraging performance of industry to an increase in private investment would be an incomplete inference. The new growth-oriented policy was discernible and it was underpinned by higher rates of investment and an improvement in the efficiency of investment. It was the changing policy context during this phase that that began to pave the way for a macroeconomic environment that would be less strictured and more conducive to higher growth rates. Notably, in spite of the increasing budget deficits during the 1980s, the government kept up the pace of public investments and this helped to increase growth by boosting demand. It is interesting to note that easing supply-side constraints, which had arisen mainly because of infrastructural bottlenecks that existed across a number of sectors such as coal, power and railways, in conjunction with reducing the restrictions of capital goods imports, foreign exchange and other scarce inputs removed some of the deterrents that had impeded higher levels of productivity. Overall, this resulted in a better economic performance.

Perhaps even more vital than the quantitative measure of changes initiated was the underlying implication that it conveyed: a fast-increasing degree of openness was on the cards and it was not to be constricted by the quasi-socialist framework that had almost overwhelmingly conditioned industrial policy till the 1980s. As explained earlier, cognizance of this fact had begun to influence decision-making from the early 1980s, but it was acted upon more decisively and whole-heartedly by a segment of the political establishment after the mid-1980s. At a glance, the changes that occurred during the 1980s may not have seemed wide-ranging from the perspective of enabling a noticeably enhanced extent of external economic liberalization; however, for the country's internal policy and macroeconomic environment the initiatives undertaken during this phase were undeniably important. It is the changing emphasis in the endogenous policies of the country that set the tone and conferred on the economy a greater preparedness to make the adjustments that trade and foreign investment liberalization would usher in its wake in 1991.

Importantly, if the Indian economy had its fair share of endowments by that time, it was the outcome of the emphasis that had been accorded to building a diversified industrial sector, the presence of a reservoir of skilled technical and management professionals, a variety of producer and supplier networks, an adequate tax base and a sizeable middle class.

India's pursuit of liberalization is markedly different from that of many developing countries because, in the instance of the latter, removing trade barriers and easing the curbs on foreign investment was mainly the outcome of structural adjustment, which was compelled by borrowing from international financial institutions, the International Monetary Fund being among the most important lenders.

It was the extraneously induced policy change that led to the opening up of markets. There is a lesson herein, one that becomes apparent in retrospect from an analysis of the empirics of economic liberalization in India. Adjustment that is compelled regardless of whether a particular national economy is prepared or not without damaging ramifications in other more vulnerable and less protected sections of society needs to be differentiated from structural transformation. Over the four decades preceding 1991 the country had undergone a deep-seated process of transformation, and it had what could be termed as a degree of economic maturity by the early 1990s.

In its initial stage the impetus to liberalization in India was endogenous as it comprised mainly of measures that were directed towards the process of internal deregulation. Demonstrably this proved to be an advantage. Subsequently, the implementation of reduction of barriers on trade and foreign investment in 1991 should be viewed as the continuity of a process that began in the early 1980s. Undoubtedly, the pressures exerted by the scarcity of foreign exchange reserves in the country acted as a catalyst in the adoption of faster and more comprehensive external economic liberalization. Equally true is the fact that India's turnaround consisted of three important points – 1980, 1987 and 1991. In a sense, this means that the adjustments to liberalization were spread over a decade.

During the post-1990s phase there has been a greater degree of openness with a reduction in the barriers on trade and foreign investment; despite this, the pace of internal policy reform has slowed down. Interestingly, during what maybe be termed as its nascent stage, liberalization in India was more broad-based than it is currently. In the present Indian context it seems that the focus of liberalization has been whittled down to enhancing the degree of openness and not much else. This is hardly unusual because a fact that is generally overlooked is that the longer required internal policy changes take the more suboptimal will be the impact of economic liberalization.

Liberalization represented a dramatic policy shift but the adjustments it brought in its wake have stretched for over a decade. During the early 1990s, the sharply divided views in the political establishment were expressed through fervent ideological lobbies that upheld or castigated liberalization. The outcome of this was procrastination over the implementation of some important projects and delays in the formulation of sector-specific foreign direct investment (FDI) policies. This meant that the adjustments entailed by economic liberalism have proceeded at a staggered pace and these discontinuities in economic reform during the initial phase explain the lags in mitigating the infrastructural constraints. Disadvantageous though this might seem on most counts, the upside is that India has avoided the pitfalls that would have inevitably arisen from an accelerated process of liberalization because haste, in this context, could have brought with it a scenario of economic volatility or even tumult.

Liberalization has taken wing in India and its impact in certain sectors has been remarkable. Notably, the gains from having markets that are more open and competitive are more evident at the sectoral level. Even a cursory glance at the IT sector and financial services would reveal the benefits of a closer integration with world markets. The foreseeable expansion in the bio-tech sector and health care is another instance of a success story in the offing. At this point it would be relevant to view the role that FDI has had on the domestic economy.

## Role of FDI in the Indian economy

Unequivocally, India and China are two of the global economy's most promising investment opportunities. The latter has had rather sizable inflows of foreign investment over the last decade and a half and India is on the threshold of an FDI surge. Plausibly, the impact of FDI will be more significant in both quantitative and qualitative terms as inflows of FDI increase into the realm of infrastructure, retail and an entire spectrum of service-sector activities, many of which already have a fair amount of FDI.

Although foreign direct investment (FDI) into India has been increasing since the 1990s, it is by no means quantitatively as massive as the amounts of overseas investment that countries in East Asia and China have been receiving. India has received FDI inflows of about US$45 billion over the decade and a half; this is a minuscule amount compared to China's massive amounts of foreign investment. The role or importance that FDI has played in the Indian economy has been an incremental one because it has driven expansion in certain spheres in the realm of the service sector, such as information technology and financial services. The significance that FDI in

India has had in catalyzing the transformation and expansion of certain areas in the service sectors, is undeniable. It is estimated that by March 2007 FDI in India could increase by US$10 billion, which is far more than the increase during any fiscal year. The process that began in India in 1991 is gaining rapid momentum as Indian industry is taking strides towards globalization. Interestingly in this regard, 2006 has been a particularly eventful year for Corporate India, which witnessed acquisitions of overseas companies by frontrunners in Indian industry. Some instances of this include: Tata Steel, which recently acquired Anglo-Dutch steel firm Corus for $11 billion; Videocon, which bought South Korea's Daewoo Electronics for $684 million; and Dr Reddy's, which purchased Germany's Betapharm for $572 million.

A concise overview of the role that FDI has played so far in the Indian economy follows.

According to some estimates, the share of service sector (including all the above) in total FDI inflows to India rose significantly from 5 per cent by 1990 to about 54 per cent between 1991 and 2004. It must be noted that over 2004–5 net exports of software services amounted to $16.5 billion and this accounted for more than half of India's total service exports.

Unlike China, export-oriented FDI in the manufacturing sector has not been the most vital facet of FDI in India; this is understandable given the stage of development at which the country found itself at when FDI began to matter significantly. When FDI as a source of investment entered the picture, insofar as the Indian economy was concerned, the country had achieved a certain degree of industrial maturity and, thus, its significance has to be seen as propelling the expansion of certain knowledge-intensive core competences in the manufacturing and service sectors.

The information technology (IT) sector, power and transportation industry and automobiles are among the sectors that have received the bulk of FDI over the last five years. As a matter of fact, the concentration of FDI in the infrastructure and tertiary sector in India mirrored the trends underlying FDI inflows worldwide, the sectors receiving a larger proportion of foreign investment including IT (comprising telecommunications, computer software, consulting services, etc.), as well as power generation, and hotels and tourism. According to the UNCTAD report (2004), by 2000 about half the total stock of FDI in developing countries was in services, more than double of that in 1990. The report attributes this shift to three main reasons: the rising share of services in practically all countries; the increasingly tradable nature of many service outputs; and liberalized entry into many service industries previously closed to foreign businesses.

As a consequence of the rapid dissemination of information and communication technology (ICT), the fragmentation of international production has emerged as a driver of export growth. Herein, FDI has played a vital role in international splitting up of the production process within vertically integrated manufacturing industries. Through this process, firms have been able to relocate not just their production processes but also service-denominated activities to other countries in accordance to the principle of comparative advantage. The application of this principle is not a recent one in the manufacture of goods such as garments, footwear, toys, handicrafts, etc. However, its utilization as a fundamental in the service sector, through business process outsourcing (BPO) is relatively recent. The outsourcing boom, as some describe the expansion in BPO industries, was an eye-opener, as it revealed the immense potential for export-oriented FDI in the service sector. Potentially, this spells a terrain of opportunities for India and an important role for FDI-linked exports. India's emergence as a hub of knowledge-intensive activity is underpinned by the presence of highly skilled and management-level manpower, which also gives it the absorptive capacity to assimilate the gains from technological diffusion and knowledge spillovers.

According to the *Asian Development Outlook* (2004):

India's human capital and R&D base has pockets of international excellence, most notably in information technology and in some defence-related heavy industry. Until recently, and in contrast to much of East Asia, its educational priorities resulted in centers of international quality alongside quite high levels of illiteracy. It also differed in that its inward-looking strategy meant that it was unable to exploit its human capital strengths in the global economy. Thus, in contrast to China, its major intrusion into the international information technology industry has been via services rather than manufacturing. Its commercial environment is broadly predictable, and the legal system cumbersome but independent. It also has the highest level of decentralized economic policy making among the six countries. A large diaspora facilitates its connections to the international economy. The 1991 reforms and their aftermath have begun to transform the commercial environment, but the unfinished agenda is large and complex, and the forward momentum appears to have slowed significantly in recent years.

Although the increase in FDI-linked service exports is still at a fairly early stage in the Indian economy, it has demonstrated that it can have a significant part to play in making India a global hub of sourcing a fairly wide range of services. In a small way this is happening but the potential for expansion is nothing short of tremendous. Some of the other spillovers that would occur from an expansion in service-oriented exports would enable firms in the sectors involved to utilize existent technology with higher levels of efficiency and to enhance productivity of employees. This is evident in certain spheres, such as banking and financial services, health and education, and has helped in enhancing levels of competitiveness.

Furthermore, a number of multinational enterprises (MNEs) have set up their software-development subsidiaries and, added to this, other multinationals are looking to set up their R&D centres (global and regional) to avail of India's cost-competitiveness across a spectrum of knowledge-related spheres, such as bio-tech and pharmaceuticals. Over the last five years, about 100 MNEs have set up their R&D centres in India, including Colgate Palmolive, Eli-Lily, Dupont and Daimler Chrysler.

## Liberalization and the dynamics of economic progress

Liberalization unshackled businesses from the binds of excessive bureaucratization and government intervention, but this was not enough to accelerate the pace of reform. The underlying dynamics of trade and investment liberalization spurred business sentiment and financial markets but, although internal deregulation should have been much faster, it wasn't. Declining levels of public investment, coupled with a deficiency of infrastructural inputs and inadequate employment creation that stubbornly persisted, bore testimony to the fact that, although the licence Raj was whittling away, the politics of underdevelopment continued.

From a macro perspective, the quantitative impact of liberalization has been moderate, exports have increased significantly, though not enough to be described as outstanding, industrial growth has not increased discernibly and total factor productivity has been much higher during the 1990s. India has posted an average annual growth rate of over 6 per cent per annum and over 8 per cent over the last two years. This makes it among the fastest-growing nations in the world. Having said this, the country's growth performance was good, but not as spectacular as it could have been.

An evaluation of the state-wise impact of liberalization brings to the fore some interesting revelations. As indicated in Table 3.3, of the 16 states in India economic growth rates exhibited discernible change (either positive or negative) in only half. It increased significantly in Gujarat, Kerala and West Bengal and decelerated in Bihar, Uttar Pradesh, Punjab and Rajasthan. The imminent question that arises is: was it investment climate, a vast expanse of untapped opportunity or the prevalent initial conditions and macroeconomic environment in a particular state that shaped the outcomes of liberalization?

Arriving at generalized inferences about the features that facilitate successful liberalization is not easy because the rise in growth rates occurred in states that are not exactly similar, except for the fact that Kerala and West Bengal have a political context that is underpinned by leftist leanings. Almost at the other end of the spectrum in terms of the ideological orientation of its political establishment is Gujarat, one of the country's richest states, which represents an instance where liberalization has worked effectively.

If one were to uphold theoretical propositions about the link between potential for growth and investment patterns, the forecast would have been

*Table 3.3*    Economic growth rates in Indian states, 1980–2004

| States | 1980–90 | 1990–2004 | 1980–2004 |
|---|---|---|---|
| Andhra Pradesh | 4.81 | 5.33 | 5.10 |
| Assam | 3.91 | 3.00 | 3.40 |
| Bihar | 5.20 | 4.20 | 4.60 |
| Gujarat | 5.70 | 8.11 | 7.10 |
| Haryana | 6.68 | 6.63 | 6.65 |
| Himachal Pradesh | 6.10 | 6.44 | 6.30 |
| Karnataka | 6.10 | 6.38 | 6.30 |
| Kerala | 4.50 | 5.69 | 5.20 |
| Madhya Pradesh | 5.18 | 4.74 | 4.90 |
| Maharashtra | 5.98 | 5.92 | 5.95 |
| Orissa | 5.85 | 3.94 | 4.70 |
| Punjab | 5.14 | 4.14 | 4.60 |
| Rajasthan | 7.17 | 5.68 | 6.30 |
| Tamil Nadu | 6.35 | 5.70 | 5.97 |
| Uttar Pradesh | 5.88 | 3.76 | 4.64 |
| West Bengal | 5.20 | 7.12 | 6.32 |
| All India | 5.60 | 5.90 | 5.80 |

*Source*: Atul Kohli, 'Politics of Economic Growth in India 1980–2005, Part II', *Economic and Political Weekly*, 1 April 2006.

that the poorer states and those that had not received much investment, either public or private, would be the biggest beneficiaries of liberalization. This was hardly the case. Given the reduction of public investment across all states it is those that managed to elicit inflows of private investment (domestic and foreign) that have been able to boost their levels of economic progress. Now comes the crux of the point being discussed: those regions that had either a conducive investment climate or a better situation insofar as infrastructure was concerned, or preferably both, could attract higher levels of investment. This means that the relatively affluent states were able to benefit much more from liberalization than those that were poorer. Furthermore, even those among the more prosperous states that did not witness a discernible increment in growth rates, such as Maharashtra, Karnataka and Tamil Nadu, did not witness a deceleration of GDP growth (even in Tamil Nadu the decline in growth rate was marginal). The poorest states witnessed both a decline in the levels of private investment and a deceleration in economic growth. Thus, empirical findings that may have seemed puzzling or confusing at times reveal a clear trend. Liberalization did not provide an impetus to either private investment or growth in the poorer regions, which required it the maximum.

Evidently, liberalized markets could not induce an increase in the inflows of investment in regions that lacked a minimally conducive macroeconomic environment and the other prerequisites for it to be considered a relatively safe bet or a less risky investment proposition by prospective investors. In the Indian context, thus, liberalization has borne benefits for those states that had already achieved certain a level of economic progress. Alternately expressed, states that crossed a threshold of well being could reap the advantages of liberalization. Poorer states that had a disappointing scorecard on economic progress were almost bereft of any increase in public investment during the post-liberalization era. Not surprisingly, their growth rates declined and they found themselves below the threshold required to be a beneficiary of liberalization. Notably, increasing levels of private investment corresponded to rising levels of public investment, a fact that should not be overlooked in an evaluation of present trends in economic liberalization in India.

An overview of economic progress in the Indian states during the post-liberalization era provides yet another affirmation that high levels of GDP growth does always translate into commensurately significant improvements in the ambit of development. The highest gains on the human development frontier are in states where per capita incomes are moderate. Kerala and Tamil Nadu are the best performers insofar as human development is concerned and, as indicated, the per capita income in these states is much lower than that of Gujarat. The nature of governance at the state level was among the key determinants of whether liberalization would work, it was not the specificities of its ideology or how market-friendly it may have inherently been but how proactive state governments were in spearheading measures that would make a particular state an attractive investor destination. This was certainly the case in Gujarat and in Kerala. Notwithstanding their distinctly different political leanings it is highly probable that the two states will adopt policies that will make them more investor-friendly.

Economic liberalization in India did not change the ground rules significantly in relation to the political economy of underdevelopment. This is revealed most unmistakably by the patterns of economic progress and the rising levels of regional and income disparities (between various socio-economic groups) that liberalization could not do much to alter. The existing endemic underdevelopment in certain states really has remained unchanged during the post-liberalization era. It is not income inequity alone but a host other socio-economic inequities that can prevent the gains of 'smart policy' percolating to those who find themselves in a gridlock of deprivation, with a lack of livelihood options. For instance, the initial measures towards setting up special economic zones in India did encounter resistance from farmers, particularly in certain rural regions (Singur and Nandigram) of West Bengal. This was inevitable given the absence of a comprehensive land acquisition act. As the Indian government is putting into place policy safeguards to protect peasants and other lower-income groups it is yet another reminder that 'compromised development' is really no development at all.

# 4
# Economic Reform: Moving Beyond Liberalization

India's growth prospects are extremely encouraging and one can realistically envision that the country's growth rates will be on the upswing for the next few years. An 8 per cent growth rate of GDP per annum, which may well climb to 10 per cent, very simply means that India has crossed the growth barrier, entered the league of the fastest-growing nations and is poised to consolidate itself as an economic power.

The nation can certainly extol its achievements; however, this should not lead to complacency about the unattained goals if economic progress is to be sustained over the longer term. Issues of sustainability define an unequivocal need for a continuous process of economic reform. As in any other nation so also in India economic reform in contemporary India may be succinctly described as a process that would facilitate the integration of growth objectives with the larger goal of development.

According to the National Sample Survey (2006), the incidence of poverty in India has declined over the period 1993–4 to 2004–5. It is important to note the fact that this reduction has been extremely gradual and insufficient in magnitude, estimated at 0.74 per cent per annum over the period 1993–4 to 2004–5 and 0.79 per cent over 1999–2005.

The immediate priority is that economic reform in India should be directed towards facilitating patterns of growth that are more inclusive and pro-development than these prevalent at present. Prosperity, where it occurred, was a selective phenomenon, as evidenced by the 300 million people who live on the margins of existence. Liberalization that was tempered with gradualism during its initial stages was prudent; however, the current hindered and slowed down the trajectory of poverty reduction, and it has to be surmounted if the momentum of progress is to continue unabated. Although the country's growth performance has improved significantly over the last decade, it still represents a level of output and employment that is much below what the nation is capable of achieving. Theoretically, India's current situation may be described as one that does not represent full employment. (Full employment output may be defined as a country's supply determined output.) Notably, full employment is a useful concept not because it is a goal that most countries find tenable but because there are very few nations that have achieved full employment levels of output. Thus, it can be used as a gauge or measure of how proximate or distant a country is from attaining its optimal level of output and employment.

## Sustainable growth and economic reform

A decade ago, India was an emerging market with unbridled potential; now it is an emerging economic power with immense untapped capacity for opportunity creation. Having embarked on economic liberalization in 1991, India's reforms in the financial and capital markets have been successful. This is evidenced by the emergence of a fairly competitive and rapidly expanding banking sector, vibrant equity markets and foreign exchange reserves, which were about US$ 180 billion as of February 2007, giving the country a balance of payments situation that can be described as reasonably comfortable. Over the last decade and a half, the country has certainly made discernible strides towards increasing levels of efficiency, particularly in industry, and entrepreneurs have certainly found a business environment that was more conducive than what prevailed during the licence Raj.

It is not as if liberalizing financial and capital markets did not elicit opposition; dismantling curbs, unbundling bureaucratic shackles was not an easy option. However, throughout the early 1990s economic reform was limited to initiating the steps that would propel liberalization. Evidently, the structure and content of economic reform in the subsequent era will have a far-reaching impact on development. The highlight of the next phase of economic reform would be its transition from being an appendage to liberalization in the precedent phase to becoming a full-blooded development strategy. There is a consensus about economic reform in India, one that has fortunately transcended political factions. However, despite this crucial issues pertinent to these continue to be topics of fervent debate, which, more often than not, erupts into disruptive squabbles in the Indian parliament.

Thus, during the ensuing phase the country's reform agenda would have to take on a role that is certainly more broad-based and with many more ramifications than its precedent one. This would entail steps that extend beyond the purview of implementing the policies of deregulation and privatization because its central objective would be to ease the constraints that restrict economic development.

Basically the challenges currently confronting the nation can be viewed as three:

1. The political economy of underdevelopment.
2. The alarming inadequacy of human capital formation and infrastructural provision.
3. The transformation of the public-sector enterprises.

It must be noted that the first has perpetuated inadequacies in both infrastructure and human capital formation.

## The political economy of underdevelopment: its ramifications

A simply stated unambiguous fact: at every level, conceptualization and implementation of strategy and policy encounters a major hurdle – the political economy of underdevelopment. The next phase of economic reform has to spearhead the evolution of a political economy that is rooted in fundamental considerations of economic development. This is an integral process that is already underway; however, it needs to be expedited and it is a faster process of economic reform that will catalyze development.

At the core of the country's political economy of development is the apparent divergence in the concerns and priorities of two distinctly disparate socio-economic strata in India. One consists of the urban or metropolitan community, with its international donor and investor component, and the other comprises those individuals at the grassroots (urban and rural) and powerful anti-reform vested interests in the politicians' constituencies. It is the perceptible conflict of interests between these two realms that stokes the country's political economy of underdevelopment and enables it to rear its head from time to time. Reform is seen as a tool of populism for one strata of the electorate and it is precisely those measures that undermine or deter the processes this entails that are used to woo other sections of the polity.

Regardless of the short-term gains to some powerful clusters of individuals, over the longer term the costs of having a fragmented approach to the reform process is monumental. Over the last decade or so the political economy of underdevelopment has shrunk, and yet it continues to weigh down a faster pace of economic reform. It is not difficult to cite instances of a staggered process of reform. As will be demonstrated in the next section, the consequence of this is a costly fall-out that manifests itself through the inadequacies of infrastructure provision, the inefficiencies of some public-sector enterprises and a piecemeal approach to much required labour legislation that has not occurred. It is this reality of contemporary India that defines an inextricable link between surmounting the challenges that confront it and ensuring that the political economy of development is resilient and extensive enough to expedite the process of economic reform.

Despite the widespread cognizance about the unequivocal need to transform most public sector enterprises and limited progress towards disinvestment and privatization of some enterprises, India has a considerable distance to cover before it can boast of having a public sector that can be considered viable. As for the impending change in labour legislation, the country has a situation where not much has been done to set the ball rolling towards reform in labour laws. An illustrative instance of this is the manner in which the plans for airport modernization in the country's metros have proceeded at a staggered pace. In the larger context, the most widely used pretext for stalling reform in a number of public-sector enterprises are apprehensions about the impact that privatization and restructuring of public-sector enterprises would have on the interests of employees in the institutions concerned.

The attempt to preserve job security and all the remunerative advantages that go with it is a valid one provided it is linked to productivity and efficiency. This obvious fact was often lost sight of (particularly by a number of public-sector enterprises) during the licence Raj, an era where employment accretions were at the expense of potential increases in labour productivity in public-sector enterprises. Protecting the interests of the workforce is an imperative; however, as was the case in an earlier era, frequently attempts to do so get disembodied from the need to increase levels of productivity and efficiency.

It is evident that the country requires the formulation of a comprehensive and transparent exit policy, which takes into account the extremely feeble state of millions who are at the lowest rung of the employment hierarchy. It is precisely the glaring absence of a safety net that has been a 'trump' card of sorts for a certain faction of politics. Sadly, the culmination of this has been that the exit policy has been veritably held to ransom by the indiscriminate politicization of the interests of the country's labour force.

It is rather perilous to politicize socio-economic objectives but this has been a recurrent feature of politics in India, as it is in many countries. Moreover, this would not have been adverse if it enabled the attainment of developmental targets. Instead, this was not the case. On the contrary, it deterred the process of development during the licence Raj and it plays a similar role in economic reform. Not surprisingly, the consequence of this has been to perpetrate the political economy of underdevelopment.

Ironically, the most vulnerable sections of the country's workforce employed in the unorganized and informal sectors continue to live on the margins of existence without any bargaining position at all. Regardless of whether protecting the interests of this segment of the population force falls within the purview of the exit policy or not, there is a compelling need to formulate policies that will take into account the requirements of the weakest sections of the employee strata (in the organized and unorganized sector), for insurance job security or compensatory relief.

Notably, any exit policy that is not accompanied by measures to address this issue can at best be described as a half-baked attempt at resolving the problem of labour legislation.

## Infrastructure provision and human capital formation: a story of unaffordable paucity

The pace of economic progress was held back in pre-liberalization India by a rising degree of decadence and inefficiency that beset the licence Raj. During its post-liberalization phase there were gains, tremendous in certain sectors, that accrued to the country. Expressed descriptively, the economy has just begun to tap into its economic potential and in this context the bottom line is that India could have had growth rates that were higher and a pace of development that was much faster if it were not shackled by highly inadequate infrastructure provision.

According to a study undertaken in 2000 and 2003 by the World Bank and Confederation of Indian Industry regarding the manufacturing sector, it was the availability of power that represented the most severe deterrent to expansion and productivity. The study estimated that if the power constraint was removed it would raise the value added per worker by 79–80 per cent. Despite the passage of the Electricity Act in 2003, the country is confronted with a shortfall of 7.1 per cent of its energy requirements and 11.2 per cent of peak demand over 2003–4. Not much has changed in this context.

*The McKinsey Report: When to Make India a Manufacturing Base*, by Shashank Luthra, Ramesh Mangaleswaran and Asutosh Padhi (2005) states:

> When multinationals evaluate India as a hub for offshore manufacturing and sourcing, its engineering capacity and existing network of suppliers and related companies are important inducements. But before the manufacture of electrical and electronic products can take off, the country must address three issues, low domestic demand, a lack of manufacturing clusters and an unreliable transport infrastructure.

According to the approach paper of India's 11th five-year plan (2007–11) the total investment that was ploughed into infrastructure during 2002–6 was well below the potential that was provided by the domestic savings and the manageable current account deficit. Over the next five years the total investment required for the expansion and building of ports, highways, power plants and civil aviation and other segments adds to about US$ 320 billion. The estimated investment outlays would be raised through a combination of public and private investment. Importantly this also dovetails the formulation of practical public–private partnership solutions so that both the government and private sector can work in unison to resolve the inadequacies that confront the vital sectors of the Indian economy.

It is the expediency and efficacy with which the estimated investment outlay needed to bridge the infrastructure shortfall is disbursed that will have the most critical role in determining the consistency of growth and the impact that it will have on poverty reduction and employment. The rapid proliferation of infrastructure in the telecom sector, particularly mobile telephony, typifies the multiplier effect that increasing the supply of a single infrastructural input can have. Undeniably this illumines the crucial consequences of a rapid expansion in the infrastructure sector. The extent and quality of infrastructure provision in India over the next few years is also the litmus test of how resilient its political economy of development is.

Current levels of productivity indicate the ability of the Indian economy to perform reasonably stably amid the existent constraints. However, the rather large gap between actual performance and expansionary potential is a outcome of constraints imposed by the infrastructural sector. As a matter of fact, there are certain spheres in the agricultural and service sector that have not even begun to scratch the surface of their intrinsic capacity for growth or opportunity creation.

Human development is not a competing priority; it is the lynchpin of sustainable growth. This fundamental tenet does get overlooked and this evidently, does reflect a contradiction between the imperatives of attaining growth targets and those facets of policy formulation that pertain to the social sector. The problem that confronts the educational sphere is not merely about the quantity of resources allocated but the manner in which these are utilized. Many parts of rural India are without any form of school infrastructure and even where there seems to be some kind of an arrangement for schooling either there is a shortage of teachers or it is simply a matter of non-attendance by teachers and students.

We begin this enumeration with a concise description of how the phenomenal expansion of the software industry in India exemplifies an instance of the phenomenal pay-offs that can accrue to a country from its investments in human capital formation. During the 1950s, the emphasis on setting up tertiary institutes of learning and research and development seemed lopsided to many because of inadequacy of primary school infrastructure. However, the existence of certain technical core competences, of which information technology is one, cannot be separated from the importance assigned to creating a large pool of skilled manpower. Around 350,000 engineers graduate in India annually, which is on a par if not higher than the number of the same in the US per annum. There are about 1675 technical training institutes and even this is perceived as inadequate given the rapidly increasing demand for technical and managerial personnel in number of fast-expanding knowledge-intensive sectors, which range from information technology and bio-tech to banking and financial services.

Reverting to the software industry, it should be noted that the IT industry did not exhibit any discernible sign of taking off until industrial policy prioritized the achievement of self-reliance in the creation of hardware capabilities. Import tariffs on hardware and software were high (135 per cent on hardware and 100 per cent on software), besides which software developers did not have easy access to finance in the banking sector. As a matter of fact, there was an oversupply of IT-trained professionals during the 1980s and it is worth mentioning that about 59 per cent of graduates in computer science and engineering from the Indian Institute of Technology emigrated in 1986.

The inception of partial liberalization in India occurred in 1984 and this gave the software industry its much needed shot in the arm with the reduction in import tariffs on hardware and software to 60 per cent; software exporters became eligible for bank finance and, in 1985, all export revenue was exempt from income tax. Furthermore, the establishment of a chain of software parks in the early 1990s also eased some infrastructural constraints.

The cumulative consequence of these measures was to kickstart the expansion of the IT industry, particularly its software segment in India. The growth of this industry happened on a scale that may have surpassed even the most optimistic expectations. Over the period 1995–2000 it grew at a rate of over 35 per cent annually and during 2003–4 the value of software and other allied services was US$12 billion. It must be noted that software exports account for a large proportion of industry sales, comprising 80 per cent of industry sales over 2001–2. Employment provided by the software industry stood at 345,000 persons in 2004. India's software industry is a phenomenal success story, a fact that prompts the question: does it have applicability to other developing countries?

The Nasscom report (2005/6), by India's National Association of Software and Services Company, states:

> We believe that India can sustain its global leadership position, grow its offshore IT and BPO industry at an annual rate greater than 25 per cent and generate export revenues of about US$60 billion by 2010. Additionally export growth can further be accelerated by deep and enduring innovation by industry participants. Such extensive innovation could generate an additional US$15–20 billion in export revenue over the next 5–10 years.

The crucial point is not whether the growth of the IT industry in India can be replicated in another country, but more importantly whether a particular developing nation can harness its ability and endowments through policy and non-policy measures to create core competences that can spell great success for the global economy.

India's IT industry finally began to steal a march when certain conducive features came together. Undoubtedly, policies in the mid-1980s propelled its progress but this was possible because India had a reservoir of talent and technical expertise. This tells us something vital: be it the software industry, financial services, bio-tech or any other core competence, the basic and most fundamental input is education, training in human capital investment.

India's ascent in the global economy was possible largely because its leadership managed to create a base of both technical and non-technical expertise. Among other things, it underscores the critical nature of enhancing and expanding human capital formation at an increasing rate. The costs of opportunities foregone and potential core competences that are not built upon due to an inadequacy of human capital accumulation typify an instance of growth prospects that remain unexploited. Can sound economies let this happen? Not really.

India's competitive advantage because of its endowment of skilled manpower is the legacy of policies pursued in the early stages of modernization; this was an era during which resource constraints could get fairly acute at times. Despite this, policy formulation emphasized setting up of institutes and centres that would create an underpinning of talent and skill. The irony at this point in time is that an India that is more affluent has not prioritized human capital the way it should have done, given its strengths and imperatives.

Policies and measures directed towards the vital goal of building infrastructure should be implemented more expeditiously and more effectively. India wants to consolidate itself as a service hub; this is hardly surprising given the skill-intensive core competences that have evolved in the country. However, in the light of its comparative advantage in knowledge intensive spheres an anomaly that continues to characterize the Indian economy is the glaring inadequacy of capital formation. Despite this it is obvious that not enough is being done to remedy the situation and there is a severe paucity of educational institutions at every level.

Furthermore, there is a mismatch between the curricula that exist in most universities and the prerequisites for a higher degree of employability. The consequence of this is an alarming contradiction: on the one hand, four million educated Indians find themselves unemployed and, on the other, there is a paucity of certain categories of skilled professionals, in the spheres of information technology, management and engineering. It is wonderful to note that salaries for this educated strata have skyrocketed and may continue to do for some time.

However, over the medium and longer term a developing country where employment provision is a major issue cannot afford a situation where the existence of opportunities in certain spheres is not matched by a sufficient number of those who can take advantage of these opportunities. One might argue that it is not unusual for a developing country to be saddled with shortages of skilled labour. Be this as it may, in the case of India its competitive edge emanates from a wide range of skill-intensive activities. This fact itself sets it apart from the quintessential developing nation, which usually carves out for itself a competitive edge in activities that do not have a high skill or technical content.

In the broader context of ensuring sustainable growth this demand-supply mismatch has to be tackled over the medium term. The antecedents of this problem of demand and supply mismatch can be traced to the prevalence of rather low social-sector expenditures over the last five decades. This feature

*Table 4.1*   Trends in public expenditure and infant mortality in South Asian countries

| Country | Public expenditure on health (% GDP) | | Infant mortality (deaths/1000 live births) | | Change* per annum |
|---|---|---|---|---|---|
| | 1990 | 2001 | 1990 | 2001 | |
| India | 0.9 | 0.9 | 94 | 67 | 3.13 |
| Sri Lanka | 1.5 | 1.8 | 26 | 17 | 3.94 |
| Maldives | 3.6 | 5.6 | 61 | 58 | 0.46 |
| Bangladesh | 0.7 | 1.5 | 114 | 51 | 7.59 |
| Bhutan | 1.7 | 3.6 | 123 | 74 | 4.73 |

*Average annual rate of reduction in infant mortality rate.
*Source*: UNDP, *Human Development Report* (2004).

cannot be attributed merely to a scarcity of resources because countries such as Sri Lanka, China, South Korea, Taiwan, Malaysia and Indonesia had, at one time, lower per capita incomes than India; this did not deter them from allocating a higher proportion of their GDP towards the provision of social infrastructure. (This is indicated in Table 4.1.) Efficient and productive allocation of social-sector outlays have facilitated substantial improvements in capital formation and the crucial role that this has had in catalyzing technological dissemination and upgrading in East and South-East Asia is an obvious one.

Ironically, Indian planning assigned considerable importance to having policies that would enable an improvement in human development indicators. By the 1970s it was evident that, despite the rhetoric, social-sector imperatives were sidelined. Furthermore, poor delivery, deficient and delayed implementation and low productivity of resources dampened the impact of the allocations deployed towards this sector.

Throughout the post-liberalization era so far social-sector allocations have not improved significantly in quantitative terms and neither has productivity of the outlays deployed. For instance, even as the need for educational inputs seems to becoming more acute it should be noted that the National Policy of Education, which was formulated by the Indian government in 1968 and 1986, had as its central objective the eradication of illiteracy and providing universal elementary education in the minimum possible time. The clear intent of the education policy that was launched in 1986 was to provide free and compulsory education to all children until the age of 14 by 1995. The reality falls far short of attaining this target, and predictably an important reason for this is that the expenditure allocated to education has not exceeded 4 per cent. A developing country that set out to increase the pace of development should assign at least 6 per cent of its GDP to education.

Despite policy concurrence about the problems confronting the educational sector, initiatives directed towards expanding the sphere could be obstructed or delayed by superfluous political interference. In this context, however, it was rather encouraging to note that the recent attempt by the some sections of the government to thwart plans by the Indian Institute of Management to set up a campus in Singapore was not successful. The institute's expansion plans seem to be proceeding on course.

The larger context is one where decision-making on matters that pertain to the liberalization of the educational sphere in India should proceed expeditiously. It is very likely that there will be a discernible expansion of the educational sector, the imminent question that arises is about the time that will elapse before the shortfall is bridged. As a matter of fact, despite all the imperfections and inconsistencies that pervaded the licence Raj, it is undeniable that India's present core competences evolved or were built upon a base that was created during the pre- liberalization era.

On the subject of the educational sector, reservations in the institutions of learning provide us with another illustrative instance of politicization in the realm of education provision. It demonstrates that sound rationale and good intent can get sidetracked by the politics of underdevelopment.

The premise for caste-based reservations appears straightforward; in essence it is the predominance of upper castes that constitute about 20 per cent of the population in educational institutions, the ambit of skilled professionals and in relatively privileged spheres of economic activity. On the other hand, the oppression of the lower castes, particularly the scheduled castes and tribes, has been a historical feature of the social polity of India. The presumed corrective for this pronounced disparity has been the advocacy and impending implementation of caste-based quotas in educational institutions. The announcement has elicited intense opposition among certain sections of the academic community and professional categories. Understandably, it also had a fairly wide support base among the lower caste groups.

There have been a slew of discussions and debates about the issue, and it is inherently a subject that can elicit an emotive response because it concerns a basic humanitarian issue of access to education. However, retaining objectivity is the key to having a balanced perspective and the aim should be to elucidate some basic considerations and questions that arise in the course of making a priori assessments about the possible impact of reservations.

At the outset it must be emphasized that it is not the intent or purpose of reservations that is in question. As outlined, the rationale underlying caste-based reservations is not an ambiguous one, neither is the indisputable need for having a system that would enhance accessibility of the lower income groups to education. The important question that arises is whether the provision of these caste-based reservations will correct the skewed access to educational institutions. Even at this point, in the light of previous evidence pertaining to reservations that have been enforced over the last few decades there is no categorical affirmation that reservations would serve the main objective for which these have been formulated. However, it is not just past experience that underlies scepticism about whether caste-based quotas will be able to bridge the undoubtedly blatant inequities in the access to education. At the core of most doubts that have been evoked about the impact of reservations is the premise of quota provision that assigns a preponderant emphasis on the caste that the person concerned belongs to. Observably, this implies that that the economic status of the individual is of secondary importance. Making caste the most important criteria of defining the beneficiaries of caste-based quotas does not have a positive connotation and it reflects demonstrably yet another instance of vote chasing politics.

Principally, the constrained access by the lower caste groups is the outcome of low incomes. Undeniably, those belonging to backward and scheduled castes have found that their access to education and employment opportunities is restricted by their weaker social backgrounds. This is a disadvantage that a number of individuals belonging to higher caste groups also have, a fact that cannot be overlooked but seems to have been insofar as reservation policy is concerned. Conversely, there are affluent sections within the backward caste groups and, despite their higher incomes, allowing the 'highest layer' of backward caste groups to avail of the quotas primarily because of their caste origins would be diluting the purpose and impact of these quotas.

One of the arguments that has been used to support the non-exclusion of this highest layer from the ambit of quota provision is that affluence has not eliminated other forms of caste-based discrimination insofar as backward castes are concerned. The fact cited is a reality but equally true is the fact that the remedy for certain social discriminatory practices with regard to backward castes does not stem from extending the purview of quotas to the affluent in this group. As a matter of fact, this would be discriminatory vis-à-vis poor individuals in the upper caste groups. Thus, the attempt to mitigate one form of discrimination in a manner that could result in another is a misjudgment and certainly not sound economics.

Second, the glaringly inadequate school and university infrastructure (both physical and manpower) deters access for all social and economic groups. Bridging this does entail sizable government expenditure and the entire allocation required does not seem forthcoming over the short term. Thus, the limited access to education is not merely the outcome of upper-caste privilege; there are other infrastructural constraints for which reservations are not the cure. Regardless of the efficiency with which the quotas are implemented, the insufficient availability of institutions will continue to deter access to education and not just at a higher level but at the primary and secondary level. The presumption underlying this discourse has been that the recipients of the quota will belong to the category that it is supposed to benefit. There have been more than a few instances in the past where this is not the case.

Thus, the prioritization of economic criteria should have been the core principle that reservation policy embodied if the singular most important purpose of reservation was to reduce the socio-economic disparities that result from a pronouncedly unequal distribution of education. Instead, so far the inclusion of backward-caste individuals who belong to the higher income groups and the exclusion of those upper-caste individuals who are poor, however small a proportion this may comprise, evidences that the reduction of socio-economic disparity is not an unencumbered objective of reservation policy. There are undeniably other reasons, which lie outside the purview of socio-economic concerns, that have had a discernible role in the formulation of the reservation policy.

Reservation can be potentially an effective tool in enhancing access to education; however, if the political connotations that underpin caste-linked quota provisions override its economic rationale its impact will not be very encouraging. It is, thus, the principles that guide the formulation of reservations that will have a crucial part to play in determining their impact; this is a point that is underscored by the outcome of reservations policy in the past.

## Privatization: an overview of its impact in India

By the 1990s, a backdrop of intensifying competition, increasing fiscal deficits and the sagging levels of productivity and profitability across a wide range of public-sector enterprises began to matter enough for disinvestments to be discussed as an option that would transform public-sector units (PSUs) in India into commercially viable units. (Table 4.2 indicates the public-sector units that have been privatized over the period 1999–2005.)

In the Indian context, so far governments have not been able to raise half the revenue that it had planned to through privatization. A rather gradual pace of disinvestment in a developing country, one in which the public sector has been an important player in steering economic policy, is not necessarily an unfavourable feature. Empirical evidence also points to the fact that privatization has not been able to remedy the ills arising from a wide gamut of factors, ranging from underperformance, overcapacity and declining levels of operational efficiency to the manager – politician nexus. Changing patterns of ownership may not alter the mode of functioning in a public-sector enterprise, even the instances where it has been able to revitalize the companies concerned are certainly not enough to substantiate that privatizing a public utility will ensure an increase its levels of viability and efficiency. The recurrent point that comes forth from recent empirical

*Table 4.2*   Privatizations with strategic partners in India, 1999–2005

| Name | % government equity sold | Profit/loss |
|---|---|---|
| Modern Food Industries | 80.0 | Loss making |
| Bharat Aluminium Co. | 51.0 | Profit making |
| CMC | 51.0 | Profit making |
| HTL | 74.0 | Profit making |
| Lagan Jute Machinery Corp. | 74.0 | Loss making |
| India Tourism Development Corporation 19 hotels | 90.0 | All loss making |
| IBP Co. | 33.5 | Profit making |
| Videsh Sanchar Nigam | 25.0 | Profit making |
| Paradeep Phosphates | 74.0 | Loss making |
| Hindustan Zinc | 44.9 | Profit making |
| Maruti Udoyog | 4.2 | Profit making |
| Indian Petrochemicals Corp. | 26.0 | Profit making |
| Jessop and Co. | 72.0 | Loss making |

*Note*: A significant proportion of the PSUs that have been disinvested over the period mentioned are profit making.
*Source*: Department of Disinvestment of India, Government of India.

literature about privatization is that it is the macroeconomic environment that is a distinct determinant of the outcomes of privatizing.

At the outset it is necessary to differentiate between successful and effective privatization because the two might be related but are not identical. If the government is able to raise the revenue it planned to from disinvesting a PSU, the endeavour to privatize the unit can be deemed as successful. Having privatized a PSU, either partly or in its entirety, how effective the process will be in enhancing performance, viability, efficiency and, finally, the expediency and continuity of the product or service delivery to the end user is a facet that would have to be evaluated subsequently. Thus, what maybe perceived as successful privatization might not always exemplify an instance of effective privatization.

Privatization may have been advocated as a panacea for the inefficiencies that usually characterize a public monopoly; however, the problems that confront public utilities in India cannot be dissociated from the larger context that prevails. Regardless of whether an organization is a public monopoly or a private one, its performance is impacted (and rather adversely so) in a milieu where pressures exerted by political compulsions are given precedence over economic imperatives. When the sphere concerned is infrastructure provision, the results can be detrimental.

Privatizing a PSU in haste would have a negative fall-out and, in any case, relinquishing the government's stake in a particular public-sector corporation is not always the antidote to revitalizing poorly performing units. Besides this general fact, integral to this discussion is the improvement in the profitability and efficiency levels of PSUs in India. It must be noted that the profitability of central public-sector enterprises has increased from 8 per cent in the mid-1970s to 21 per cent in 2003–4. It must be mentioned that this estimate of profitability is partly the result of high mark-up cost-based administered pricing in the petroleum companies. Excluding the petroleum companies from the calculation of profitability gives us a lower estimate of 18 per cent return on gross capital; however, this does not alter the observation that performance in central PSEs has improved. Befuddling though this may sound, despite the improvements in profitability at one end, the financial position of the Indian public sector is not satisfactory. This fact could be explained largely by the declining revenue – cost ratios of the state electricity boards (SEB) and the road transport corporations. The revenue – cost ratio has declined from 82.2 per cent in 1993–4 to 68.6 per cent about a decade later. Insofar as the road transport corporations are concerned, there has been a reduction in the revenue – cost ratio from 91.4 per cent in 1992–3 to 88.7 per cent in 2000–1.

The prevalence of lower levels of efficiency has not been cited as the chief reason for the present problems confronting the Indian public sector, particularly in the infrastructural sphere. For instance, findings indicate that over the last 30 years thermal efficiency levels in SEBs has risen, this is denoted by the increase in the plant-load factor in SEBs from 55 per cent in 1975–6 to 75 per cent in 2004–5.

The underlying cause for the present situation in the state-run public utilities and infrastructure services has been cited as inadequate pricing and the lack of recovery of dues. Over the preceding four decades, public-sector prices have never exceeded the overall price level and in 2003–4 the relative price was about 83 per cent of what prevailed in 1960–1. This is hardly unusual given that PSUs consist mainly of decreasing cost industries; however, it still does not detract from the point made by some recent studies that pricing is the main cause of the current financial situation of the most PSUs.

Even if one were to accept that the underpricing of public utilities is an important cause for the losses that have accrued, it is also true that much more than an increasing level of profitability is entailed for there to be an overall discernible and continued improvement in the public sector. Ceteris paribus given the present financial position of PSUs, if the delivery of its goods and services had been more efficient the social and developmental benefits that stemmed from this (over the longer term) would have to be taken into account in the evaluation of its performance. Furthermore, given the current pricing patterns of public goods, if the beneficiaries of the subsidies on public utilities and services comprised primarily individuals from the lower income groups it would still mean a higher social gain. Although this may not have reflected in a better financial status, it certainly would mean lower levels of inefficiency insofar as allocation and delivery of utilities are concerned. Instead, a misuse of subsidies and the prevalence of a fair extent of misallocation indicates that there are other leakages. Plausibly, if underpricing is also accompanied by resource leakage or diversion it will inevitably result in an unsatisfactory financial situation.

For instance, the attempts at restructuring the power sector in India tells us that transforming a public monopoly from a loss-making enterprise to one that can function in a commercially viable manner is considerably eased by a state that accords primacy to having both an efficient governance and bureaucratic administration. However, the main beneficiaries of the subsidies in the power sector are a small group of rural elite, namely the electric pump-using farmers. Despite the fiscal drain that this has caused, it is hardly surprising that this is a tricky deterrent and, unsurprisingly, measures to reduce subsidies have been rather superficial. The power sector is straddled between the need to appease and placate those interest groups that play a crucial role in political preservation and the obvious imperatives of economic reform. The link between political patronage availed of by certain powerful lobbies (and this also includes sections of the bureaucracy who are opposed to reforms) and vote chasing politics has had its ramifications in the power sector as it has in other public utilities. Thus, the subsidies provided or corrupt rent-seeking activity that persists despite the precarious financial state of most state electricity boards in the country are a manifestation of the vested interests that have entrenched themselves in the power sector.

This is yet another instance of the political economy of underdevelopment that has impeded almost every sphere of infrastructure provision and it is an affirmation that the transformation of the power sector or, for that matter, other public-sector enterprises may involve privatization but this is certainly not the only element the turnaround, or restructuring strategy, would need to encompass.

The functions and responsibility of public-sector enterprises does constitute a distinct social component and, thus, the advocacy of expeditious and large-scale privatization would be misleading; however, this should not detract from the significance of privatizing in bolstering levels of efficiency. It is the nature of privatization rather than its extent that constitutes the more important aspect in the Indian context.

Thus, amid a rather gradual process of disinvestment the Indian government seems to be moving in the right direction, and it is likely that the competitive pressures emanating from private-sector participation in certain spheres (telecommunications, aviation) that were earlier dominated by the PSUs, along with the onslaught of consumer dissatisfaction and the inherent need to adapt and adjust for survival amid intensifying competition, will compel the evolution of an appropriate pattern of disinvestment. It is heartening to note that some elements of this have been put into place. For instance, the establishment of a fund called the National Investment Fund in early 2006, the main purpose of which would be to channel the proceeds originating from the sale of minority shareholdings of profitable PSUs to the fund. The National Investment Fund would be managed by public-sector financial enterprises and returns from this will be ploughed into investments in health, education, employment and possibly other spheres of social infrastructure, and towards the support of profitable or revivable PSUs. Observably, the proportion of funds that will be allocated towards expanding social infrastructure provision remains to be seen.

The case by case approach adopted by India to evaluate every prospective proposal of privatization seems prudent given its larger context and in the light of the experience in developing countries such as Eastern Europe and Latin America.

A discussion on the disinvestment in public-sector enterprises takes us to the situation in fiscal policy over the last decade. Fiscal policy has made considerable strides towards tax reform. Although there does remain some scope for widening the tax net, this is a sphere that has witnessed some extremely positive measures. The outcomes of what may be described as the first phase of fiscal restructuring have been partly successful; however, the second phase has yet to gather to momentum. During what maybe termed as its subsequent phase, fiscal policy restructuring has to align itself, or do so more overtly, to the developmental imperatives with which the country is confronted. The unfinished agenda of fiscal policy in the next few years concerns reducing the fiscal and revenue deficits; the rather contentious political debate and acrimonious differences that this continues to evoke has caused procrastination in the process of fiscal restructuring. This process entails much more than cutbacks in government expenditure.

Over the last two decades, savings from the household and private corporate sector have risen; the former has increased from 16 per cent of GDP in the 1980s to about 22 per cent in 2002–3 and the latter has risen from 18 per cent of GDP to 26 per cent over the same period. As indicated in Table 4.3 gross domestic saving has increased to 32.4% (2005–06) The laggard has been public saving, which has declined from 2.4 per cent of GDP to −2.3 per cent in 2002–3. Thus, on aggregate, there has been a modest increase in gross domestic savings; however in effect, the surplus generated in the private sector has been partially offset by the downslide in public investments.

Fiscal deficits that arise as a consequence of investments in infrastructure expansion, which would have enhanced the productive capacity of the economy, need to be differentiated from those that persist because of the proliferation of non-developmental expenditures. This included rising government and debt and interest payments, increases in government wages and pensions, weak tax revenue performance, rising subsidies for fertilizers, power and water. A noteworthy point that needs to be reiterated insofar

*Table 4.3*  Savings and Investment in the Indian economy (%)

|  | 2000–1 | 2003–4 | 2004–5 | 2005–6 |
|---|---|---|---|---|
| Gross Domestic Savings | 23.4 | 29.7 | 31.1 | 32.4 |
| (a) Public | −1.9 | 1.2 | 2.4 | 2.0 |
| (b) Private | 25.3 | 28.5 | 28.7 | 30.4 |
| (i) Household | 21.0 | 23.8 | 21.6 | 22.3 |
| Financial | 10.2 | 11.3 | 10.2 | 11.7 |
| Physical | 10.8 | 12.4 | 11.4 | 10.7 |
| (ii) Private Corporate | 4.3 | 4.7 | 7.1 | 8.1 |
| Gross* Domestic Investment | 24.0 | 28.0 | 31.5 | 33.8 |
| Public | 6.9 | 6.3 | 7.1 | 7.4 |
| Private | 16.5 | 19.4 | 21.3 | 23.6 |
| Valuable | 0.7 | 0.9 | 1.3 | 1.2 |
| GDCF* | 22.8 | 24.8 | 26.3 | 28.1 |
| Change in stocks | 0.6 | 0.8 | 2.0 | 2.9 |
| errors and omission | 0.7 | 0.9 | 1.3 | 1.2 |
| Savings and Investment Gap | −0.6 | 1.6 | −0.4 | −1.3 |
| Public | −8.8 | −5.2 | −4.7 | −5.4 |
| Private | 8.8 | 9.2 | 7.4 | 6.9 |

*GDCF: Gross Domestic Capital Formation
*Source*: Central Statistical Organization, Government of India.

as subsidies are concerned is that if the beneficiaries consisted of lower income groups it would have to be viewed as a developmental expenditure. However, this is not the case. Similarly, if the increases in the wages and salaries (excluding pensions) of government functionaries are matched by increments in productivity, it would have resulted in a better performance in the public sector. Furthermore, although fiscal deficit over the period 1999–2000 to 2002–3 was slightly higher than in the preceding period of 1987–8 to 1990–1 and yet primary and capital expenditure was much lower.

The fundamental objective of reducing the deficit is often sidetracked by the fervent and intense lobbying of a melee of vested interests pitted against each other. If fiscal restructuring is to act as an instrument for development, then it is absolutely essential that the recommended reduction in the deficit is not achieved at the expense of development. This means that reducing non-developmental expenditure should be accompanied by the expedient redirection of resources released therein into developmental activity, for instance, infrastructure provision.

Sadly, fiscal adjustment in the post-liberalization or, as some would call it the post-reform era has partly been facilitated by the reduction in public investment. Social-sector expenditure stood at 2.7 per cent of GDP over 2000–1, even ten years after liberalization. This is certainly not a feature that one would anticipate in a country that has set out sustainable growth as one of its fundamental goals. Social-sector allocation remains too low; during 2005–6 the allocations to health (including family welfare) and education stood at a meager 0.263 per cent and 0.451 per cent of GDP respectively. Furthermore, the allocation made towards women and child development stood at 0.097 per cent and the provision for rural development accounted for 0.602 per cent of GDP. For that matter, budgeted expenditures for urban development (including urban poverty alleviation programmes) was only 0.072 per cent of GDP.

The enactment of the Fiscal Responsibility and Budget Management Act in 2004 targeted a reduction in the fiscal deficit to 3 per cent of GDP by 2009; it also targets a reduction of the revenue deficit to zero in this year. This measure could have been hailed as fiscal prudence if the brunt of the slated reduction had not been borne by the social sector.

The fact that there is a significant component of non-developmental expenditure in the fiscal deficits, which can be reduced, is a consideration that cannot be overlooked. Over the year 2004–5, the estimated allocation towards planned capital expenditure, which is generally utilized for building infrastructure, was brought down from Rs537 billion to Rs477 billion. On the other hand, items of non-planned expenditure, which is generally used to finance government consumption, has increased significantly over the last decade or so. Assigning more importance to non-planned expenditure than to public investment represents a lopsided order of priorities that economic reform has to address.

Preserving the political economy of underdevelopment costs and the decline insofar as public saving is concerned represents a fraction of this; however, even more costly are the repercussions of this and the limits that it imposes on productive capacity. Perhaps it would be apt to revisit a central proposition of Keynesian theory, which elucidated that public investment

*Table 4.4*  Gross domestic saving and investment

| Country | Gross domestic saving | | | Gross domestic investment | | |
|---|---|---|---|---|---|---|
| | 1971–80 | 1981–90 | 1991–6 | 1971–80 | 1981–90 | 1991–6 |
| China | 35.8 | 30.8 | 40.3 | 33.9 | 30.5 | 39.6 |
| India | 20.5 | 21.2 | 22.2 | 20.5 | 22.4 | 23.6 |
| Indonesia | 21.6 | 30.9 | 30.2 | 19.3 | 29.3 | 31.3 |
| Korea | 22.3 | 32.4 | 35.2 | 28.6 | 30.6 | 37.0 |
| Malaysia | 29.1 | 33.2 | 37.6 | 24.9 | 30.6 | 38.8 |
| Philippines | 26.5 | 22.2 | 16.5 | 27.8 | 22.0 | 22.2 |
| Singapore | 30.0 | 41.8 | 48.1 | 41.2 | 41.7 | 35.1 |
| Thailand | 22.2 | 27.2 | 34.6 | 25.3 | 30.0 | 41.0 |

*Source*: Reserve Bank of India, *Report on Currency and Finance* (2004).

would result in an increase in incomes that would be a multiplier or multiple of the initial investment outlay.

Economic progress may be abounding in certain sectors of the Indian economy but, in aggregate, it is far below the country's economic potential. India has a multitude of growth opportunities, of which only a proportion have been tapped. A major reason for this is a declining rate of net capital formation in the public sector.

It is interesting to note that at a similar stage of economic progress savings and investment rates in East Asia were much higher than the prevalent levels in India. This is indicated in Table 4.4. It is unlikely that the East Asian 'miracle' would have stretched for over a decade if public investments did not increase.

## Conclusion

Efficient, effective and expedient strategy implementation is among the most vital inputs that the country requires. It is not weaknesses in strategy formulation but delivery systems though which measures are implemented that need to be strengthened. This is at the heart of economic reform in the ensuing phase. There are umpteen instances that would corroborate this point; among the most recent and apt examples is the National Common Minimum Programme which was announced in 2004, that targeted an increased allocation towards public expenditures on health and education.

The National Employment Guarantee Scheme will require Rs650,000 million per annum. The National Common Minimum Programme (NCMP) also envisages that the expenditure on health and education should increase from 1.5–3 per cent in the instance of the former and from 3–6 per cent in the instance of the latter. Allocations for the Department of Health and the Department of Family Welfare have been increased from Rs84,200 million in the year to Rs10,2800 million. The imminent question that arises is whether resource mobilization on the scale required would be feasible at least over the short term.

Understandably, attaining this objective will not be easy; the simple, unequivocal and uncomplicated fact is that it is among the most essential investments that need to be made to sustain growth. Commercial enterprises and corporate houses invariably manage to raise investments to fund their projects, however difficult a proposition mobilization of finance may seem at the outset. Regardless of the dissimilarities in the incentive structures underlying business houses and infrastructure provision and other development schemes, the moot point is that an unstinted endeavour to harness resources is something that is likely to require an innovative approach (without increasing the tax burden) towards fund mobilisation.

Furthermore, the productivity of existent outlays in the social sector should be increased and allocative and other forms of inefficiencies should be minimized. On the subject of outlays, an aspect of strategy formulation that is overlooked pertains to the design of procedures that would help facilitate the cost-effective and efficient implementation of projects and programmes initiated. This is a measure that would considerably reduce the leakages from the actual disbursements made towards social-sector outlays and this would translate into a discernible improvement insofar as project completion is concerned.

The National Common Minimum Programme is by no means sufficient to tackle the inadequacies in social infrastructure provision but if effectively implemented it would be a stride in the direction of reducing the shortfall in the social sector. Furthermore, it may be a precedent for similar subsequent programmes. The problems that it is confronted with are not so much to do with resource mobilization as with inefficiency and, in certain instances, inexpedient implementation.

Prior to the NCMP, the targets were set out by the tenth plan, some of these goals included:

- Reduce infant mortality rates to 45 per 1000 by 2007;
- Reduce maternal mortality rates to 2 per 1000 live births;
- Ensure that all children complete schooling by 2007;
- Reduce gender disparity in literacy by at least 50 per cent by 2007;
- Reduce poverty by 5 per cent by 2007 and another 15 per cent by 2012.

Progress made so far falls short of the targets specified.

Electoral support for reform measures is also divided. There are substantial factions of the population that do not see or are not aware of the inextricable link that reform has with propelling development. It seems rather absurd that even after liberalization has entered the second decade (since its inception in 1991) there exists, particularly at the lower end of the socio-economic hierarchy, a blatant lack of awareness about the crucial role that reform has in economic progress. This information gap cannot be described as an inadvertent outcome and set aside as a fact that can be wished away. Undeniably, reform is seen by certain segments of society as inimical to their interest. Herein, a distinction needs to be made between those groups that have at stake certain gains (in terms of subsidies, power theft, rent-seeking) in stalling the process of reform and those socio-economic categories that have either misperceptions or are almost clueless about the what is meant by reform. It is vital that the information gap is bridged by the media, as well as certain pressure groups in civil society, including citizen's groups, NGOs, academics and all those in the well-informed echelons of society whose role in expanding and consolidating the political economy of development is a critical one.

## Appendix

The exigency of resolving supply–side constraints has become all the more evident with the recent rise in the prices of essential commodities such as food grains and vegetables in the Indian economy. As such during the second week of February 2007 it increased to 6.78 per cent when compared to the inflation rate of 3.98 per cent during the same period last year. The apparent causes that may have fuelled this price rise may be the increasing economic growth rate and the recent oil price rise, however the fundamental reason that underlies this are supply-side constraints which arise because of the generic inadequacy infrastructure provision and the shortage in the production of wheat and other cereals which has stagnated over the last few years. Thus reining in inflation through monetary or demand management policies which involve restricting the supply of liquidity by raising interest rates would, at best, be a quick fix.

According to the Economic Survey (2006–7), 'In India, with unemployment, both open and disguised, concerns about overheating are connected more with capacity utilization and skill shortages. Rapid growth in capacity addition through investments can avert the problem of capacity constraints.'

In the context of inflation the survey says that a durable solution would be to increase the yields and domestic output of pulses, edible oils, rice and wheat. Furthermore it mentions the tremendous scope there is in raising yield levels through technology diffusion.

# 5
# India: Unleashing Opportunity Creation

## Introduction

India has finally broken through the boundaries of the Hindu rate of growth of about 4 per cent per annum but, over the last decade, although the country's growth has increased significantly employment has lagged far behind.

In the Indian context, achieving sustainable development becomes even more exigent even as India's tremendous economic potential becomes increasingly manifest in the global economy. The imminent question is: will its rising growth rates propel development and employment creation at a pace that is fast enough to transform it into a developed nation within the next few decades? The previous chapter analyzed the role that the political economy of underdevelopment has had in deterring economic progress and the pivotal significance of economic reform in propelling development. This takes us on to an analysis of the fundamental issues that concern employment and opportunity creation in the Indian context. Chapters 5 and 6 will analyze fundamental issues pertinent to stepping up the momentum of opportunity creation.

India has a larger proportion of its population in the working age group of 15–64 than any other country in the world. This gives it what may be termed as a demographic dividend and the Goldman Sachs report and some other projections suggest that India will, as a consequence, have a declining dependency ratio. According to Rodrik-Subramaniam's study, the country's dependency ratio will decline from 0.62 per cent in 2000 to 0.48 per cent in 2025. Furthermore, it cites that the 14 per cent decrease in dependency ratio will translate into an approximate increase in private and aggregate savings from about 25 per cent of GDP to 39 per cent.

When a country has among the youngest populations in the world it means an expanding consumption base. All's well if the country reaps the favourable demographics; at this point in time it is poised only partially to do so because of the rather sluggish growth in employment. Over the period

1993–4 to 1999–2000 the Indian economy had an average growth rate of over 6 per cent per annum; however, according to the tenth plan estimates employment grew at hardly 1 per cent per annum. It should be noted that the labour force was increasing by over 2 per cent during this period. Notably, even if employment registers a modest increase it would result in significant market expansion and this would boost the country's commercial prospects, including its attractiveness as a foreign investment destination, even further. Having said this, from the perspective of development it is absolutely essential that employment is provided to the maximum in the minimum possible time.

There have been several studies about the reasons for this rather slack uptake in employment in the Indian economy: some of these include a rather capital-intensive mode of production in the manufacturing sector, exigently required labour reform (that is still waiting to happen) and an overall decline in the growth rate of the agriculture sector, which is so far the largest provider of employment. Added to this, measures that stifled entrepreneurship, a political economy that did not do much to increase levels of efficiency and staggered the implementation of large-scale projects, along with a host of antiquated laws are among some of the numerous reasons underlying the slow pace of employment creation. Thus, singling out a cause for present problems of unemployment would be a partisan interpretation.

Fundamentally, the rather lacklustre performance in the ambit of job creation is the culmination of a policy framework and macroeconomic environment that has inadvertently slackened investment in employment-intensive activities, such as infrastructure provision.

Juxtapose the current unemployment situation with the fairly pronounced intent of India's planners to create employment. As a matter of fact, one of the objectives of the public-sector enterprises was to provide employment and, although this goal was served in the initial years, it became evident that there was much more to creating jobs than specifying targets and filling vacancies. In any case, by mid-1970s it was rather obvious that the scope to do so was determined mainly by the growth rates and productivity levels, both of which were at best moderate.

The reality is that, more often than not, policies pursued have a rather disembodied or myopic view of either employment or growth. The consequence of this was pronouncedly manifest prior to liberalization, apparent against a backdrop of compressed demand and low productivity. Inevitably, as is the case with other developing countries, India continues to be confronted with the problem of rampant unemployment, the prevalence of which results in growth compression over the longer term.

As the adage goes, the market always gets it right; however, sometimes we, as individuals or companies, do not read the market as accurately as we should. Employment provides us with one such instance where we have not grasped or rather not responded in consonance with market signals. The manifestation of this has been the phenomenon of compressed demand. (The prevalence of low demand could be the outcome of many factors. In a developing country that has a growth rate such as India's, it is very probable that a deficiency of demand, particularly for essential goods, is the result of a lack of purchasing power.)

When companies undertake market surveys one of the objectives is to find avenues for tapping potential demand or increasing demand where it is found to be insufficient. In the context of development it is absolutely vital that we pursue a similar principle. It is obvious that we haven't. Delving into the main causes for sluggish demand holds the key to understanding what would constitute the solutions for employment. The following section will elucidate important aspects about trends in opportunity creation and employment in the Indian economy.

## Growth creation and slackened employment growth in the Indian economy: an analysis

Arthur Lewis's theory of economic dualism presents a vivid enumeration of the processes involved in the structural transformation of an economy. Lewis's model was a two-sector model, consisting of an industrial sector and subsistence (agricultural) sector. Simply expressed, the defining tenet/principle was the absorption of surplus labour from the subsistence agricultural sector by the expansion of the industry. The process continues until the supply of excess labour in the former is exhausted, after which wage rates in the agricultural subsistence sector begin to increase. Trends in most advanced countries during the emergence of their industrial economy were fundamentally similar to what Lewis described.

In the Indian context, although the pattern of structural transformation does corroborate some elements of the Lewis model, there are certain fundamental differences between the transitional pattern that the model describes and the Indian economic experience. At the outset, the most obvious point of difference is that only a fraction of its 'surplus labour' has been absorbed by the country's industrial sector. At the lower end of the income hierarchy, in the rural economy, there is a sizable segment that were simply not absorbed by either the agricultural or the manufacturing sector.

India is a highly industrialized country and, according to the precepts of conventional economic thought (many of which have been validated), this should have meant a receding importance of the agricultural sector. Although for all practical purposes we may say that India has made the transition from an agricultural to an industrial economy this has certainly not meant that agriculture was relieved of its role as an important provider of employment. This feature stands in veritable contrast to the experience of a number of advanced countries where the emergence of an industrial sector absorbed the surplus labour released from the agricultural sector.

Furthermore, as we have seen, unlike in the developed world the transition (in terms of sectoral importance) made by the Indian economy and some other developing countries from an agricultural to an industrial and then to a services sector was certainly not fuelled by a generalized increase in per capita income across all socio-economic categories.

In essence, the impetus that would come from a surge in demand for products of the agricultural sector and for those from the manufacturing and services sector will unequivocally propel an increase in employment creation. This was a sequence that occurred in a limited way and not as a pervasive phenomenon in the Indian context.

Engel's Law states that, as a consequence of rising incomes, the share of expenditure on food declines. It must be noted that Engel found, based on surveys of families' budgets and expenditure patterns, that the income elasticity of demand for food was relatively low. The resulting shift in expenditures affects demand patterns and employment structures. Engel's Law does not suggest that the consumption of food products remains unchanged as income increases. It suggests that consumers increase their expenditure for food products (in percentage terms) less than their increases in income. Thus, understanding changing consumption and demand profiles as incomes rise could aid analysis about the link between sectoral transition and the shift in employment patterns. Income elasticity of demand for food declines when incomes rise.

According to the latest National Sample Survey, expenditure on food items accounted for 43 per cent of total consumption expenditures in urban India (during 2004–5). This represents a significant decline from the share of 64 per cent that food expenditures had in total expenditures of urban India over the period 1972–3.

In rural India too, the proportion of spending on food has reduced from 73 per cent over 1972–3 to 55 per cent over 2004–5. Although the survey indicates that Engel's Law does apply in certain income groups of the country's population, it also cites that 10 per cent of India's rural population lives on just Rs9 per day and 10 per cent of its urban population subsist on a slightly higher Rs13 a day. Furthermore, the expenditure on food as a proportion of total consumption is lower in states with a higher per capita expenditure and vice versa.

Thus, unlike in advanced countries, Engel's Law does not apply to a fairly significant proportion of the low-income groups in developing countries. Although it would be convenient to describe a landless labourer who can barely afford two square meals as someone with a low elasticity of demand, it would be outrageous to consider this to be the result of Engel's Law operating. By no means does the subsistence and small farmer comprise a small minority of India's agricultural economy; as a matter of fact that group constitutes a significant proportion of the rural population.

For those in the primary sector that are unemployed or employed at wages that are highly inadequate it would take some time for Engel's Law to operate because incomes would have to increase by a certain extent before the proportion of expenditure allocated to food and other agricultural products declines. Those who currently live on the margins of subsistence will have a higher income elasticity of demand for food in the initial stages of a rise in income. When demand for food is low as a result of a lack of purchasing power it represents a potential for growth that will obviously remain untapped until incomes among the poor increase.

The story of compressed demand continues even as we view the manufacturing and services segment. Over the last four decades the strides taken by Indian manufacturing have been remarkable. Even as it traversed a phase during which its progress was dampened, when it was not as competitive and efficient as it is in current times, there was at some stage a declining demand for manufactured goods and an increasing one for the output of the services sector. Once again, the transition to the services sector, in terms of its 50 per cent contribution to the GDP at this stage of the country's per capita income growth, is rather unusual.

Economic experience has demonstrated that the emergence of the services sector as the most important one occurs when a country's per capita incomes are high because, although India's per capita incomes have increased significantly it cannot be considered high (at this point in time, India is a middle-income country). As might be expected, in the higher income categories individuals would allocate a higher proportion of their incomes to services. Consonant with this, an increase in the employment absorption of those who comprise the skilled and educated segments of the population by the services sector is hardly surprising.

However, what is rather unique is the importance that the service or the tertiary sector has had in providing employment to those in the lower income groups. The service sector has acted as a safety net of sorts. At the lower end, this sector has provided an avenue of livelihood to millions (who would otherwise have been without any means of sustenance) and it consists of a fairly diverse spectrum of service providers that have little or no skill. As a matter of fact, a sizable proportion of this segment constitutes the informal economy of the country. More often than not, the wages that the labour force in country's informal economy receives are highly inadequate and frequently lower than the minimum wage prevalent (for the same task in the organized sector). Thus, constrained or compressed demand for products of the agricultural sector does place limits on the demands for manufactured goods.

When demand for food is low as a result of a lack of purchasing power it represents a potential for growth that will obviously remain untapped until incomes among the poor increase. Consequently, employment growth has been far from satisfactory and it is this feature that has spawned the expansion of the country's vast unorganized sector. Herein, we have an instance of compressed growth, which arises from the deficiency of purchasing power

*Table 5.1*    Trend growth rate in employment (%)

|  | Manufacturing | ASI total |
|---|---|---|
| 1973–4 to 1990–1 | 1.6 | 1.6 |
| 1990–1 to 1997–8 | 3.1 | 3.4 |
| 1997–8 to 2001–2 | −3.3 | −5.8 |

*Source: Economic and Political Weekly*, 20 November 2004. Estimates are based on the annual survey of industries in India.

and not from a natural decline of expenditure allocations towards food and related products. This accentuates the imperatives of achieving an expansion of income across an entire gamut of socio-economic categories in India. Given that it is likely that India will have an average growth rate of 7–8 per cent per annum over the next few years, in this context the imminent question that arises is whether this will result in employment or not. Even if one were to be cold-bloodedly pragmatic, a fundamental fact is that the Indian economy cannot afford the option of jobless growth.

During the initial years, the measures used to increase levels of employment were unfortunately at the expense of efficiency. In the years during liberalization the compelling need to become competitive meant an increase in the levels of efficiency across practically every category of industry. Unfortunately, this meant a decrease in the rate of employment. The efficiency–employment trade-off is not unique to India alone, it is a feature that has emerged in a number of developing countries. More often than not, the flip side of being competitive is reducing levels of employment.

The broad conclusion that emanates from trends in the manufacturing sector during economic liberalization and subsequently is that the score on employment creation has been rather disappointing. The expansion and an enhanced extent of technical upgrading in the manufacturing sector did lead to a rise in industrial productivity but it did not result in a commensurate increase in employment. (Table 5.1 indicates the trends in employment creation in the ambit of Indian manufacturing.)

At this point it would be relevant to present an overview of the impact that liberalization has had on the Indian manufacturing sector.

## The impact of liberalization on the manufacturing sector in India: trends in productivity, output expansion and employment creation

There was a decline in total factor productivity (TFP) during the 1970s and it was a reorientation of business and trade policies that resulted in an increase in total productivity during the 1980s. Some studies indicate that total factor productivity accelerated in the country's industrial sector during the 1980s and there are other estimates that reveal that this is an exaggerated inference insofar as the extent of total factor productivity growth is concerned. However, undoubtedly the 1980s was a phase during which productivity that had slackened in the preceding decade began to rise. Furthermore, the results that a changing macroeconomic environment would have on productivity became rather obvious with the initiation of partial liberalization.

Total factor productivity did increase during the 1990s and, although a number of studies corroborate this rather anticipated outcome, there are some that refute this inference. According to a study that was undertaken by Unel, TFP growth in aggregate manufacturing and many subsectors accelerated after the 1991 reforms. Unel estimates that the annual average growth rate in TFP in aggregate manufacturing was 1.8 per cent per annum over the period 1979–80 to 1990–1 and 2.5 per cent per annum for the period 1991–2 to 1997–8.

An increased growth in TFP in the ambit of the Indian manufacturing sector was also the inference of a study undertaken by Tata Services (2003). This study estimated that the average annual growth rate of GDP in manufacturing stood at 0.68 per cent over the period 1981–2 to 1992–3. It was 0.97 per cent over 1993–4 to 1999–2000. (Estimates of TFP calculated by various studies, including those by Unel and Tata Services, are indicated in Tables 5.2.)

However, unlike the inference of the two studies mentioned, the study undertaken by Goldar and Kumari concluded that the trend growth rate of TFP in Indian manufacturing reduced from 1.89 per cent per annum during the period 1981–2 to 1990–1 to 0.69 per cent over the span 1990–1 to 1997–8.

A recent report by Goldman Sachs (January 2006) about India's rising growth potential cites that India's 'growth acceleration since 2003 represents a structural increase rather than simply a cyclical upturn'. The study explains that it is the turnaround in manufacturing productivity growth that has been one of the main drivers of the country's improving growth performance. It must be noted that the report estimates that TFP has increased from 1.3 per cent during 1990–9 to 3.5 per cent over 2003–5.

*Table 5.2* Total factor productivity growth in Indian manufacturing

| Years | Unel estimates (2003) |
|---|---|
| 1979–80 to 1990–1 | 1.80 |
| 1991–2 to 1997–8 | 2.50 |
| Tata Services study (2003) | |
| 1981–2 to 1990–1 | 0.49 |
| 1991–2 to 1999–2000 | 1.20 |

*Source*: Tata Services Study, *Economic and Political Weekly*, 20 November 2004.

Productivity improvements have been the cumulative outcome of increased competition that has been the result of liberalization, advances in information technology and, financial sector reforms. The report cites that the movement of surplus labour from agriculture to more productive sectors of industry and services contributes about 1 per cent of the GDP increase. It is the expeditious and extensive expansion of productive capacity that will step up the rather constrained employment absorption by industry and services.

One reason for differing inferences of research findings about the same subject is the variety of methodologies on the basis of which estimates are arrived at. If calculations made differ but inferences arrived at are similar it does corroborate a proposition. There is also a distinct possibility that if inferences are divergent there are aspects of an issue or a parameter that need to be scrutinized. In the instance of TFP in Indian manufacturing during the post-liberalization phase, even if one accepts the plausible contention that productivity in Indian manufacturing increased, it is evident that the increase could have been much higher if infrastructure provision expanded. This, however, was not the case. Alternatively, if one accepts the apparently unlikely conclusion that TFP declined it underscores that, from a macroeconomic standpoint, the next turnaround in the country's productivity would be propelled by a large-scale provision of infrastructure.

Trends in output (value added) and employment creation are indicated in the Box 5.1.

---

## Box 5.1    Broad trends in the manufacturing sector

### 1984–90: Partial liberalization

The upswing in India's industrial economy that occurred during the partial liberalization phase over 1984–90 did achieve a fairly high growth rate in value added output in the organized sector, along with an increase of capital by 6 per cent and there was a rather meagre increment in employment of 0.65 per cent. Some of the industries that witnessed an increase in growth included clothing, paper and paper products, intermediate goods (such as chemicals and their by-products, coke and refined petroleum, rubber and plastic products), consumer goods (such as accounting machinery, radio, television and communications), medical, precision and optical instruments.

The reason for the rather encouraging performance of the spheres mentioned was the high rates of protection accorded to the chemicals industry. Furthermore, as the tariffs on most capital goods declined the protection availed by certain other industries reduced and this led to a slowdown in the realm of electrical machinery, fabricated metal products, transport equipment and motor vehicles.

Not surprisingly, the unorganized sector was dealt a blow during this phase. It had a negative growth in capital and employment. Interestingly, as was the case in the organized segment of Indian industry, chemicals and chemical products, along with rubber and plastic products, comprised the most rapidly growing spheres of the unorganized sector.

Evidently the partial or pre-liberalization phase marked the beginning of an adjustment that Indian industry has had to make towards gearing itself to higher levels of competitiveness. Employment increased marginally; employment elasticity in the organized sector was only 0.09 per cent and in the unorganized sector it was negative.

## 1989–90 to 1994–5: The first phase of liberalization

Quite unlike the previous phase, employment in the organized sector rose by an average of 2.1 per cent during this phase. As a matter of fact, over the period 1992–3 to 1994–5 employment increased by 4 per cent per annum in the organized sector. Interestingly, a sizable proportion of labour absorption occurred in smaller and medium-sized factories and the maximum employment growth was in clothing, rubber products, petroleum products, paper products and coke. Employment elasticity in the organized sector increased from 0.09 per cent to 0.26 per cent during this phase.

The scenario in the unorganized sector of manufacturing was not a positive one through this period and, with a negative growth in value added output and employment, this was a sector that bore the adverse effects of liberalization. Manufacturing in the unorganized sector witnessed a negative growth of employment of −1.7 per cent and the growth in value added output was also negative.

Importantly, a similarity between the organized and unorganized sectors that became observable during this phase was that both were characterized by an increasing capital intensity of production, which was not accompanied by a rise in capital productivity.

This was attributable to the capital-intensive pattern of production that was adhered to even in a labour-intensive industry such as the consumer goods sphere. Reliance on imports, antiquated labour laws and labour unrest in the textile sector, which led eventually to the closure of the textile mills, created a situation where capital utilized was labour-displacing rather than employment-enhancing in most industries. Those spheres that had a high employment elasticity did

## Box 5.1   (Continued)

not generate an increasing number of jobs. Thus, although overall industrial performance was encouraging, the impact it had on expanding employment was marginal.

On the whole, manufacturing had a growth in value added output of 8.3 per cent during this phase. Easing the curbs on imports of raw materials, intermediate inputs and capital goods and an increased access to better technology facilitated policies that made technology transfer easier. This meant that companies were not compelled to rely on suboptimal inputs and obsolete technology.

The highlight of this encouraging performance during the first phase of liberalization was the expansion of an entire range of consumer goods industries, such as clothing, watches and clocks, radio, television and other communication devices, and some others. Evidently, this was a sphere that had been a laggard in the phase preceding liberalization as a result of policies that were directed towards encouraging the creation of a base for the expansion of heavy goods industry.

When the situation changed the immediate benefit of this was apparent in the consumer goods sector. Interestingly, this was not merely a matter of correctly timed neo-liberal policies but largely the result of continued restrictions on the imports of consumer goods, even after the inception of liberalization. There are many who castigate this as a measure that distorted resource allocation in favour of the protected consumer goods sector. Although this is a contention that can be debated, even if one concurs with it for a moment the protection accorded to this sector had an upside. This becomes evident if we visualize a scenario where the imports of consumer goods were not restricted. Plausibly, this would have resulted in lower growth in value added output and a smaller increase in employment.

During the first phase there was ostensibly a political consideration in postponing the implementation of measures that would have dealt a hard-hitting blow to employment. Although this did elicit opposition from certain groups there was an economic rationale in adopting a cautious approach during the initial phase of liberalization.

### 1994–5 to 2000–1

The organized sector witnessed a slowdown in the high growth of value added output during this phase. Some infrastructural constraints and the vestiges of what had been an over-bureaucratized system did limit the expansion of the industrial sector. The reduction in tariffs continued and an important measure during this span was the delicensing of 15 small-scale industries. This facilitated the entry of larger firms into this sector. The performance of the unorganized sector was discernibly better; possibly, the expansion of the organized sector spilt over onto this segment, which had by this time reoriented itself to the changing scenario. The unorganized sector registered an employment growth of 2.1 per cent and value added output increased by 6.9 per cent. In the organized sector employment increased by 0.7 per cent and employment elasticity declined to 0.10 per cent; in the unorganized sector it was 0.45 per cent.

In the context of the Indian manufacturing sector it is evident that the employment absorption in most industries has ranged from low to moderate. The under or non utilization of labour-intensive patterns of production even in spheres that were labour intensive in industrial sector is a feature that did not change. Furthermore it would be unrealistic to expect the factor composition of industry to change over the short or medium term, however. The role that the unorganized sector has played insofar as employment provision is concerned cannot be deemed as insignificant and therefore it is necessary to incorporate this segment of industry into the mainstream so that it is provided with increased access to credit and training facilities. Plausibly, an impetus to a particular industry, if large enough, could provide a fillip to the expansion of the organized and unorganized sectors of the industry concerned.

## Conclusion

As India's economic experience demonstrates the causes that impede productivity and those which obstruct employment growth may be not be entirely similar. This explains the rise in productivity and a rather negligible increment in employment over the last decade. At this juncture, productivity and employment creation are prevented from increasing substantially as a result of the slow pace and paucity of infrastructure provision.

In his study Unel also cited that the share of labour's income in value added output reduced to 25 per cent from 40 per cent in the 1980s. At the sectoral level, the utilization of labour-saving technology was one reason that explains the rather weak link between improvements in the manufacturing sector and job creation. However, from in a wider context, when we bring in the role that the macroeconomic environment has in determining economic performance it is evident that an impetus to demand fuelled by an consistent increase in incomes would have led to a much better score on employment, even if technology used was labour-saving.

Among other benefits that stem from a more broad-based pattern of economic growth, it enables the expansion of sectors that are intrinsically labour intensive. A fair proportion of these are in the agricultural sector, which has been virtually excluded from the economic gains of liberalization. As demonstrated in this chapter, the employment elasticity of GDP growth in India has been rather low; this is an unfavourable feature that can deter sustained economic progress. Plausibly, it is likely that infrastructure provision and increasing demand for labour-intensive manufactured goods, particularly in the rural economy, would result in a rise in the employment elasticity. Importantly, the rise in employment elasticity needs to occur as expediently as possible and by an extent that is as substantive as possible. A gradual small increment in the employment intensity of GDP growth would have an impact that is observably far less significant than a faster and larger rise in employment elasticity.

Instead of assuming that the momentum of India's present levels of progress would result in an increase in labour intensity of production it is paramount that a concerted attempt is made, through policy and non-policy measures, to expand labour-intensive production.

# 6
# A Multisectoral Pattern of Economic Growth: Important Issues

The phrase 'service-led growth' has been used rather frequently in the post-liberalization era of the India's economy. A wide range of estimates corroborate that the contribution of the service sector has been increasing and steadily so over the last decade and a half. Concomitantly, there has been an increased usage of inputs of the service sector during liberalization. As mentioned in earlier chapters, it is a widely acknowledged fact that some of the country's cutting-edge core competences in the spheres of finance and information technology emanate from the service sector.

It would be tempting for us to underscore the commonly cited conclusion that it is the service sector that is the most important driver of growth in the Indian economy. Having said this, it is evident that a scenario where high growth rates in the service sector are not accompanied by significant growth in the manufacturing and agriculture spheres is certainly not conducive to equity and balanced economic development.

At the outset of this discussion it would be useful to view the empirical findings of a study by Sanjay Hansda about the intersectoral linkages between agriculture, industry and services. The study analyzed 115 activities across the three sectors and the aggregate level and the main empirical findings of this were that the intersectoral linkage was measured by the computation of direct and indirect measures of intensity for spheres in the agricultural, industrial and services sectors.

(i) In terms of the direct measure of intensity 34 out of 115 activities (30 per cent of the activities) had an agricultural intensity that was above 7 per cent of the gross output. Furthermore, the agriculture sector itself was of course the most agriculture intensive, with 68 per cent of the activities from this sector having an intensity that was above the average of 7.

(ii) 23 per cent of the activities in the industrial sector and only 8 per cent of those in the service sector had an agriculture intensity that was either average or above.

Hotels and catering was the only activity in the service sector that had an agriculture intensity that was above the average.

(iii) Notably, not a single agricultural activity had an industrial intensity that was above average. 57 of 80 industrial activities included in the study, or 71 per cent, had an industrial intensity that was above average. Three service activities, i.e. medical, health and railway and other transport services, had an industrial intensity that was above average. 56 out of 80 industrial activities are service intensive. Six out of 13 service activities had a service intensity that was higher than the average of 15 per cent of gross output. In terms of direct and indirect measures of service intensity, the most service-intensive industrial activities are computing, ships and boats and coal tar products.

(iv) Out of ten categories at the aggregate level, four including agriculture, allied activities, manufacturing and construction, are relatively agriculture intensive. Notably, the study depicts that none of the aggregate categories of services is agriculture intensive (in terms of direct and indirect measures of sectoral intensity).

(v) Three industrial categories – electricity, gas and water supply; manufacturing and construction; and of transport, storage and communication – have an industrial intensity that is above the average. At the aggregate level the economy can described as one that has a high industrial intensity; 50 per cent of activities analyzed in the study had an industrial intensity that was above average in terms of both direct and indirect measures of sectoral intensity.

(vi) Three industrial categories out of four – manufacturing, construction, electricity gas and water supply – and the two service categories of transport, storage and communication and trade, hotels and catering are found to be service intensive in terms of the direct measure. In terms of direct and indirect measures only the service category of transport, storage and communication has a services intensity that is above the average. Notably 63 out of 115 activities had a services intensity that is above the average.

The agricultural categories were neither industry nor services intensive.

On the basis of the findings of the study on intersectoral linkages certain crucial observations come to light. These are as follows.

There is an inextricable link between the manufacturing sector and the expansion of the service sector. Understandably, liberalization ushered in its wake the compelling need for Indian industry to tighten its belt and increase levels of efficiency and productivity. As manufacturing expands and adapts to a competitive environment it unleashed demand for a wide spectrum of services, some of which embodied highly specialized skill-intensive inputs.

An increased demand for services involving a higher degree of specialization, improvements in the co-ordination of production processes and delivery resulted in a boom in the services sector and an increase in skill-intensive employment. This was a positive outcome; however, it is also true that spheres with the highest employment elasticities, such as hotels and catering, tourism, personal services, construction, transport, storage and communications, have not expanded as much as some other spheres.

One fundamental reason for this is the lack of infrastructure provision, which has, as with other sectors, impeded the expansion of certain segments of the service sector. It should be noted that although existent patterns of growth are based on and have reinforced certain intersectoral linkages it is evident that a quantum increase in the level of investment made in the ambit of infrastructure provision, along with the expedient implementation of projects, would provide the much needed fillip to an entire gamut of products and services. A plausible outcome of this would be that existent sectoral links will be accompanied by new linkages. This is a critical point in the context of employment creation.

For instance, regardless of the rather weak linkage that may exist between agriculture and the services sector, the provision of certain services (a proportion of which can be described as infrastructural inputs) will certainly propel the expansion of the rural economy. In the light of this, I contend that there exists a definite intersectoral linkage, one that has remained largely untapped, between the rural economy and the services sector. Let's explore this point further.

If the rural economy (by which I mean the agricultural and non-agricultural sector taken together) had achieved significant growth rates over the last decade it would certainly have generated demand for a host of services spanning banking, finance, warehousing, storage and so on. The employment that this would have provided would have been substantial.

In rural regions there exists considerable scope for provision of other infrastructural inputs and, added to this, plugging the blatant lacunae of service-related inputs in a large proportion of the rural economy will have a discernible impact on employment generation. There exists a pressing need for a wide range of services, from micro-finance to health care and education, in practically every village of the country. Taking this point further, I delve into two important facets of the Indian rural economy. The first pertains to current trends in the agriculture sector and the second pertains to the emergence of the non-farm sector in a number of villages.

As indicated in Table 6.1, low levels of growth in the agricultural sector since the mid-1980s should not suggest that we have exhausted the potential for opportunity creation in either agriculture or the larger context of the rural economy. As a matter of fact, in a nation where agriculture continues to be the provider of employment, this is a rather dangerous inference to arrive at. The pronouncedly slackened pace of economic progress across many rural regions has partly been the result of lack of public investment in the agricultural sector. In spite of the increased allocations to irrigation by the tenth plan, the share of agriculture and rural development in the total plan outlay declined from 20.1 per cent by the ninth plan to 18.8 per cent by the tenth plan. Furthermore, there has been a reduction in private investment over the last few years and the inadequacy of rural infrastructure has persisted.

The mid-term appraisal of India's tenth five-year plan (2001–6) stated:

*Table 6.1*    Annual growth rate in agriculture and GDP

| Period | Growth rate in GDP of agriculture | Rate of growth in overall GDP |
|---|---|---|
| 1985–90 | 3.2 | 6.0 |
| 1990–2 | 1.3 | 3.5 |
| 1992–7 | 4.7 | 6.7 |
| 1997–2002 | 2.1 | 5.5 |
| 2002–3 | −7.0 | 4.0 |
| 2004–5 | 1.1 | 6.9 |

*Source: Economic Survey of India (2004–5).*

The objective of accelerating GDP growth to 8 per cent in the years ahead and achieving a more inclusive spread of benefits depends critically upon a reversal of trends in agriculture where growth has decelerated sharply from 3.2 per cent between 1980–81 and 1995–96 to a trend average of 1.9 per cent.

The average gross fixed capital formation in the economy was 26 per cent and in agriculture it was 16 per cent. Exigently required irrigation systems and an obvious dearth of marketing and storage and distributional facilities have eroded (literally speaking) the attractiveness of this sector.

This is one aspect of the problem; the other stems from a slow process of adjustment by the sector to market realities. As the per capita income of a nation increases there is usually a change in the composition of demand for agricultural products. On aggregate, the demand for non-cereal products increases and for cereals, particularly wheat and rice, it reduces. Having said this it must be noted that the lower income groups have positive income elasticities for wheat and rice. Although crop diversification is an imperative in this sector, however, the prerequisites that would facilitate this are either not available or unaffordable by the small farmer.

Another anomaly was that minimum support prices of wheat and rice were certainly out of alignment with what prevailed in the international market. At a time when the prices of these cereals were declining in world markets, the domestic prices of these products were much higher. In a developing country there are certain valid considerations that form the basis of having minimum support prices. This rationale may have held true for India about two decades ago but in present times a sizable proportion of the beneficiaries of this measure are the affluent or large-scale farmers. There could have been a countervailing advantage of the rather distortionist price structure that prevailed in the agricultural sector if rural infrastructure building had proceeded on course. As we know this was not the case. Instead, as it turned out, rats benefited immensely from the high minimum support prices of wheat and rice because of the huge surpluses of these grains that piled up as a consequence of the misaligned prices. Unfortunately, the 'surfeit' of food grains was not adequately distributed among the 260 million poor.

One of the major achievements of the country's primary sector has been its attainment of self-sufficiency in the production of food; this is evidently one of the main tenets of poverty reduction. However, an overtly skewed incentive system without an equal and opposite developmental dimension has resulted in an emerging disconnect between self-sufficiency and poverty reduction. The country cannot afford to stoke this.

Not surprisingly, minimum support prices remain one of the few levers through which politicians can extract mileage from the agricultural sector in India. The imminent question is whether it remains pragmatic to constrict the economic progress of the rural economy because of the vested interests of a few. The answer is no, because unleashing the forces of opportunity creation is, among other things, undoubtedly a more viable option.

Cognizance of a problem should fructify into attempts to resolve it; however, the agrarian sector in India continues to be characterized by an entire gamut of inadequacies that include: the absence of a proper crop insurance; spurious seeds and pesticides; serious water problems connected to drying up of ground water; lack of extension services, particularly for commercial crops; exploration of marketing; and lack of non-farming activities.

Measures directed towards overcoming these constraints would create a host of opportunities and yet not much is being done, even as the peasant economy in many parts of the country veers from one crisis to another.

The Economic Survey of India (2005–6) stated that, 'Agriculture suffers from low yields per hectare, volatility in production and wide disparities in production over regions and crops.' Furthermore, the survey enumerated that some of the emerging areas of high growth potential in this sector included horticulture, floriculture, organic farming, genetic engineering, food processing, branding and packaging. Despite the need for the agricultural sector to grow at a rate of 4 per cent per annum, its present average growth is 1.5 per cent per annum. As discussed earlier, rural infrastructure building will provide an impetus to the creation of employment either directly or indirectly. A noteworthy point is that calculations about the investment required for this purpose will hopefully take into account that the allocations made towards the minimum support price and the proportion of subsidies that are not availed of by the poorer sections of the agricultural community. It would be practical to consider redirecting a fraction of these resources towards the outlay required for rural infrastructure building, as it could very well expedite the process.

The emergence of the non-farm sector is another aspect that concerns the rural economy and employment generation. According to a study undertaken at the beginning of the 1990s, this segment of the rural economy provided 18–20 per cent of employment in the rural economy. Some instances of these include retailing, businesses related to wood products, furniture, land transport, textiles and other personal services.

Although at the aggregate level there is no clear evidence of growth in non-farm employment rates, studies at the village or district level reveal an expansion of non-agricultural employment. The proliferation of tea or foods stalls by the bus stop in villages and semi-rural areas and an increase in the number of bicycle and tractor repair shops over the last decade represent some instances of non-farm employment. Regardless of the amount of employment that has been generated by this sector, it holds considerable potential to create opportunities in the rural economy. Once again, the lack of infrastructure provision and the rather limited access to educational facilities has deterred the expansion of this segment of the economy.

The options for remunerative non-farm employment are negligible in the absence of education. It is interesting to note that, relative to those individuals who have no education at all, even primary education can improve the prospects, for tapping into the opportunities that exist in this sphere. In states characterized by low farm productivity, lack of social capital and consequently low living standards, the need for non-agricultural employment opportunities is pronounced and it is precisely in these regions that poorer sections are either not equipped to participate in the non-farm sector or they manage to enter into the lowest category, which would obviously constitute unskilled activities.

There should be more studies about the country's non-farm sector but, even at this point, the limited data available reveals two fundamental facts. Over the last decade, India's rural economy had a pace of economic progress that can at best be described as tepid. This was not an inevitability because a faster expansion of the non-farm sector and a quicker adjustment of the agricultural sector to the changing profiles of food grain consumption, coupled with better distributional facilities, would have provided the momentum for higher levels of opportunity creation.

Second, the expansion of skill-intensive activities did not happen out of thin air; the precedent to the boom in certain segments of the service sector was preceded and facilitated by the creation of a certain base of technical and managerial expertise. Taking the underlying principle further, if the rural economy was not confronted by the glaring inadequacy of physical and social infrastructure it would have witnessed the growth of an entire spectrum of services. The non-farm sector has demonstrated instances of a number of activities that are providing livelihood to some, and there exists the imminent possibility that these services could provide avenues of incomes to many more if basic infrastructural and organizational inputs are provided. Furthermore, it is pivotal in ensuring that forays of retail majors into the rural economy should not impede job creation.

India needs an employment revolution. In this context the issue is not merely about expanding the employment-absorption capacity of agriculture, but about increasing the options of non-farm employment. The scope for doing this is considerable (to say the least) and it would entail rural infra-structure provision, better systems of credit delivery, improving the supply of inputs to the smaller farmer and concerted initiatives in research and development that would enable crop diversification and soil conservation.

## The skill development paradigm

As mentioned earlier, the solution is not an ambiguous one: it would be tapping the immense opportunities that this country has for employment intensive projects. The proposition sounds a simple one but the fact that it has not happened as much as is required tells us that we have a distance to go before we start making inroads into job creation. The challenge that confronts India at the present juncture is to strengthen the currently weak nexus between employment growth and efficiency.

The tenth plan (2001–6) speaks about the creation of 40 million jobs and this would entail that the service sector grows at the rate of 82 per cent and the manufacturing sphere increases at the rate of 18 per cent. Once this happened, the promise of plenty would be delivered and we would have realized our growth potential. Agriculture's rather lacklustre performance, which was predictable, cannot become the pretext for wishing away the role that it has in ensuring that the country attains the slated growth projections.

The revival of rural economy continues to be largely reliant on agriculture; this should not be lost sight of. In this context, the extremely encouraging performance of manufacturing and services should not detract us from the crucial role of the agricultural sector.

India is evolving a skill development paradigm. The process began with tapping certain technical and knowledge-intensive core competences and we are beginning to witness the immense potential of a wide range of opportun-ities, some which have been explored, yet others that have been identified but remain untapped. There exists in absolutely every sector the opportunity to build a skill paradigm that is based on the expansion of core competences that exist and the identification of new ones.

Thus, it is the evolution of what maybe termed as multiple micro-skill paradigms in every sector of the Indian economy that will contribute to the building of a macro-skill development paradigm. When viewed in isolation, there are certain core competences that do not embody a potentiality for expansion that is immense. However, when taken in conjunction, building upon a wide range of existent untapped core competences will contribute significantly to employment provision and growth. India has managed to identify a host of opportunities that occupy the higher echelons of the skill development paradigm.

Policy and industry now need to sustain the expansion of the industries that conferred on it a distinct edge in technologically intensive manufacturing and services; however, policy and non-policy measures should extend its purview to those spheres that have an expansionary potential, even if these include a spectrum of moderately knowledge-intensive and non-technical opportunities.

It would useful to describe the inputs entailed for the evolution of the skill development paradigm. Be it at a sectoral level or at the organizational level, putting into place the paradigm mentioned requires three basic inputs; we could refer to these prerequisites as parameters. These are innovation, institutions and infrastructure provision. Thus, this paradigm may be termed the 3Is skill development paradigm. In the Indian context, as in the case of other developing countries, expediting the pace at which innovation occurs depends on having an appropriate institutional framework (and this includes policy measures) and on the presence of infrastructural inputs. Fundamentally, the impediment to stepping up the extent of opportunity creation results either from an inadequacy in the ambit of policy, such as its staggered formulation, or weaknesses in the process of implementation or from the dearth of physical and social infrastructure. Plugging deficiencies that arise as a result of weaknesses in these variables will most certainly facilitate a pattern of growth that is inclusive and sustainable.

India's present outsourcing boom and expansion in the services and manufacturing sectors are essentially based on the presence of knowledge-intensive skills, which were provided at a lower cost. India's present economic performance is the result of measures that were adopted decades ago. At this point in time the objective would be to ensure that that the current level of economic progress is sustained.

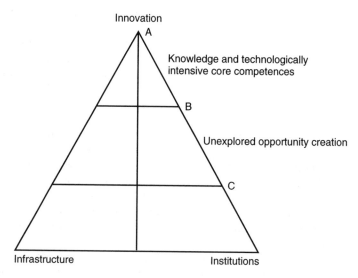

*Figure 6.1*   A diagrammatic depiction of the skill development paradigm

This means that government and industry in India has to set the stage, build the platforms for harnessing subsequent opportunities that would give to it the advantages that its present core competences do.

For purposes of analytical convenience I have drawn a diagrammatic depiction of the skill development or 3-I paradigm (see Figure 6.1).

# 7
# India's Economic Ascent: Insights and Issues

Lessons in retrospect are a valuable legacy that the past gives us and learning from them helps in the evolution of an effective strategy, which would be useful not merely in the Indian context but also for other developing countries.

It is obvious that geopolitics is a pivotal consideration in the present era of fast-paced globalization; however, even during earlier times, global circumstances wielded an influence on the policies that a country pursued. In 1947, when India had obtained independence, the world was recovering from the damaging onslaught of the Second World War, global markets were hardly functioning and the sharp ideological divide had a profound role in shaping foreign policies of most countries. Undoubtedly, this exerted a decisive influence in determining the economic strategies that India and other developing countries pursued. The challenge confronting India at the time was an immense one, not merely because it had resource constraints but because it had to handle the stupendous task of organizing and managing the inputs it had. Amid the scenario that existed at the time, the emphasis on industrialization was inevitable during the post-independence era in India.

It must be noted that India's bid to make progress was not taken very seriously Given the constraints (some of which were acute) and challenges that she had to grapple with, the appropriate path for the country seemed to be a production pattern that would prioritize the production of primary goods and light consumer goods. The advocacy of this, particularly by the advanced nations, was based on the rationale that India was better endowed to have a production structure that focused on the spheres where she had a comparative advantage. It is not as if Indian planning overlooked this line of thinking; the fact that it assigned importance to the attainment of self-sufficiency in the production of food-grains corroborates that it didn't. However, the policy agenda looked beyond the purview of what the country could have attained with greater ease to what it needed to attain to become self-reliant.

*Lesson*: As was suggested by a number of eminent economists in the initial phase of policy formulation, visualize for a moment that post-independence

India had not built the industrial base that she did and instead assigned importance mainly to primary-sector production and light consumer goods. Inevitably, the consequences for the nation would have been divergent and not nearly as promising. Given the geopolitical context that prevailed at the time, if India had relied exclusively on the imports of industrial goods it would at best become an exporter of primary commodities and not much more. The terms of trade are weighted against most agricultural commodities and if this had been the main thrust of the country's economic agenda it is extremely unlikely that India would have its present position in the global economy.

Two decades after independence there was economic progress but the fact that stood out and shouted itself hoarse was that the policies pursued and the resources allocated for the purpose could have had a more decisive impact on underdevelopment if processes of implementation and delivery systems functioned with a higher degree of efficacy. Having said this, time underscored the merit embodied in the projections and policies that had initially envisioned the crucial need to create a well-diversified industrial base. However, if this had happened in a milieu that fostered higher levels of efficiency, expediency and entrepreneurship the outcomes generated would have probably have been outstanding. Plausibly, India's goals would have been achieved over a decade ago.

*Lesson*: A partial inference from this would be that inward orientation and protectionism are the 'baddies' that resulted in the build-up of inefficiencies, distortive pricing and the regressive impact that the licence Raj had in subsequent years. Empirical evidence tells us that inward protectionist regimes can elicit higher levels of efficiency if the institutional framework and functioning therein is solidly based on high standards of integrity and transparency. In India, these standards existed at the time of independence and a few years thereafter; however, the political economy of unproductive rent-seeking yielded pressures that ultimately led to a systemic lapse so far as accountability was concerned.

Higher standards of accountability would have ensured that an entire gamut of incentives, concessions and privileges granted to certain sectors and industries, particularly those that operated in the public-sector domain were delivered to the intended recipients. This was not the case, and some instruments that could have been effective tools of development planning were rendered either partly or completely ineffective. One such instance was the subsidies allocated to the agricultural sector. As far as the private sector was concerned, the curbs on entrepreneurship were almost stifling. Excessive bureaucratic intervention at every stage of the production process involved in any industrial unit was a defining trait of the licence Raj; it was only a handful of businesses that could survive and thrive. Predictably, the absence of competition bred monopolies and the outcome of this was inefficiency, accompanied by technological obsolescence. The important issue that confronts developing countries in current times is to ensure that institutions, governance and politics are not completely outweighed by the entrenched vested interests of certain powerful rent-seeking lobbies. Thus, the pronouncedly inward orientation of the kind that existed in many developing countries about two decades ago or, more recently, the pursuit of neo-liberalism does not exonerate nations from having to cope with the rather dangerous possibility of having their institutions and governance predominated by vested interests that are inimical to economic progress. As a matter of fact, there is ample evidence that demonstrates that development is held to ransom by agendas that seek to promote short term political gain. This is a difficult obstacle that continues to slow the pace of development in India.

India may have unshackled itself from the licence Raj but the evolution of its political economy of development continues to be obstructed by the considerable number of 'special' interest groups that have thrived on the prevalence of underdevelopment. This is a fundamental ill that confronts many other developing countries and, thus, observing the manner in which India's developmental processes continue despite the deterrents that exist and may arise could very well be useful.

An integral aspect of the India story pertains to the impact that economic liberalization has had on India. It is interesting to note that, in the course of making the adjustment to liberalization, the country has evolved its own variant of liberalism. The IMF prescription of neo-liberalism that the nation may have agreed to conform to in the initial stages has taken on a much a broader dimension in the ensuing years. It is this that differentiates India's economic experience in the preceding decade from that of other developing nations. This certainly adds a useful perspective to empirical evidence about the features that will determine the outcomes of liberalization in any country. This fact takes us on to the reasons that made liberalization a positive instrument for the national economy.

First, India did not opt for liberalization too early; as a matter of fact, some would contend that the process was significantly overdue. Furthermore, despite all the setbacks that compelled the country to opt for market-friendly policies, when it did India was, by then, a mature industrial economy. However, when adjustment programmes and the conditionalities that comes with loan disbursements from international financial institutions dictate decision-making pertinent to a country's policies, production structures and in some cases even political trends, the form and content of liberalization is almost divergent from what exists in countries where pro-market policies are not the only cards on the economic agendas. The former has characterized a number of African and some Latin American countries, such as Argentina. For instance, regardless of the differences in India, China and East Asia's economic strategy, the similarity that comes forth is that liberalization was an important but not the only aspect of their policy formulation. Second, having liberalization serve the purpose of a corrective in an environment that is riddled with distortions in pricing and other denominators of the incentive structure, as was the case in India, does make it a constructive constituent of the growth process. In contrast, having it as the main thrust of a country's economic policy for a prolonged period of time can prove disastrous.

Excessive bureaucratic delays and vacillations in decision-making, particularly about important projects, is an irritant that continues to stall progress in the country. However, expediency does not imply an environment where decisions are taken in a hasty manner. It is amusing when one recalls that there are instances when the propensity of the country's governments to procrastinate has been advantageous, albeit inadvertently so. For instance, in 1997 when the East and South-East Asian market reeled under a financial crisis it certainly laid to rest the debate about whether India should opt for capital account convertibility at the time. Instead, if the nation had conceded to the pressures for having full convertibility on the capital account, the country would have been faced with the imminent possibility of financial instability and even crises. It is obvious that the nation was less prepared to tackle the problems that this would usher in its wake on the eve of the new millennium. Expediency, in the Indian context, means minimizing the lag between decision-making and implementation and it is this input that would propel economic progress to a much higher level.

Cutting across party lines, Indian governments have had a rather cautious approach towards permitting liberalization in the country's agricultural sector. The reason for this is obviously not rooted entirely in developmental considerations; there are rather influential vested interests that wield clout and attempt either to stagger the process of liberalization or have a policy package that would enable large-scale commercialization of agriculture.

However, even more important than the benefits that might accrue to some from liberalization of the agricultural sector are the measures that have not been taken or at least not implemented adequately to safeguard the interests of the smaller farmer, the landless labourer and all those who find themselves at the lowest levels of the socio-economic hierarchy. Shutting out Indian agriculture from the winds of liberalization does not seem a feasible option, even over the longer term. Although it is true that this is a sector that is replete with misallocated incentives and distortive pricing, liberalization could play a role in eliminating or at least reducing these. India's stand about issues related to agricultural liberalization at the WTO negotiations reflects that policy makers (regardless of their political affiliations) are cognizant of the importance of ensuring that any strategy of agricultural liberalization does not dampen poverty reduction. Formulating policies that would liberalize segments of India's agricultural sector and, in doing so, supplement and strengthen poverty reduction efforts would certainly be an achievement for the country. From the perspective of other developing countries, this would certainly embody some useful lessons in the context of chalking out pro-poor agricultural liberalization.

Some countries in the global economy contend that India remains one of the most protected countries, even after 15 years of liberalization; the reason underlying this claim is that the country's imports currently constitute less than 1 per cent of world imports. However, this would detract from one of the main lessons that emanates from the country's experience over the last decade. All in all, liberalization has worked successfully, and this despite being, as some say, among the most protected markets. This rather quirky fact could bear relevance to the contemporary developing world, particularly where liberalization hasn't delivered. India has demonstrated quite illustratively that liberalization does not deliver its promise of plenty merely because trade barriers are dramatically reduced at the drop of a hat or because every element of protectionism is relinquished.

As we have seen, the consequences of this in most underdeveloped countries (be this in Africa or Latin America) have been to exacerbate vulnerabilities, worsen imbalances in foreign exchange reserves and disparities of income and all of these culminate in an observable deterioration of well being. During the early 1990s the rather tumultuous effects of liberalizing markets in Russia and Eastern Europe, which were reasonably developed countries at the time, underscored that Big Bang liberalization brings with it a rather costly transitional process. Furthermore, it is important to differentiate a country that wraps up its economy in layers of protectionism, the impact of which is invariably detrimental, from one that protects the interests of its economy. Moreover, it is not as if nations that have had relatively free markets for over 50 years have relinquished every element of protectionism. Thus, India should not be castigated merely for having what some describe as a protectionist stance in certain crucial sectors.

India had, by the 1960s, managed the first major transition to modernization. Two decades after independence, the country had an the edifice of a development. This would consist not just of diversified domestic industry it would have the institutions: legal, constitutional, a judiciary that would not be a political appendage but be a distinctly independent entity. Added to this were its institutes of higher learning that placed considerable emphasis on science and technology and political structures that were ensconced within democratic systems. Evidently, these were elements that prevailed in the relatively advanced First World; it could be said that in a sense India had a superstructure of development – the lacunae that existed was the social and physical infrastructure. Despite having the prerequisites for development in almost full measure India continued to be a developing country. The lesson herein is important. Development is not merely about getting together a package of the required constituents (tangible and intangible), although undoubtedly this in itself is not a mean feat. Perhaps even more vital than harnessing the requisites for development is the task of effective utilization of inputs acquired. Be it the allocation of capital as envisaged by the national or state plans, or the implementation of projects, particularly infrastructure or optimizing the efficiency of resources deployed towards poverty reduction schemes, there were rampant inefficiencies. The reason stemmed from what can be described as an imbroglio of corruption, superfluous politicization and institutional inertia.

Although the fundamental task of putting together adequate infrastructure is a compelling and a difficult one, it is also true that if India did not have the superstructure that it had, economic reform would have been much more complex than it is at this point in time. Regardless of the some of the inherent weaknesses that strategies formulated may have had, it is unequivocal that making industrialization an overarching priority was based on sound economic rationale and much more. India's progress in certain sectors is the consequence of policies it pursued to lay the foundation of indigenous industry. The impact of measures initiated could have been more positive had these been properly implemented; however, to fault the formulation or conceptualization of the strategy itself is an incorrect inference.

Furthermore, it is unlikely that India would have been among most the important nations in the global economy if it had waited for a certain level of economic advancement before it had a democracy. It is interesting to note that even when the country was partly socialist it had certain attributes that would quintessentially be associated with neo-liberalism. Economic liberalization in the absence of concomitant or commensurate political liberalism was not an option that India had; as a matter of fact, this is a fundamental point of differentiation between India's and China's economic experience.

The conventional assumptions about what course and sequence economic transition will follow are only partly validated by the empirics of the growth experience in India and China. Among the most important insights that arise from the Indian economic experience is the possibility that a developing nation can evolve knowledge-intensive core competences; and have a competitive edge in technology-intensive products and services. Furthermore, the sizable contribution that the services segment makes to GDP in the Indian economy denoted that the tertiary sector can play an important role at a much earlier point in a nation's economic progress than conventional theory would have indicated.

Even the emergence of a rather sizable industrial sector is not necessarily accompanied by a contraction of the agricultural sector to a point where it becomes an insignificant sector. The coexistence of a relatively technically advanced industrial sphere with a primary sector that continues to be an important source of employment provision in India has some decisive implications, some of which have been overlooked. The model of development that was pursued in Northern Europe and the United States may have a certain degree of applicability to the urban and other industrialized segments of the Indian economy; however, it is hardly relevant insofar as the primary sector of the country are concerned. In the context of other developing countries, the lesson is that increasing levels of economic progress and industrialization does not mean that the agricultural sector will cease to matter. Recent empirical evidence that pertains to India and, to a lesser extent, China demonstrates that sustainability of growth entails higher levels of progress in the rural economy. Thus, the assumption that an expansion of the manufacturing sector and liberalization of trade alone will propel development or eliminate dualism is questionable.

For instance, India will remain a dualistic economy even though one can plausibly contend that the significance of the primary sector will reduce over the next few years, but this still does not mean that it would be rendered a miniscule sphere of insignificance. Present and foreseeable trends in the Indian economy have indicated that economic dualism is strength and not a weakness because it means more sources of growth, larger markets and the existence of more potential core competences. In the larger context of development strategy, this means that assigning importance to the industrial sector should not be tantamount to disregarding the significance of the agricultural sector in countries where it plays an important role in the economy.

Mitigating economic backwardness has been associated with the predominance of the industrial sector. However, empirical evidence in a number of developing countries also demonstrates that taking the focus away from the primary sector impedes poverty reduction initiatives and limits growth. Thus, although transition does bring with it a shift in sectoral importance this should not result in marginalization of the primary sector. India is an instance of a country with a vibrant industrial economy and yet this does not take away from it the imperatives of economic progress in the primary sector. This fact accentuates the importance of not overlooking this sector amid initiatives to expand industry in those countries that do not have a well-diversified industrial sphere.

*Lesson*: Thus, economic advancement in the Indian context does not require a gradual convergence to the pursuit of a particular prescription or model of growth. Unleashing economic progress in a particular sector would entail an approach that may possibly be distinct from the measures required for the expansion of another sphere. As India's growth strategy evolves it would in all likelihood be an amalgam of elements and principles derived from a range of growth models and economic prescription. Interestingly, a common deterrent encountered by practically every sector and subsector in India is the lack of infrastructure provision and it is this that constitutes the major impediment towards rapidly tapping other potential core competences. As India finds itself in the midst of a 'growth boom', the task that lies ahead is to ensure that this phase of economic buoyancy is sustained for as long a time as is possible. This requires that it puts into place a scenario that enables it to harness the maximum number of core competences in an expedient manner. Thus, when viewed in the context of sustainable development, the tenet of economic convergence takes on a wider connotation: for a developing nation it means converging to a situation where its economy finds itself proximate to the point of its maximum potential economic growth. Furthermore, an expedient pace of internal economic integration needs to accompany a brisk pace of external economic liberalization if the benefits of globalization are to accrue to a larger proportion of the country's population. A pronounced gap between the levels of economic progress across different regions, which would inevitably result in the prevalence of rather acute income disparities, is symptomatic of a lack of internal economic integration and it is tackling this that denotes an aspect of liberalization that is as important as the need for the country to rapidly integrate itself with the global economy. As a matter of fact, the momentum with which India will proceed towards globalization will be largely determined by the pace at which internal economic integration proceeds.

The presumption that effective liberalization and reform depend on a minimization of government control conditioned policies of liberalism for almost a decade and a half. Recent empirical evidence has demonstrated that whittling down the role of the government per se may, in fact, not be conducive to higher levels of development. It is reducing the superfluous interventionist role of the government rather than pursuing a course that will result in an indiscriminate reduction of the government's role that is an important objective of economic reform in India as it is with other developing countries. Liberalization in India never took on a form that would make minimizing the role of the government a possibility.

*Lesson*: The existence of a blatant deficiency of infrastructure provision in India itself spells out that the role of the government is a fundamental input in economic development; however, the country's economic experience also underscores that reform does entail changing the composition of state control. The lack of infrastructure provision in India has not been plugged by private investment, this fact alone corroborates that it is the prevalence of a collaborative endeavour between the private and public sector that will facilitate not just a faster pace but more continuity in the progress made towards development.

A group of visionaries and pragmatists formed the government in post-independence India. These individuals had foresight and the principles and priorities that they chalked out reflected a fair degree of erudition. One such aspect accorded importance was the proposition that the basic organizational structure of the Indian economy would be in conformity with what was termed as the mixed economy. The practical wisdom embedded in this has become all the more evident in contemporary times because it prevented policies from being conditioned by ideological extremism. The country had a socialist orientation and the licence Raj was characterized by excessive red tapeism and certain policies that were unduly interventionist;

However, given that the preponderance of state control was accompanied by a democratic system of governance and the existence of a private enterprise sector, the politico-economic organization of post-independence India did epitomize a fusion of ideologies. This was observably consonant with the rationale underlying the pursuit of the mixed economy tenet, which was to fuse the strengths of socialism with those of capitalism. The stated objective of this may have been only partly attained; however, it did avert a transitional process that could have been tumultuous.

The concept of mixed economy is more relevant in the larger context of a globalizing world, where the fervent adherence to a particular ideology is almost an anachronism. As will be elucidated in the subsequent chapters on China, it is blending the features of communism with those of capitalism, which can be illustratively termed as Com-Cap or Cap-Com, that seems a more practical ideological option.

India stands on the threshold of an era that could bring it abundant prosperity; its impediment is not the paucity of resources. Perhaps in a sense this makes the problem it is confronted with slightly more complex. Development is not merely about garnering huge amounts of financial capital; it entails the presence of an institutional framework and delivery systems that support and catalyze an expansion of productive investments. The present core competences that India has were facilitated by putting into place a certain framework of which accumulating capital comprised a single albeit important aspect.

Minimizing the slip between resource mobilization and its deployment is a challenge that requires the prompt execution of development-oriented measures. The pursuit of measures that were development-oriented in a milieu that did not encourage economic growth had its disadvantages, which became apparent in India by the 1970s. It is also true that the adoption of growth-oriented measures relegating developmental considerations to the background is not a favourable outcome. Once again, present trends in India are a reminder that economic growth is a necessary but not a sufficient condition for development. The emphasis on resource mobilization needs to be accompanied by initiatives that are directed towards maximizing the productivity of resources raised. It is basically the insufficiency of such inputs that needs to be remedied in the Indian context.

The insight that this lends development economics is that the nature and magnitude of constraints that confront a country are determined largely by the stage of economic progress at which it finds itself. Against a backdrop of rampant underdevelopment and negligible economic progress it is a severe paucity of financial resource that obstructs an increase in economic growth rates. When economic growth rates and levels of progress increase, the constraints that manifest relate to the qualitative aspects of economic organization, such as the institutional framework, the effectiveness and efficiency of governance and all those inadequacies that impede productivity. Systemic adjustments cannot be couched merely in terms of numbers because it requires building transmission mechanisms from growth to development.

In retrospect, the considerable strides in economic progress that India made after its independence and until the 1970s was possible despite its annual average 4 per cent growth rate because of the higher proportion of developmental gains that stemmed from its economic growth. Certain macroeconomic adjustments initiated in the 1980s and during the 1990s paved the way for higher and faster levels of economic progress. Sustaining this requires one major adjustment: the creation of the mechanisms that would enable the benefits of increasing economic growth to percolate to sectors such as the agricultural sector and the lower income groups.

# 8

# China: The Emerging Superpower

China's three greatest strengths can be illustratively termed as the 3Ms – manpower, manufacturing and market. It was the deft utilization of an abundance of labour supply and a massive market that were the two main attributes with which it was innately endowed that led to the emergence of a competitive and low-cost manufacturing sector.

China's remarkable ascendancy as one of the most important nations in the global economy has been one of the highlights of the preceding two decades. Whether this blend of systems, invariably referred to as one country two systems, is called market-based socialism, neo-Leninism or anything else does not matter significantly, certainly not as much as the ramifications and implications that it has for other developing countries and the world. On a theoretical plane, ideological demarcations become rather ambiguous when we consider the country's rather successful but peculiar combination of communism and market-based economy. China's economic experience does compel a rethink, not just about watertight ideological demarcations (categorical assertions about which will be highly questionable) but also about a wide range of firmly held assumptions related to economic growth, trade, employment and the free market.

Chapters 9–15 will delve into various issues relating to China's economic experience, and the aim once again is to extract from the country's rapid ascent insights and lessons that are applicable to other nations in the developing world.

# 9
## China: Its Ascent as an Economic Powerhouse

Communism premised its existence on utopian egalitarianism. Such idealism is wonderful in theory but its attempted enactment had rather turbulent and painful consequences for China. The immediate aftermath of communism in China was nearly not half as tempestuous as what ensued about a decade later. The advent of the Great Leap Forward (1958–60) and the Cultural Revolution (1966–77) unleashed a period of tumult and uncertainty that drove the country to catastrophic outcomes (even if one takes into account some of the gains that emanated from the Great Leap Forward).

Deng Xiaoping took on the mantle of China's governance 1976. It was not that Deng Xiaoping drew out a line of priorities that was distinctly different from Mao Zedong and it would also be misleading to suggest that Mao was not aware of the importance of decentralization. He was, but his approach to the issue was not quite as pragmatic as Deng Xiaoping's. (A concise description of Mao Zedong's approach to centralization and the purpose underlying the inception of the Great Leap Forward has been enumerated in the Appendix.) The disadvantages of centralization were obvious to Mao and, conversely, so were the advantages of decentralization. In his speech on ten important relationships (in 1956), he stated:

> our territory is so vast, our population is so large and the conditions so complex that it is far better to have the initiatives come from both the central and local authorities than from one source alone. We must not follow the example of Soviet Union concentrating everything in the hands of the central authorities, shackling the local authorities and denying them the right to independent action.

Modernization was also accorded importance by Mao but, once again, his avowed bid to achieve this without assigning any importance to market forces was inherently unrealistic, when viewed in retrospect even more so.

China during the Maoist era alternated between phases of decentralization and recentralization; it was clearly an all-pervasive, rigid authoritarianism that was the predominant influence on policies and structures. It was not that Deng Xiaoping was not authoritarian, he was, but he was tactical enough to strike a balance between authoritarianism and liberalism.

Deng Xiaoping could be theatrically hailed as the architect of China's reform and be credited with the tremendous progress that the country has made over the last two decades. Even in more realistic terms, this statesman can be described as the man who had the most crucial role in shaping the country's destiny. In a larger global context he can also be seen as among those who had the most profound influences on the global economy in the previous century.

Deng Xiaoping was, more than anything else, a political strategist who knew how to balance opposing forces. If one were to pick out the most fundamental point of differentiation between Mao's regime and Deng's it was that, while the former subordinated the economy, society and all else to a specific ideological orientation (or, as it turned out, hedonism), the latter realized that the centrality of economic progress could not be sidelined for any other imperative. In any case, at the time that Deng Xiaoping assumed the reins of control the country had plunged into turmoil and the obvious causes leading to this gave Deng no option but to recognize the imperatives of economic progress.

Over a decade and half ago, China's economic growth rates gathered momentum and its immense potential began to resound in the global economy. At the time, it seemed that this was East Asia's next success story in the offing; by the mid-1990s it was becoming rather obvious that China was an emerging economic superpower. Box 9.1 provides some instances of the country's economic achievement and potential. Table 9.1 indicates its growth performance over 1990–2001.

## Box 9.1   China's market: its potential – some indicators

It has the largest mobile phone network and among the fastest-growing markets in this sector.

Boeing Corporation predicts that China will be the largest market for commercial air travel outside the US in 20 years.

In 2002 China replaced Japan as the world's second largest PC market.

The Chinese government projects that, by the year 2020, there will be 140 million cars in China.

The sum of income and reinvested earnings from US FDI in China increased from US$543 million in 1998 to US$2 billion in 2000.

US exports more to its foreign affiliates in China than it imports from them.

Over the period 1990–8, US exports to China tripled and the sales of its affiliates in the domestic market increased by 21 times.

According to Morgan Stanley, between 1994 and 1998 exports from non-United States foreign affiliates in China to third markets (including the United States) surged by nearly seven times.

Exports by foreign investors in China have increased from 2 per cent of total exports in 1986 to 48 per cent in 2000.

In 1999, of China's total processing trade amounting to US$127 billion by foreign-funded enterprises, US$53 billion-worth of material and other inputs were imported.

Processing trade continues to be an important component of its total trade.

*Table 9.1*   China's economic growth rates (1990–2001) (%)

| Year | As first published | As in *Statistical Yearbook* (2002) | Keidel* real GDP growth rate |
|------|-----|------|------|
| 1990 | 3.9 | 3.8 | 6.8 |
| 1991 | 8.0 | 9.2 | 10.1 |
| 1992 | 13.2 | 14.2 | 10.9 |
| 1993 | 13.4 | 13.5 | 10.7 |
| 1994 | 11.8 | 12.6 | 14.6 |
| 1995 | 10.5 | 10.5 | 11.4 |
| 1996 | 9.6 | 9.6 | 9.8 |
| 1997 | 8.8 | 8.8 | 7.3 |
| 1998 | 7.8 | 7.8 | 6.1 |
| 1999 | 7.1 | 7.1 | 5.5 |
| 2000 | 8.0 | 8.0 | 7.1 |
| 2001 | 7.3 | 7.3 | 8.7 |

*Notes*: Estimation of China's economic growth rates has evoked debate; there are studies that suggest that published statistics from official sources could be an overestimate of the country's actual growth performance. Having said this, it is an indisputable fact of recent economic history that China has exhibited a spectacular economic performance for almost two decades.

* In an attempt to remedy the flaws underlying the calculation of China's GDP growth rate, Albert Keidel used the expenditure approach to calculate the country's economic growth rate over the years 1990–2001. As can be seen, Keidel's estimates are lower than official estimates for the period 1997–9. Interestingly, its estimates were higher than the official estimates for the years 1994–6 and 2000–01.

*Sources*: China Economic Quarterly Special Report (2003); *Statistical Yearbook*, Government of China.

*Table 9.2*   China's GDP growth (2002–6) (%)

| Year | China's GDP growth |
| --- | --- |
| 2002 | 9.1 |
| 2003 | 10.0 |
| 2004 | 10.1 |
| 2005 | 9.8 |
| 2006 (January–November) | 10.7 |

*Source*: National Bureau of Statistics of China, *Statistical Year-book* (2004).

Deng had unequivocally critical role in spearheading China's transition from communism to its present market-based socialism. This was a process that emanated as the leader steered through rather extenuating circumstances. Circumstances and policies that had misfired laid out the rationale for economic reform in China by the mid-1970s. This heralded a new era in China's history, one that began with a 15-year span, which is the time it took for the policies of reform to gain a firm foothold in China's economy. This period can be divided into three phases, the first of which began in December 1978 when the third plenum of the 11th Party Congress formally announced and initiated the process of economic reform. The second phase began in 1984, which witnessed the enactment of the Decision on the Reform of the Economic System, and the third was after the Tiananmen Square revolt in 1989.

The following section will enumerate a concise review of the measures that were implemented for about a decade until 1989.

## Economic liberalization

The 1980s was an important phase in the economic transition of China, it would be viewed as the interim between centralized communism and market-based socialism. As will be demonstrated subsequently, despite the promulgation of crucial measures of decentralization in the financial, industrial and agricultural sectors, the process was not a smooth-sailing one; it was inevitably obstacle-ridden and there were interruptions. The need for economic reform was undeniable but the course that it should take and the initiatives that it should encompass did not elicit undivided support. It was only after 1992, or more specifically after Deng Xiaoping's 'historic tour of the South', that economic reform gained momentum a well-defined form.

Agriculture had been collectivized in 1955 and the people's communes were established in 1958. The commune was the basic unit of production and distribution and initially it consisted of 50 households that were vested with a certain degree of decision-making authority. Two decades later peasants in some poor counties began to adopt a different system whereby the land would be divided among the households who had managed to obtain almost all control rights over production with the exception of private ownership of the land. This practice was officially formalized during 1980 when the Communist Party allowed the pursuit of the household responsibility system (HRS) in poor areas.

However, it was only during early 1982 that the political establishment began to promote the HRS as a reform initiative in China's rural economy. Consequently, peasants who were bound to the commune were liberated. It was not as if they were conferred with private property rights or the ownership of land, however; the land was leased out to families for a rent (the lease was renewable and had a tenure of 15 years and in some instances 30 years). In effect, the peasants became the de facto owners of the land and this provided a spur to the rural economy.

Notably, the origins of rural reform in China were not policy-led; instead they sprang from a response to the rigidities that characterized the commune system. The people's communes did have the discernible advantage of being at the centre of a social security system in rural China but the flipside of this was that they lacked mechanisms that would incentivize the peasant. Subsequently, the declining levels of yields and productivity in the agrarian sector paved the way for HRS.

Another aspect of rural reform pertained to the setting up of village and township enterprises during the early 1980s. As a matter of fact, the Central Committee Circular on Agricultural Work that was issued by the government in January 1984 encouraged peasants and collectives to invest towards the creation of village enterprises. Consonant with this the commune and brigade enterprises were renamed as town and village enterprises (TVEs). This was a sphere where the principle of liberalization applied maximally, relative to other sectors, because insofar as TVEs were concerned there was a distinct easing out of administrative restrictions. Thus, the expansion of this sphere was not constricted by curbs on the entry of new enterprises, the closure of existent units or by the imposition of stringent controls on price setting and employment. TVEs could not afford slackened levels of efficiency because they did not have the easier access to bank credit that state-owned enterprises (SOEs) had. Unlike enterprises in the state-owned sector, TVEs did not have a soft budget constraint to rely upon and this meant that their productivity or efficiency could not slacken. In the instances where performance was poor the enterprises would cease to function.

As decentralization gathered pace local governments provided an impetus for the setting up of TVEs. Consequently, over the period 1979–92, the number of small enterprises increased by an average annual rate of more than

26 per cent. Fiscal reform that began in 1980 was also an integral facilitator of decentralization in China. The enactment of the fiscal contracting system (also referred to as *fenzao chifan*, which means eating from separate kitchens) entailed that budgetary revenue would be divided or allocated between the central and local government. Revenue income was to be divided into two constituents – central fixed revenue and local revenue. The former constituent was the amount or proportion of revenue remitted to the centre and the latter was the fraction that would be shared between the provincial and central authorities. There were different kinds of sharing schemes, for instance, over the period 1988–93 six types of sharing arrangements were adopted.

The implication of fiscal decentralization was far-reaching because it enabled provincial governance and lower levels of administration in China to have a decisive role in the development of their respective regions. Inevitably, this meant a wider range of responsibility in the ambit of providing education, health, housing and local infrastructure. Over the period 1978–83, total rural industrial output nearly doubled. Undeniably, rural reform was successful, perhaps even more than was anticipated, and it was undoubtedly an instrument in the creation of a market-based economy within the larger precinct of communist control. Interestingly, in 1987 Deng Xiaoping remarked, 'The greatest achievement that was totally unexpected is that rural enterprises have developed.'

State-owned enterprises in China stood at the commanding heights of its industrial production. The expansion of enterprise autonomy began as an experiment that was initially undertaken with six enterprises in Sichuan province in 1979. Subsequently it was extended to 100 enterprises in the same region. A higher degree of autonomy included the right to produce and sell products to the market (after a certain proportion was allocated towards the fulfilment of plan quotas) and the right to appoint middle-level managers without approval from the government. Furthermore, enterprises were allowed to retain some of their profits.

By 1980, enterprise autonomy had been granted to about 60 per cent of the SOEs in China. This was not unexpected given the positive impact of the decentralization in the agricultural sector also encouraged the pursuit of similar policies in the industrial sphere. By 1985, the central government controlled only 20 per cent of the total industrial output. In 1987, the government promoted the contract responsibility system, which delegated a wider extent of control to managers of SOEs. This meant an enhanced role in decision-making that pertained to important matters, such as investment and technological upgradation. More importantly, SOEs were allowed to retain a sizable proportion of their profits and contracts between the government and enterprises were finalized for a period of three years, thus avoiding the rounds of annual bargaining between the two entities. By 1987 about 80 per cent of large and medium-scale SOEs had adopted the contract responsibility system and by 1989 almost all had done so.

From a political perspective the coexistence of enterprise autonomy and centralization seemed a rather tactical formulation because it seemed advantageous not just for the enterprises but also for the various tiers of government. Observably, SOEs given the larger degree of autonomy would have found themselves with a better chance of increasing levels of profitability. Furthermore, by determining the extent of flexibility granted the government ensured that marketization of the enterprises would proceed without a dilution of the main embodiments of centralization.

However, by the mid-1990s, despite the positive effects that decentralization had on the state-controlled industrial sector, the proliferation of loss-making SOEs underscored the imperative for chalking out a larger and more comprehensive reform package.

Setting up special economic zones (SEZs) was smart economics; it was also among the most decisive initiatives taken in the context of propelling the emergence of a market-based economy. However, China, as other developing countries, also had a resource constraint and, thus, it was more realistic to envisage that the process of modernization and technology could be achieved in certain designated areas, most which were located on the eastern coast. The attempt to modernize the entire country in one sweep would have been detrimental. Expectedly, the economic zones attracted inflows of investment, the bulk of which came from Hong Kong and Taiwan. However, instead of becoming production centres that would use advanced technology, an outcome that the leadership had envisaged, these regions became an attractive hub for investment in cheap processing, toys, textiles and other light consumer goods. These zones had a distinct advantage that Hong Kong and Taiwan did not have. This was cheap labour.

The objective of the SEZs was a clear-cut one: to usher in market forces in a selective and region-specific manner. These export promotion zones would utilize relatively modern technology and managerial expertise and were exempt (almost) from the administrative interference of local authorities. SEZs were granted tax concessions; an instance of this was the tax holiday that was granted to foreign investors for a period of five years. It must be noted that a differential tax rate applied: 5 per cent for SEZs and 20 per cent for the rest of the country. Furthermore, these zones also received considerable funding for infrastructure projects.

Box 9.2 enumerates the cities and regions that have been granted the status of SEZ since the early 1980s.

## Box 9.2   Cities and regions with SEZ status

The two provinces of Guangdong and Fujian were opened in 1979. These were allowed the adoption of special policies and flexible measures that would enable them to avail of certain tax and non-tax concessions, which would encourage the expansion of exports. Proximity to Hong Kong, Macau and Taiwan was the main reason for making Guandong and Fujian the country's first special economic zone. In consonance with this, the government conferred the status of SEZ to Shenzhen, Zhuhai, Shantou (three of which were located in Guangdong) and Xiamen in 1980.

In February 1985 the Yangtze Delta, the Pearl River Delta (that encompasses Xiamen, Zhangzhou, Qianzhou), the East Shandong Peninsula and the East Liaoning Peninsula were turned into economically open areas.

In 1984 the Chinese government decided to open 14 coastal cities, which would grant foreign-funded enterprises certain preferential incentives and concessions akin to what was being offered by the SEZ. These cities included Dalian, Ouinhuandao, Tianjin, Yantai Quingdao, Lianyungang, Nantong, Shanghai, Ningbo Wenzhiu, Gangshou, Fuzhou, Zanjiang and Beihai (including Fangcheng port).

In April 1988, the government decided to turn Hainan into a SEZ.

Since 1990, the Chinese government decided to develop and open the Shanghai Pudong New Zone and a number of cities along the Yangtze River open belt.

Since 1992, the Chinese government has opened a number of border and capital cities in all the inland provinces and autonomous regions. In addition, by 2005 it had set up about 49 state-level economic and technological development zones and 53 technological development zones in large and medium-sized cities.

By the late 1980s it was envisioned that the entire coastal region of eastern China would become an important extension of the international division of labour. Herein, China would make use of the distinct labour-cost advantage that low labour costs endowed it with and assume its role as an increasingly significant producer of labour-intensive goods, which also included electronics.

There was a flurry of economic activity, intense in some SEZs and not so buoyant in others. Xiamen and Zhuhai, for instance, did not become the scene of action that Shenzhen in Guangdong province was becoming as the 1980s drew to a close.

The consequences of setting up SEZs were manifold, not merely from the economic perspective but also from the social one. It lured not just investors and businessmen but individuals from various walks of life, such as peasants and intellectuals, who flocked to this enclave of liberalization. Proverbially, the grass was greener on the other side of the bamboo curtain and people resorted to rather imaginative ways to take advantage of the gold rush. For instance, peasants in Shenzen built houses on the land that had been leased out to them and rented these to individuals that came into the region. There were also ideological connotations to economic liberalism, even though this came in relatively small doses to China at the time. It was becoming evident that SEZs would, among other things, be an escape from what were perceived as the oppressive pressures of the system on the other side of the divide.

Predictably, the communist establishment castigated the tide of commercialization that sprang from the emerging growth centres. The inception of SEZs provided employment to hordes of villagers in the region and this trend gathered pace for many years after the creation of the economic zones.

Perhaps the most crucial propellant of the expanding role of SEZs, despite the mounting anti-liberalist political ideology, was Hong Kong. The economic momentum of this island had implications for China; these manifesting in an entire gamut of spillover effects, which included investment inflows into the mainland and the impartation of certain skill-based and knowledge-related activities. However, this was not all. China's trade strategy was veritably anchored in Hong Kong's role as one of the leading financial and trading centres of Asia. China was a beneficiary of Hong Kong's rising costs and Hong Kong could retain its competitive edge because of China's low wages. Notably, during the initial stages of opening up, 60 per cent of investment into Guandong came in from Hong Kong and, by the early 1990s, Shenzhen emerged as the largest source of exports after Shanghai.

Understandably, by the early 1990s a sizable proportion of manufacturing activity had been relocated out of Hong Kong. Call this the hand of fate or a geopolitical dividend, it is unequivocal that the presence of Hong Kong was instrumental in the impressive economic progress that China would garner in subsequent years. As reform initiatives gathered momentum, they brought with them the implementation of measures that result in a higher degree of decentralization in both the rural and industrial sectors of China. This was the beginning of a new direction; in no way did this mean that centralization would be reduced. In a sense, the forces of the command economy were redirected towards encouraging the attainment of higher rates of economic growth. The Maoist-Stalinist economic model that seemed to underpin the Mao era was restructured.

I do not use the term 'done away with' because there were obvious similarities between the Soviet model of development and the course that economic strategy took in post-Mao China. It was not as if China had moved from being a planned economy to a market oriented one. However, within the larger framework of a planned economy that had its priorities determined or stipulated by the government, market forces had a distinct role to play in certain production, investment and trade decisions. This did reflect a cognizance by Deng's leadership that authoritarian planning could not supplant market forces. Attempts to do so had been inimical to economic progress during Mao's era and this was a realization that permeated decision-making at all levels during the subsequent phase.

Furthermore, if communism did not disintegrate in China as it did in Eastern Europe it was because its transition began in the early 1980s, at the outset as a process that was selectively applied to certain regions. China's economic transition embodies among the most illustrative instances of gradualism, a feature that has elicited criticism from certain quarters but is indisputably a feature that spared the country from the rather disruptive effects of Big Bang privatization.

From an international perspective, the China story had begun at the inception of the 1990s, but it was not until Deng's historic tour of the South in 1992 that the country began to spiral towards its emergence as a leading investor destination in the global economy. The initial phase of liberalization in China was largely a regional phenomenon, fuelled as it was not only by Hong Kong but also by Taiwan, Macau and South-East Asia. Investment inflows into Guangdong and other zones came mainly from the overseas Chinese diaspora.

One country – two systems: this was the defining principle of the direction towards which the country had begun to move but initially liberalization was not exactly smooth-sailing. China found itself straddled between the predominance of the state-owned sector, shackled, as it were, by the binds of centralized planning, and the emergence of a market economy. Undoubtedly, the initiatives taken were well timed but the larger context within which these were enforced was one that had a weak legal system and an institutional framework that found itself rather unsuitable for the adoption of reform. Inevitably, autonomy granted to bureaucrats not only enlarged their scope within the SOEs; for some it also meant that they had the freedom to indulge in all kinds of rent-seeking activity such as pilfering state funds and increasing investment in non-essential goods. The consequence of this was an import boom, which resulted in increasing budgetary deficits and foreign exchange reserves.

Inevitably, there were political connotations. Deng Xiaoping had envisioned the economic agenda but it was becoming increasingly obvious during the 1980s that economic reform would bring in its path split ideological factions, power struggles within the party ranks and geopolitics that was not always conducive to China's economy. Thus, even though Deng was aware that the ideological demarcations between capitalism and communism were hardly sacrosanct, grappling with the implications of reform was a task that the leader became rather adept at in the course of tackling the obstacles that appeared.

Deng attempted to take reform beyond the periphery to the political mainstream on four instances, first in 1980, then in 1984, 1986 and 1988. Predictably, this encountered considerable opposition, particularly from the elders of the party. Deng was not able to quit the political centre-stage, even with the appointment of pragmatic, reform-oriented leaders, whom he designated should succeed him. For instance, relatively young and pragmatic leaders such as Hu Yaobang and Zhao Ziyang could not push reform beyond the limits that had been set by the hardliners, and eventually both had to step down.

The hardliners in the Communist Party had an extremely conservative stance insofar as matters of reform were concerned. A rather vivid reflection of this came to the fore when Zhao Ziyang, who was the Chinese Communist Party leader from 1988–9, was ousted amid the crackdown on pro-democracy protesters at Tiananmen Square in 1989. Zhao epitomized the liberal and pro-reform faction of China's avowedly totalitarian political echelons and the circumstances that finally culminated in his fall from power were rather dramatic. Having been successful in implementing market reform at the provincial level during the early 1980s, his attempts to steer the forces of political liberalism resulted in his being ousted. Some say that Zhao Ziyang was ahead of this time, but the fact remains that, even at the beginning of the 1990s, it was evident that economic liberalization in China did not have to translate into commensurate political change.

At the time there were sceptics, many of them who thought it unlikely that China would be able to manage the coexistence of centralized authoritarianism and the emerging consumerist, market-based economy. The rationale for this forecast was a sound one but in more ways than one it was not validated.

Veering from one slant to another, Deng toughened his stance on reform in 1992. At the 14th Party Congress in 1992 it was declared that economic reform would be the principal focus of party policy for 100 years. The octogenarian had accomplished what he had set out to; this was undeniably an achievement, one that had taken him almost two decades of a tenuous exercise that proceeded in fit and starts. Deng's famous tour of South China was clearly a moment of reckoning for the country because it underscored in unequivocal terms that economic reforms would continue. On the subject of reform in the ideological orientation, the leader stated, 'Do not debate on this issue any more. Carry out a reform so long as it is beneficial to the increase of social productivity, the country's overall strength and the people's living standard.'

In 1993, the Communist Party's Economic and Finance Leading Group, headed by Party Secretary Jiang Zemin, and a team of economists worked on the formulation of a comprehensive strategy that would pave the way to transition.

The result was the Decision on Issues concerning the Establishment of a Socialist Market Economics Structure, which was adopted by the third plenum of the 14th Party Congress in November 1993. This rather multivariate Decision advocated four principal measures. First, it advocated the implementation of a package of measures that would enable a sequencing of reforms. Second, it proposed the creation of a rule-based market system that would create a level playing field. Third, it stated that the focus would have to be on building institutions that would support the market-based economy and would facilitate the adoption of international best practices. This would include putting into place a centralized monetary system, formalizing fiscal federalism and having a social safety net. The fourth integral element of this pertained to addressing the issue of enterprise reform in the context of transforming state-owned enterprises into modern enterprises that have a clearly defined responsibility and authority.

## Conclusion

Deng Xiaoping's historical ideological breakthrough mapped out the path that China would traverse for a decade. Consequently, China has moved far beyond the phase where reform was viewed in the rather limited context of controlled decentralization. Insofar as specifics of the Decision are concerned, China is in the process of attainment of the third and fourth principle of the reform agenda. For instance, although large and medium-scale SOEs have been corporatized, this has not resolved the prevalence of inefficiency and sagging levels of productivity that characterizes a number of loss-making enterprises. The enactment of policies with the purpose of tackling the rather contentious issue of ownership still leaves the situation rather ambiguous with regard to conferring private property rights. China has enforced some important policies, which has ensured a continuous process of reform; however, by no means has this eliminated the rather obvious tussle between the politics of centralization and the emerging neo-liberalism. By the early 1990s it was evident that the focus would be on the implementation of growth oriented measures. Despite this there still exists an underlying disharmony between the vestiges of the ideological under-pinnings that had determined China's policies until the early 1980s and the country's present and future economic imperatives. As will be demonstrated in subsequent chapters, political ideology continues to exert a significant influence on various aspects of the country's economic agenda, such as state-owned and banking sector reform. Its role, however, is discernibly different from the rather unflinching, authoritarian one that it played during the pre-1990 era.

# Appendix

The underlying intent of the Great Leap Forward was grandiose; it was an attempt by Mao to achieve modernization and do so without the free play of market forces. This was the rationale for the reorganization of state and collective farms into huge communes. Furthermore, the peasants in these communes were ordered not only to work the land, but also to make their own tools out of the iron that they were to smelt into steel.

Diluting the preponderant influence that the USSR was having on various aspects of China's economic and political affairs was also one of the main objectives of the Great Leap Forward. This explains why, by January 1959, China's military reportedly numbered 220 million and constituted about one-third of the population.

It seemed almost inevitable that the Great Leap Forward would have near catastrophic consequences. The attempts to create the rudiments of an iron and steel industry by the creation of small-scale steel mills dealt a heavy blow to the agricultural sector. While some positives emerged from the incentives that were provided for industrialization, the extreme decentralization of economic control led to problems in co-ordination and distribution. There were shortages of investment and severe shortfalls in production, which were further exacerbated by bad weather and crop failure. Evidently, the Great Leap Forward fell far short of being either an economic or for that matter a political strategy. It culminated in some serious adversity, including the ravages of a widespread famine, which led to the death of millions (some estimates go as high as 30 million out of a population of some 500 million, i.e. 6 per cent). Strict rationing had to be imposed in 1959–61, and this helped to reduce the loss of life.

Mao Zedong was not unaware of the flaws of centralization; he was cognizant of the limitations that would arise from the replication of the Soviet model and this resulted in an attempt at decentralization in 1957. This dovetailed delegating nearly all state-owned enterprises to the local governments such the share of industrial output to be controlled by the central government was to be reduced from 40 per cent to 14 per cent. Besides this, revenue-sharing schemes were fixed for five years and the share of central revenue decreased from 75 per cent to 50 per cent. Overall, measures to decentralize led to serious problems with co-ordination and misallocation of investment, stoked as it was by the soft budget constraints.

Consequently, recentralization was undertaken in 1959. The Cultural Revolution was another bid by Mao to induce decentralization. During 1967 and 1968, planning at the level of the central government stopped. The national economy contracted in these two years but there was a recovery in industrial and agricultural production by 1969. The implementation of decentralizing measures continued through the early 1970s. There were two main considerations underlying decentralization during this period. First was attaining the high growth target that had been set by the fourth five-year plan (1971–75), which required that steel production should double. Mao realized the attainment of this goal entailed the harnessing of local initiative and resources. Second, the looming possibility of a confrontation with the Soviet Union entailed that the country be in a situation of preparedness, and for this the country was divided into ten co-operative regions. Each of these precincts would have a complete and self-sufficient industrial system so that these would be better equipped in the event of a war with the Soviet Union.

Yet again, as was the case prior to the Great Leap Forward, most large-scale SOEs were delegated to provincial and municipality governments. In 1970 the central government retained the supervision of 142 enterprises, as against 10,533 enterprises in 1965.

# 10
# State-owned Enterprise Restructuring in China: Issues and Challenges

If economic transition is a bumpy ride, reform is a tightrope walk. China's pre-eminent challenge of sustaining economic progress impinges on its ability to expedite the implementation of reform initiatives. Undoubtedly, this task entails a rather tricky balancing act because it involves retaining the main elements of socialism on the one hand and inducting the principles of the market economy on the other.

The centrality of state-owned enterprises in absolutely every aspect of production, distribution and welfare in China is an integral feature of its economy. This could not override the compulsions of increasing the levels of profitability and efficiency in this sector and could not, as a result, avert restructuring of state-owned enterprises. Understandably, economic and political considerations did temper the pace and nature of reform of the state-owned sector in China.

During the initial stages of enterprise restructuring, which began during the early 1980s, there were some job losses and, although the state stipulated the benefits that the pensioners and those rendered jobless should receive, the responsibility of funding these programmes was assigned to the individual firms. In the absence of state support or subsidy it was extremely unlikely that loss-making firms would be able to compensate the workers laid off in accordance to norms prescribed by the government.

Added to this was the economic experience of some Eastern European countries, which demonstrated that measures that would encompass a rapid overhaul of the state-owned sector had left in their trail a sizable loss of employment and political tumult. Furthermore, given the conspicuous lack of a unified welfare system, the creation of which is currently being undertaken, China could not risk having similar consequences.

The prelude to the process of restructuring began with two important steps, which were implemented during the 1980s.

(i) The entry of new firms, a significant proportion of which would be in the realm of the non-state-owned sector, marked the beginning of what may be described as one of the most fundamental changes in China's economy.

It brought into the fold of a heavily centralized production system a key characteristic of the market economy. Firms entered China's industrial sector through three routes. The first was through the setting up of collectives, which consisted mainly of township and village enterprises (TVEs). The second avenue consisted of individually owned enterprises (*getihu*) and the third medium of new enterprise formation was through foreign investment.

The antecedents of the existence and subsequent expansion of the private sector in China were sown during this period. Although the production and investment parameters of firms in this sphere had to conform to the norms stipulated by the government to a greater extent than their counterparts in countries that had a distinct capitalist orientation, China's non-state-owned sector would, in the ensuing years, account for a significant proportion of the production.

By 1994, although China's state-owned sector continued to have its predominant position in terms of ownership, there existed a sizable non-state owned segment. Over a span of 14 years from 1980, there were millions of individual enterprises and the total number of industrial enterprises had multiplied, according to some estimates, 25-fold.

(ii) Besides allowing the entry of new firms, the other measure that came into effect during the 1980s was the implementation of the enterprise contract responsibility system. The main objective of this was to incentivize the managers of SOEs by granting them a higher degree of autonomy and strengthening and clarifying the system of rewards. This empowered the managers of SOEs to take important decisions about a fair range of matters concerning the acquisition of technology and managerial capability.

Thus began the decentralization of decision-making within state-owned enterprises wherein managerial control was considerably enhanced; this also meant enlarging the role for workers' councils and party secretaries. SOEs could sell more output at market-determined prices and retain a higher share of profits for investment, welfare programmes and bonuses. The outcome of the steps taken towards having a higher degree of market orientation was positive, particularly insofar as the larger SOEs were concerned; however, the performance of a number of the smaller SOEs worsened.

The Modern Enterprise System (MES) reform was introduced during 1993–4 and it was an important step towards the corporatization of the state owned sector. Apparently, the main objective of MES was to address the institutional weaknesses of all SOEs. Under this programme, most enterprises were converted into *gufenzi* companies, which were either companies with limited liability (CLL) or stockholding companies with limited liability (SCLL). The key difference between the two company categories was that the CLLs were relatively small, with a minimum registered capital of RMB100,000 and a minimum of two shareholders, and SCLLs were much larger, with a minimum registered capital of RMB10 million and a minimum of five shareholders.

During 1996 a massive net loss in the state-owned sector compelled the enforcement of stronger measures to tackle the problem of loss-making enterprises. Having begun as a rather generalized programme that would define the framework for SOE reform the MES was specifically targeted towards large and medium-scale state-owned enterprises from 1998–2000.

Grasp the large and release the small was the guiding principle of reform and, in consonance with this, MES was to be implemented in 514 key state-owned enterprises in crucial sectors by the end of 2000. (According to official estimates at the inception of the reform programme, these key point enterprises accounted for two-thirds of the state industry's assets, 67.4 per cent of the sales revenue and 68.4 percent of the pre-tax profits.)

Evidently, this demonstrated that the path to restructuring would be a cautious one, which was certainly not directed at an overt transformation of the sector. Understandably, an important consideration was the implementation of a process of reform that would minimize the loss of employment. A concise enumeration of the measures that were adopted to reorganize and restructure the large and medium scale SOEs follows.

(i) Large SOEs were corporatized into national enterprise groups (NEG), which would be limited liability companies with stock listed and, most importantly, be wholly state-owned.

(ii) Existent SOEs were allowed to create new spin-off or subsidiary firms by utilizing their advanced technical equipment, more skilled labour force and more profitable product lines. The obsolete technology, less skilled labour force (including those who were retired) continued to remain the responsibility of the parent firm. These new firms would become listed as private limited liability companies, which would be allowed to raise capital from the market. It should be noted that the parent firm would also be one the shareholders in the new firm and it would receive dividends for its stake in the same.

(iii) The debt–equity swap involved the inception of four state-owned management companies that would take over the non-performing loans from the state-owned commercial banks and help in the restructuring of state-owned enterprises. The SOE concerned was turned into a shareholding company and the asset management company (AMC) issued shares commensurate with the size of the debt. The AMC would buy the non-performing loan (NPL) at face value and, at the end of four years, they must sell their shares into the market. The objective of this was to achieve as high a recovery ratio as possible; 30 per cent was considered acceptable. According to Sheng Huaren, the President of the State Economic and Trade Commission, the debt or loan to equities swap had been implemented for 580 enterprises by October 2000. The amount that this involved was RMB405 billion. Over the ensuing period, as will be enumerated in the next section, the restructuring of SOEs would prove to be a rather costly exercise

(iv) The China Securities Commission made taking over, or a merger with, a loss-making SOE a qualifying condition if an enterprise was to be accorded priority for having initial public offering (IPO) and stock market listing. The inclusion of a poorly performing firm into an enterprise group, or *jituan*, did enable some weaker firms to turn around. When gauged in terms of profitability, this did not seem the most prudent initiative because it increased the burden on the efficient SOEs. The question that arises is whether revitalizing one segment of the state-owned sector should be at the expense of the more profitable sphere. The rationale underlying this initiative was the need to prevent further job losses. On the whole, this did not appear to be smart economics but it was good politics. Perhaps this measure could be justified on the grounds of a step that would have prevented a decline in the well being of a certain proportion of workers.

(v) Medium-sized SOEs, which constituted about 15 per cent of the state-owned sector, opted for the formation of joint shareholding companies. This entailed the transfer of a certain percentage of shares from the government to workers and managers, who would become shareholders along with the state or collective. This measure diversified the ownership pattern but in doing so it did not result in a dilution of control by the government. Acquiring a stake in a particular SOE did not assign to the stakeholders the option to utilize the shares in a manner that they deemed appropriate. This was because they acquired what could be described as limited property rights, which would give shareholders dividend payouts, the right to sell shares and a negligible (if any) role in decision-making about matters pertaining to the SOE in which they had invested. The drawbacks of this measure were accentuated by the fact that some workers who were unwilling to buy the shares of loss-making SOEs were pressurized to do so. There were instances of local governments that stipulated that 90 per cent of the workers of a SOE must become shareholders when this particular shareholding pattern was adopted.

## The impact of enterprise restructuring

The objective of enterprise reform was to achieve a turnaround in the state-owned sector so that it would consist of independent, profit-oriented businesses, which would have clearly defined property rights and adhere to the principles of sound corporate governance. Even more important than the goal of increasing levels of profitability was to ensure that the route of restructuring pursued would not leave in its trail high levels of unemployment and other social dislocations that would certainly have arisen if it had gone in for the long haul.

Thus, the impact of state-owned reform has to be evaluated in terms of two criteria – profitability and its implications for welfare and poverty. I begin with a discussion on the effects of reform measures on profitability and efficiency.

At the close of the three-year MES campaign to revitalize the state-owned sector, despite some improvements in this sector, some new loss-making large and medium-sized state-owned enterprises had emerged.

At the end of 1999, 41 per cent of industrial SOEs were loss-making compared with 19 per cent of collectively owned enterprises. Despite the fact that the state sector's share in total assets stood at 68.8 per cent and in employment it was 54.5 per cent, its share in total gross industrial output was 28.2 per cent. As a matter of fact, during the first half of 2000, the liability to assets ratio of this sector was 62.3 per cent.

Evidently reform has not conferred on the private sector an extent of control that comes anywhere near that exerted by the state. Despite diversified forms of public ownership, which have an element of private sector participation, the state continues to retain the dominant share.

Regardless of ownership classification there are, at most, a miniscule number of domestic firms that can be categorized distinctly as privately owned firms. Stake-holding by the state may vary across industries and enterprise groups but the fact remains that the government is a shareholder across a wide gamut of firms. Thus, quantifying the exact extent private-sector participation would be difficult and using it as a basis to review the impact of corporatization would itself lead one to half-baked inferences. There exists a pattern of pluralized, institutionalized ownership, where a multiplicity of government and quasi-government agencies are shareholders and other apparent private sector entities shareholders in joint stock companies. (Interestingly, although Article 4 of China's company law stipulates that the state should hold controlling stocks key industries and subscribe to at least 35 per cent of total shares in shareholding companies, in most instances the state share is greater than 50 per cent.)

Furthermore, according to a report for Carnegie Endowment for International Peace by Minxin Pei, the Chinese leadership continues to appoint 81 per cent of the chief executives of the SOEs and 56 per cent of all senior corporate executives. In 70 per cent of the 6275 large and medium-sized state enterprises that have been corporatized by 2001 members of the party committee were members of the board of directors.

Thus, a precise assessment of the control exerted by the government on economic activity in China is difficult and even unnecessary; suffice it to say that the state controls the administration of all key industries, such as heavy machinery, iron and steel, energy, telecommunications, metal, automobiles, aeroplanes, space and finance. The preponderance of the government's role in determining resource (including land) allocation even after the measures of reform have been implemented is undeniable, and it reveals the manner in which market forces are steered towards serving the agenda of government authorities.

Stock market listing did not usher in a discernible improvement in the corporate governance of state-owned enterprises; however, it did enable the government to raise the substantial amount of RMB210 billion from the stock market. Plausibly, one would have expected that fulfilling the prerequisites that a company usually needs to if it intends to raise equity from the capital markets would have led to higher levels of efficiency and productivity. This was not the general outcome. The reason for this was that access to the stock market was controlled, and this was possible because the government had introduced a distinction between state-owned companies that had a minority of tradable shares and those with a majority of non-tradable shares. This ensured a predominance of state ownership and the stock exchange became an additional avenue of raising funds.

The stock market was thus set up to provide SOEs with an avenue to tap into the savings of the people and, in the initial stages of listing, the firms that would be allowed to issue shares, and the quantity, would be specified by central government, the State Planning Commission, the People's Bank of China and the China Securities Regulatory Commission. Theoretically speaking, the existence of a stock exchange is an important constituent of a market-based economy. Be this as it may, in China it has functioned as an appendage of a socialistic pattern.

Understandably, stock prices did not reflect the economic performance of the company. As a matter of fact, the role of government intervention in the determination of share prices corroborated that reform of China's state-owned sector was focused essentially on improving the balance sheets of these SOEs without striking at the root of the underlying causes. Out of 1216 companies listed on either the Shanghai and Shenzhen Stock Exchanges, only 82 were privately owned.

It was, thus, inevitable that profitability would find itself mired in the conflict between the politics of control and the need for the implementation of measures that will increase levels of efficiency and productivity. This feature was rather pronounced in the large SOEs. Furthermore, in terms of growth and productivity indicators, the impact of SOE reform on the greater proportion of the enterprises has been rather moderate.

So have the restructuring initiatives failed?

If success of SOE reform in China is denominated merely in terms of the impetus it provided to the economic performance of the enterprises concerned one could infer that it failed. However, although this was an important aspect, there were, as has been mentioned earlier, other vital objectives of enterprise reform that cannot be overlooked.

The rather guarded stance towards corporate restructuring was rooted in a sound rationale. A swift transformation of public ownership may have been one way of propelling reform but it certainly is not the only one. Thus, the fact that China did not opt for a rapid unbundling of its public utilities as the main demerit of enterprise reform distracts us from the fundamental reasons that dampened the impact of turnaround measures in the SOEs.

Restructuring, as it has been formulated, did have its disadvantages, particularly in the rather superficial manner in which it sought to tackle the problems related to inefficiency and suboptimal resource utilization. However, the upside was that if China had not pursued this process of phased restructuring, which encompassed partial privatization under the aegis of some tier of government authority, it would in all likelihood have had to deal with the huge task of formulating, within an extremely short time, a massive social security programme that would provide some compensatory relief to those individuals who could not be employed. Its inability to do so could have had disruptive effects.

In any case despite the rather measured stance and pace at which restructuring proceeded it did result in considerable cutback in jobs in the state owned sector.

According to Sheng Huaren, by 1998 SOE restructuring had resulted in job losses that amounted to 12 million, however, more than half found employment.

Those impacted by restructuring did comprise the more vulnerable sections of society such as the elderly and this does lend some credence to the underlying rationale of having a process of SOE reform that seemed at times to drag its feet.

However it is the outcomes that the pronouncedly preferential status accorded to SOEs have in terms of the limitations these place on other more labour-intensive sectors that is a serious concern and certainly not one that has been completely addressed by the restructuring exercise. Studies about the elasticity of non-agriculture employment to output growth in China estimate that it is 0.5, given this even if growth were to increase considerably in China over the next few years employment provision is a concern that cannot be overlooked.

Furthermore, full-fledged privatization was not among China's options for restructuring or SOE reform because adopting the Big Bang approach to privatizing would have weakened the core sectors of its economy. This would have unleashed an entire gamut of problems that the country was attempting to tackle and the well being of a sizable proportion of the population would have been adversely affected.

Reform may not have enabled profitability of state-owned enterprises to increase as significantly as was required, but it paved the way for the emergence of diversified industrial structure, of which private-sector participation is an important constituent. One of the distinct advantages of China's phased process of enterprise restructuring is that it has been able to introduce vital elements of a market economy against the larger backdrop of a centralized command economy, despite the absence of clearly defined property rights.

Undoubtedly, the reform of a public-sector company or corporation entails addressing a wide spectrum of considerations; enhancing levels of efficiency and productivity is one of a number of vital concerns that cannot be overridden. More often than not, increasing levels of efficiency would require steps that would result in cutbacks in employment unless those laid off are reabsorbed in other sectors. China's present levels of unemployment indicate that this is not happening as much as it needs to. It must be noted that, according to official sources, urban unemployment was about 4 per cent in 2004. Estimates based on studies and surveys indicate that it is possible that actual unemployment in China maybe higher. This is indicated in Table 10.1.

Notwithstanding the route taken towards privatizing state-owned enterprises, one of the intrinsic limitations that the process embodies across countries is that it compels choosing between increasing levels of efficiency, which would invariably result in higher levels of unemployment, or minimizing lay offs even though this might dampen efforts directed towards making enterprises more efficient.

Restructuring had another crucial purpose: that of raising capital. This was an important objective that was served, although the economic performance of a number of SOEs was hardly encouraging. During the initial stages of enterprise reform the emphasis was on broadening the access of SOEs to additional avenues of finance. Inevitably, this entailed measures that would reorganize enterprises and, as the outcomes of this unfolded, it was all too evident that, overall, there had been more restructuring and too little reform.

One of the fundamental weaknesses of enterprise reform in China's state-owned sector was its inability to harden budget constraints. Related to this were the excesses of red tapeism, embezzlement, fraud and instances of investments in the absence of adequate appraisal methods. Undoubtedly, this was the fall-out of the inherent limitations with which the process of SOE restructuring was beset.

Having said this, if existent measures had been implemented more effectively the results might have been better. First, this would have enabled capital to be utilized more productively; achieving commensurately higher levels of efficiency would then have been possible despite the intrinsic weaknesses of the initiatives taken. Arguably, even if partial privatization had been implemented with greater effectiveness it would not have averted rent-seeking activity, crony capitalism and the resultant inefficiencies and resource misallocations. However, the extent could certainly have been much reduced. Recurrent reminders underscore the fact that problems that emanate from

*Table 10.1*  Estimated real unemployment figures in China's urban areas (million)

|                            | 1993 | 1994 | 1995 | 1996 | 1997  | 1998  |
|----------------------------|------|------|------|------|-------|-------|
| Unemployed (registered)    | 4.20 | 4.76 | 5.20 | 5.57 | 5.70  | 5.70  |
| Actual/real unemployment   | 5.40 | 6.20 | 8.0  | 9.70 | 13.10 | 15.40 |

*Source*: Pingyao Lai, 'China's Economic Growth: New Trends and Implications', *China and World Economy Special Report*, November 2003.

crony capitalism are not unique to China. In this context it would be relevant to consider the Asian financial crisis under which a number of South-East Asian nations, such as Malaysia, Indonesia and Thailand, found themselves reeling in 1997–8. Although this was caused by a number of factors, an important one was a build-up of loans extended for speculative purposes.

The nexus between financial institutions, businesses and politics in South-East Asia is a good example of crony capitalism in countries that had stricter enforcement of regulatory and vigilance norms. The turmoil that prevailed in the currency and financial markets in South-East Asia was a terse reminder that the inadequacy of sound credit appraisal and monitoring mechanism could accentuate the vulnerability of developing countries to financial crises.

SOE reform has defined parameters within which enterprises can improve functionally and there exists scope for a more effective implementation of existent initiatives. If this is achieved it will provide a fillip to economic performance. The output from the state-owned sector constitutes about 20 per cent of total production in China; however, SOEs utilize a large share of national resources and it is essential that current levels of productivity rise. One recalls that, at the outset, the approach to SOE reform was influenced considerably (though not exclusively) by developmental concerns. However, if present levels of inefficiency and standards of corporate governance persist the adverse implications that this decrees for economic progress is obvious. In this context, it must be mentioned that discernible improvements in enterprise performance and relaxing restrictions on the expansion of private-sector participation in China does not entail a systemic overhaul. A substantiation of this statement follows.

The crux of SOE reform in China does not rely on the extent of privatization, particularly insofar as key sectors such as machinery, iron and steel, telecommunications, automobiles and aviation are concerned. It depends crucially on the ability of the leadership and those at the helm of affairs at the managerial and the governance levels to demarcate enterprise operations and decision-making therein from the politics of the command economy.

Despite the ambiguity about the size of the private sector in China, it has come to play an increasingly significant role in economic activity; the non-state-owned sector accounts for over 50 per cent of total output production. If the productivity and profitability differential between the state-owned sector and non-state-owned sector continues to increase it will create a disconcerting context wherein, on the one hand, the role of the private sector in China's economic progress increases and, on the other, the mammoth state-owned corporations do not contribute increasingly to the progress of the nation, despite the resources and assets that these utilize and control. Undoubtedly, this is not a comfortable situation for the political economy of centralization to find itself ensconced within.

China's transition from a centrally planned economy to a market-based socialist one is an ongoing process but it finds itself at a stage where the predominance of its state-owned sector can coexist with private-sector participation. Constricting the expansion of the private sector by the imposition of certain curbs would be inimical to its economic progress.

The private sector may not be as shackled as it was previously, given that the Chinese government has eased some of the stringent restrictions that were imposed on it. However, one needs to examine whether the measures extended to encourage this sphere are sufficient and well implemented. Moreover, providing an impetus to private-sector expansion entails much more than relaxing the restrictions that were imposed on it earlier. This does not mean that it receives the support that the state-owned sector did but it implies the design and implementation of policy that would tap the expansionary potential of this sector. Evidently, this is not happening, not enough to give to the private sector the impetus that it requires. Symptomatic of this deficiency is the constrained access of small and medium-scale enterprises to resources (financial and managerial). This is a sphere that embodies a certain potential for employment provision and expansion, and it should thus be encouraged by policies that would provide it with a stimulus. SOE reform should not crowd out initiatives that will encourage the expansion of the non-state-owned sector; if the politics of centralization constricted the number of small and medium-scale enterprises in the non-state-owned sector and by doing so reduced the emerging areas of comparative advantage the impact would be regressive.

By 2004, private enterprises accounted for 50 per cent of employment provision. The present imperatives of sustaining growth entail the identification of sectors that embody a significant growth and employment potential. As indicated in Table 10.2, since 1996 the number of individuals employed by the SOEs and the collectively owned enterprises has reduced significantly and this

*Table 10.2*   Employment in terms of ownership pattern (%)

| Year | State-owned | Urban collectives and TVEs | Private enterprises and self-employed | Other types of non-state ownership |
|------|-------------|----------------------------|---------------------------------------|-----------------------------------|
| 1978 | 77.6 | 22.4 | 0.0 | 0.0 |
| 1985 | 64.9 | 32.1 | 1.8 | 1.2 |
| 1990 | 54.6 | 35.6 | 5.4 | 4.4 |
| 1995 | 34.0 | 36.6 | 12.9 | 16.6 |
| 1997 | 25.5 | 38.1 | 17.9 | 18.4 |
| 1999 | 20.3 | 35.4 | 18.2 | 26.1 |

*Source: China Statistical Yearbook* (2000).

reduction was partly offset by the increase of employment in the expanding private sector and in the numbers of self employed individuals. It would be unrealistic to anticipate that the preferential treatment to SOEs would cease. However, the formulation of bail-out packages for loss-making enterprises has curtailed the expansion of spheres that can provide increasing levels of employment.

---

## Box 10.1   Easing the controls on the private sector

The Constitution was changed in 1999 in order to recognize the status of the private sector and this offers constitutional and therefore legal status to these enterprises and enhances property rights protection.

Banks are encouraged to finance private enterprises (in the past, it was extremely difficult for private enterprises to get finance). Private firms can be listed in the stock market.

Allowing private firms entry into an increasing number of sectors. Gradual relaxation of certain restrictions to allow private firms to have more freedom to conduct their business. For example, private firms earning foreign exchange are now able to use it for imports or overseas transactions.

---

The politics of control did have a distinct development orientation and the rationale underlying restructuring policies that were extended to support, or rather prop up, inefficient and non-viable SOEs did avert a transitional process that could otherwise have unleashed tumultuous economic and social instability.

Corporate restructuring has been implemented within the confines of political and economic constraints. The result has been the attempt to retain centralization and blend it with principles of corporatization and private-sector participation. This synthesis is in the process of evolving; undoubtedly there are difficulties in combining features from divergent systems into a cohesive and cogent system. Ensuring that obstacles that could deter the evolution of market-based socialism are overcome or minimized entails that during the ensuing phase China's reform initiatives envision a larger context. This would mean that reform would need to encompass much more than restructuring if it is to move from being the appendage to SOEs towards becoming instrumental in spearheading the momentum of sustainable growth.

SOE reform has spanned about a decade and the empirics of the process and the impact embodies important lessons. As China makes its transition from a centrally planned command towards market-based socialism it needs to have an institutional framework where the functions of regulatory authorities are not completely bound by political motive.

Have the politics of control steered its course in a direction that is more conducive to delivering the imperatives of sustainable growth? The politics of control manifests itself in the politics of lending. The state-owned sector continues to receive a bulk of the bank loans and private companies receive about 27 per cent of bank loans and it is this that represents the constraint on bank reform in China. The persistent allocation of the larger proportion of financial resources from the banking sector to loss-making enterprises reflects that the politics of lending override the pressing concerns of reform. This takes us to an evaluation of another integral aspect of reform in the Chinese economy – the impact of restructuring on China's banking sector.

## The impact of financial-sector reform in China: issues and concerns

The initial public offering (IPO) by the Industrial and Commercial Bank of China raised a record U.S$19.1 billion in October 2006. In 2006 the Bank of China managed to raise the tidy sum of US$9.7 billion after its stock market listing. These are two among other instances that unravel the promising prospects of China's financial sector. Undoubtedly, the gains of a rather extensive restructuring exercise of the Chinese banking sector have begun to fructify, but this still does not take away the compulsion for further reform in this sphere.

Since China's accession to the WTO in 2001, a total investment of US$19.03 billion (IPOs not included) has been ploughed into its banking sector. Even as it can boast of impressive performance in mobilizing investment, the scope for reform in China's banking sector is significant as it continues to be riddled with non-performing loans and allocative inefficiencies, and it continues to be characterized by a lack of stringent monitoring and risk-assessment procedures. This is hardly surprising given that China's banking sector seems to have upheld the principle 'Have money will spend'. The underpinnings of this have been consistently increasing economic growth rates, a high saving–GDP ratio and its negligible public debt.

China's rather profligate approach to lending, particularly to state-owned enterprises, had its downside; its banking sector, however, saddled as it is with problems, cannot be described as a sphere with weak fundamentals. The reason for this is that the wide range of anomalies that impede the efficiency in the country's banking were financed by its rather buoyant economic performance. This rather positive characteristic has enabled it to postpone a stronger enforcement of reform measures in its banking sector.

This does not tone down the country's compelling need for reform but it certainly differentiates the process. Unlike most of the countries in Eastern Europe, this implies that reform of China's banking sector is not about transforming a sphere with decrepit and illiquid financial systems to one that has sounder ones. Its objective would be to reduce the distortions in resource allocation and credit pricing, and to ensure, through the creation a sound regulatory framework, a mechanism that makes it difficult for irregularities and fraudulent malpractices to run rife.

China's banking sector has a fairly diversified structure; the thing that continues to remain narrow-based is its scope for unencumbered functioning.

China began to diversify its banking sector in 1979. It established three specialized banks: the Bank of China, to which it delegated the handling of its foreign currency transactions; the China Construction Bank, which focused on the construction sector; and the Agricultural Bank of China, which would handle its rural banking business. In 1984 it also set up the Industrial and Commercial Bank of China. The Big Four, as these banks are collectively known, form the apex of China's banking sector and account for a bulk of the country's lending business.

The 1980s also witnessed the inception of the China Investment Bank (1981), the joint stock bank of communication, and the CITIC Industrial Bank (1987).

By 1994 the government had in place a two-tier banking system and it transferred its commercial banking activities from the People's Bank of China to the four wholly state-owned commercial banks (WSCB). The objective of financial reforms, which began in 1994, was to demarcate commercial lending from policy-orientation and this was one of the underlying reasons that the four specialized banks were transformed into four wholly state-owned commercial banks and the urban credit co-operatives into commercial banks.

Besides the wholly state-owned banks, China's banking sector also consists of joint stock commercial banks, which include, besides the government, stakeholders from the private sector (domestic or foreign) and the rural credit co-operatives.

A concise enumeration of the measures of restructuring that have been enforced on China's banks during the 1990s follows.

i) Four asset-management companies were established during 1999–2000 and these purchased non-performing loans of RMB1.4 trillion, which constituted 14 per cent of GDP, from the state-owned commercial banks. The non-performing loans were purchased at book value and the AMCs issued bonds to the bank and, by doing so, strengthened their financial position.

ii) Other measures included allowing a limited degree of deregulation insofar as entry and interest-rate determination was concerned, an abolition of loan quotas, merging of credit co-operatives that reduced government intervention in credit allocation and tightened accounting and prudential norms.

iii) By 1998 the enactment of the law on securities provided that there would be three supervision authorities, each of which would be assigned the responsibility of supervising three types of financial institutions and their business activities. These authorities included the People's Bank of China (PBC), the Insurance Regulatory Commission of China and the Securities Regulatory Commission of China.

There has been an attempt to enhance risk evaluation of financial institutions, including the medium and small-sized financial institutions, and this was also accompanied by the introduction of procedures that pertained to the exit of financial institutions.

The China Banking Regulatory Commission (CRBC) was set up in 2003. Cognizant of the need for a sound regulatory framework, the CRBC introduced the new supervisory concepts and approaches as embodied in the capital accord or Basel II. In accordance with rules aimed at improving risk management, large banks would be required to formulate a robust internal credit risk-rating system, benchmarked to Basel II, and small banks should introduce the elements of best practices for managing credit risk. It is, thus, foreseeable that the CRBC will have a pivotal role to play in not just pushing forward banking sector reform but also making it a more deep seated process. This is a fact that is clearly elucidated by Luo Ping of the CRBC, who, in his presentation at New Delhi (November 2003), stated:

> There has been a high expectation on the CRBC at the time it started its operation. The industry expects the CRBC to be independent and accountable and at the same time demonstrate a high level of professionalism. Indeed we at the CRBC have been fully aware of the potential pitfalls and we must ensure that the creation of the CRBC is not a mere split from the Central Bank and that the CRBC will develop the right mission, and introduce new supervisory concepts and methodologies in building a strong banking sector and supervisory system.

The question that arises is: how does one evaluate banking-sector reform in China?

Once again, as was the case with evaluating SOE reform, the answer to this question is not a straightforward one that tells you whether reform has been a success or a failure. Despite the organizational restructuring of the banking sector, ground-level functional realities of financial institutions have not changed significantly.

The reasons for this are obvious: in the course of serving its economic agenda, more often than not considerations linked to viability and efficiency are relegated to the background.

The rationale of loan disbursement in China may have had advantages in the initial stages of the nation's modernization but the downside is that policy-driven lending can erode some of the gains of economic progress in ensuing years. The concomitant of this has been that restructuring, so far, has been tackled by periodic rounds of rather expensive recapitalization. For instance, the Bank of China (BOC) and the China Construction Bank were recapitalized with $45 billion from foreign exchange reserves during December 2003. The restructuring plans of these two banks entailed strengthening corporate governance and risk management, resolving non-performing loans and using external auditors for more accurate evaluation procedures of the financial position of the banks.

Estimates about non-performing loan ratios in China's banking sector hardly concur; the fact that emanates from many studies is that there has been a reduction in the NPL ratio of most banks. Ernst & Young released a report in 2006 which indicated that non-performing loans in China's banking sector had mounted to US$911 million. Subsequently Ernst and Young retracted the report. However, we cannot for a moment detract from the fact that, although there has been an improvement in the credit quality, the decline in non-performing loans has been enabled by a rather costly exercise of recapitalization.

Some estimates state that, since the late 1990s, the attempt by China's government to repair the balance sheets of its banks could have cost as much as 22 per cent of its newly revised GDP in 2005. Table 10.3 indicates the NPL ratios of the Big Four. Evidently, striking at the root of all those features that culminate in and even perpetuate high NPL ratios is essential for there to be a long-term solution to the problem. Thus, the reduction in non-performing loans needs to be sustained and it is the ability to do this that will reflect on whether there has been an improvement in credit quality and monitoring systems.

Furthermore, if reducing non-performing loan ratios is the yardstick for assessing the success of reform of China's banking sector we would arrive at a rather half-baked inference because a comprehensive, exhaustive review

*Table 10.3*  Non-performing loan ratios of the Big Four

|  | 2000 | 2003 |
|---|---|---|
| Agricultural Bank of China | – | – |
| Bank of China | 27 | 16 |
| China Construction Bank | 21 | 9 |
| Industrial and Commercial Bank of China | 34 | 21 |

*Note*: The Bank of China and China Construction Bank received a capital infusion of $22.5 billion at the end of 2003.
*Source*: China Banking Regulatory Commission and IMF staff.

entails evaluating the restructuring of the banking system in China on a broader basis and in a much larger context.

Inevitably, the process of bank restructuring has not been a smooth one; there have been discontinuities and pitfalls and it certainly has some distance to cover before its banking and financial spheres can be described as functioning optimally and with high levels of efficiency. However, given the situation that pervaded the country's banking sector during the mid-1980s, the adjustments that restructuring and a certain degree of reform have facilitated enabled China to come fairly proximate to the goal of aligning itself with the global banking standards.

Thus, at this point it would be relevant to describe some of the positive trends that one sees emerging in China's banking sector.

(i) The four WSCBs continue to predominate, given that, taken together, these banks account for 60 per cent of total assets, claims on the non-financial sector and deposits. However, these banks have been losing market share to joint stock commercial banks. Since March 2002, market share of the state-owned commercial banks has reduced by 3 per cent. Rural credit co-operatives and all other deposit money banks account for 10 per cent and slightly less than 15 per cent of the market respectively. Thus, although quintessentially the banking sector in China is not a competitive one, it is also not the domain of a few.

(ii) During 2005, an investor group, which comprised the Royal Bank of Scotland, Temasek, Union Bank of Switzerland and Asian Development Bank, announced an equity investment of over US$5 billion for a 16.84 per cent stake in the Bank of China. The Bank of America and Temasek have announced an equity investment of US$3.9 billion for a 14.1 per cent stake in China Construction Bank. Direct foreign investment participation has been announced in a number of banks including some of the medium sized ones. During 2004, five Chinese banks, including the Bank of Communications, Shenzhen Development Bank and Xi'an City Commercial Bank, have announced their alliance with foreign investors.

(iii) In quantitative terms, foreign ownership participation may not seem as important a variable as it could otherwise have been if it constituted a higher proportion of the bank's investment. This is one view. There is another perspective on this issue that upholds that it is not the amount of shares that a particular foreign investor group controls in a particular bank but the skills and technology transfer it facilitates that comprises the more crucial aspect of foreign investment in China's banks. If banks with foreign investor tie-ups are able to adopt or implement better risk management procedures, along with an improvement in other managerial practices and corporate governance procedures, these could represent a localized instance of efficient management and risk-assessment procedures to other banks and institutions that have not been unable to improve their performance levels. This measure could catalyze the process of reform in China's banks.

Delving into the larger story of banking sector reform in China provides us with recurrent reminders of the inextricable link between the policies pertaining to SOE reform and the vast amount of non-performing loans that have accumulated in the banking sector consequent on funding non-viable SOEs.

Despite the SOE reform, about half of the enterprises incur net losses, due to slackening levels of efficiency amid increasing levels of competition. Allocations to loss-making SOEs and the rather constrained accessibility of small and mid-sized companies in the private sector to bank finance represent a skewed capital allocation that limits opportunity creation in certain spheres. Another alarming consequence of this has been a declining level of investment efficiency, such that each dollar of GDP growth costs more since 2001.

According to the McKinsey Quarterly Report (*How Financial System Reform Could Benefit China*, 2006), during the early 1990s China required new investment of $3.30 for each dollar of GDP growth; however, since 2001 it needs investment of $4.90 for the same. Thus, the economic rationale for holding back reform measures is an extremely weak one, even if one accepts that it exists at all. Sustaining present levels of economic progress requires that current patterns of lending expand their priorities to include those sectors that embody a certain potential for growth.

Many enterprises in the non-state-owned sector tap funds from China's informal lending market. If a larger proportion of bank lending were directed towards private enterprises it would mean a rise in the levels of productivity and competitiveness. Estimates differ, but it is undeniable that the country's economic growth will increase when the basis of capital allocation is oriented more towards productivity gain and less to political patronage. (According to the Mckinsey Report, this could increase China's GDP by 13 per cent annually.)

Another aspect of this problem is the low return on savings that depositors in China continue to receive. On average, Chinese households save about 25–30 per cent of their disposable income and over the last ten years they have earned about 0.5 per cent (in real terms) annually. Given the rather insufficiently developed stock exchange and the volatility of equities and bonds over the last decade, the banking sector receives the bulk of household savings. Once again, this is indicative of an inefficient capital allocation because bank deposits constitute not more than 20 per cent of total financial assets in other developed countries and about 50 per cent in emerging markets.

Interestingly, the problem with banks in China does not arise from their inability to earn revenue but from their high operating costs, these being the consequence of their lending priorities. The main source of revenue for a bank is the spread between its borrowing and lending rates; interestingly this is an average of about 3.3 per cent in China's banks, which is on par with the average net interest margin of about 3.1 per cent that prevails in

Chile, Malaysia, Singapore and South Korea. Despite this, the Chinese banks have required about US$250 billion of recapitalization since the late 1990s. As was the case with restructuring of its state-owned industries, the pursuit of reform in its banking sector provides us with yet another terse reminder that when political considerations override economic rationale the costs are high.

The crux of effective reform policies vests in whether banks will be able to improve their asset quality, undertake adequate risk-assessment procedures and be able to do so without depending on periodic recapitalization packages by the government and the central bank.

Apparently, China may be able to afford its current approach to restructuring but the question is whether, as a developing country that has a compelling need to expand certain segments of its infrastructure, such as the expansion of its health care systems, China can afford the present approach to reform. Obviously it cannot. When resources are allocated towards the funding of non-performing loans it represents a diversion of resources from activities that could be more productive. Inevitably, the costs of financial restructuring are partly if not completely at the expense of enterprises that have performed better and can make a positive contribution to growth. Thus, in the absence of expeditious reform measures, every round of recapitalization represents a growth leakage.

## Conclusion

A transition needs to be systemic; in the context of China's banking sector this entails an overhaul of the financial structure, particularly weeding out those factors that deter an improvement in the economic performance of banks.

The capitalization of China's equity markets is equivalent to about 33 per cent of GDP, which is low compared to about 60 per cent or more in other emerging markets. Furthermore, the corporate bond market accounts for just 13 per cent of GDP, which is, once again, significantly less than an average of 50 per cent in other emerging markets. In fact, it should be noted that bonds account for just 1 per cent of corporate debt in China, informal loans constitute about 4 per cent and bank loans comprise 95 per cent. Having a business environment that is more competitive insofar as the SOEs are concerned requires a greater extent of diversification and more sophistication in China's financial markets. Narrow-based capital markets, particularly equity and corporate bond markets, aggravate the situation and increase the costs of financial intermediation. This feature, coupled with the predominance of banks, also nurtures the lack of competitiveness in the state-owned sector.

A broad basing of the financial markets in China, which would involve an expansion of the bond market and the deepening of equity markets, will provide companies in the private sector with other avenues through which they can raise capital. Added to this, depositors would have a wider range of investment options.

## Appendix

First, we will continue to strategically readjust the distribution and structure of the state-owned sector of the economy and improve the mechanism for ensuring rational distribution of state funds by increasing investment in some areas and pulling it out of others. We will energetically develop large companies and large enterprise groups that own intellectual property rights, have name brand products and are internationally competitive. Second, we will speed up the transformation of large state-owned enterprises into stock companies. We will improve corporate governance and change the operational mechanisms of enterprises to meet the requirements for a modern enterprise system. We will institute a system for annually assigning responsibility for enterprise performance and a system for holding enterprise executives responsible for their work during their terms of service. We will standardize the system of benefit packages for these executives.

Third, the process of relieving state-owned enterprises of the obligation to operate social programs will be accelerated. We will continue to carry out policy-based closures and bankruptcy proceedings for enterprises, and a legal mechanism will be established for declaring them bankrupt. Fourth, we will deepen reform of the power, telecommunications and civil aviation industries and continue reform of the postal and railway systems and urban public utilities by liberalizing market access and instituting competitive mechanisms. We will improve the management system and the methods of oversight for state assets and institute a budget system for the use of state capital. We will standardize the procedures for transforming state-owned enterprises and for transferring state equity to prevent erosion of state assets and protect the legitimate rights and interests of employees. We will deepen the reform of collectively owned enterprises and promote the development of a diversified collective sector of the economy.

(An extract from the Third Session of Tenth National People's Congress of China, *Report of the Work of the Government*, March 2005)

# 11
# Economic Reform in China: The Ensuing Phase

If economic liberalization in China was the only constituent of reforms, the challenges that currently confront the nation would have been much fewer. China's precedent economic experience, a subject that has been discussed in the last few chapters, demonstrates that inducting China onto a path that would take it towards liberalism was not simply a matter of easing curbs on investment and trade. It also entailed a wide gamut of steps that included decentralization, marketization and ownership diversification. In the absence of a broader understanding of the underpinnings and measures that would be required for an effective strategy of economic liberalization, it is improbable that China would have a macroeconomic environment that has enabled it to emerge as a leading foreign investor destination.

If a single element of economic reform entailed a broad-based strategy it underscores that achieving other objectives of reform requires much more than garnering huge amounts of foreign investment and increasing the rates of industrial expansion. So far, China's primary focus has been to ensure the continuity of economic liberalization and at the outset this was a point of emphasis that worked well in creating the link between liberalization, growth and development. The linkage between the three vital parameters of economic progress scored significant gains in poverty reduction and per capita income. Perhaps this was one reason that helped postponing the implementation of certain reform measures that were required but difficult to put into place.

Having traversed a path that has enabled China to capitalize on its strengths or areas of comparative advantage and taken it towards the attainment of an impressive economic performance, the nation has entered the next stage of reform, which, in essence, is about managing and sustaining its prosperity. Sustainability of growth is a tough call in the absence of institutional reform and so far this is a fundamental that the establishment has skirted around. In the Chinese context, it is not as if the institutional structures have not adapted to changing scenarios in the economic and geopolitical realm. Undeniably, the pursuit of liberalism itself was an adjustment, particularly for hardliners in the communist establishment. However, the thrust of policies and measures was towards harnessing the growth potential and institutional change was an adjunct or an ancillary constituent of this process.

In the ensuing phase of China's economic development, institutional reform will have a pivotal role to play in determining whether or not it can step up the pace of its development and concomitantly the expediency with which it can surmount its challenges. The process of institutional reform involves an extensive range of ideological, political and social adjustments, some of which have been kept at bay. Delving into all the reasons that have deterred a greater extent of institutional adaptability would be an exhaustive exercise; in essence at the root of obvious inadequacies in this ambit lies one basic reason: an apprehension by factions of the political establishment in China is that a process of institutional reform could usher in its wake the possibility (some would even contend the imminent likelihood) of political and ideological tumult. This is a fact that has elicited fervent debate and a categorical assertion about the precise consequences of institutional reform would be difficult. Equally true is the irrefutable irony that the attempt to preempt change does not prevent it, over the medium or longer term.

Once again, if one alludes to China's economic experience it tells us that liberalism and its ramifications did not herald tumultuous outcomes; on the contrary, it averted these (this point has been elucidated in Chapter 10). Perhaps, it should be reiterated that one of the advantages of the policy strategy pursued by China is that the elements of what could have heralded dramatic change have crept into the economic and social domain of contemporary China without creating a major upheaval. Evidently, the precedents of China's experience over the last three decades underscores the realistic possibility that the nation will be able to achieve the required extent of institutional reform without resulting in situations that are unmanageable or extreme. Moreover, the need to preserve certain vested interests, which have got so entrenched, should not preclude measures that China needs to implement if it is to serve its imperatives, a crucial one being the expansion of an indigenous private sector and home-grown entrepreneurship.

In any case, shutting out the winds of ideological change, particularly during an era when a nation is transforming itself, is as possible as keeping the sunlight out on a desert strip at noon. Reining it in does not do much good either. Directing it on a course that would facilitate overcoming the constraints to development is the most positive option. In 1990 there were about six provinces that had reportedly witnessed problems of rural unrest; by 2000 there were 16 such provinces. In the larger context, such instances may be sporadic; however, these are reminders that the outcomes of increasing levels of disparity may be contained for a time by the hand of draconian authority but cannot be curbed.

On the subject of ideology, economists and political scientists opine, and some fervently so, that the prevalence of democracy in China is inevitable. Regardless of how likely this may seem, an even more exigent concern relates to the developmental challenges that the nation is grappling with. Tackling these could result in systems that work more democratically (relatively speaking), but whether these would culminate in making China a democracy remains to be seen. Furthermore, even if institutional reform were to propel China towards becoming a democracy the precise manifestation and nature that this would take is another feature that only time will unravel. Thus the central objective is sustaining development; whether or not one of the outcomes of the policy and non-measures directed towards this will be a democratic political establishment continues to be a matter of conjecture. It would be particularly interesting to observe the variant of democracy that China may very well evolve. Undeniably, this is a possibility that that we cannot rule out because, if the nation can have its fusion of market-based socialism, it can have its own variant of democracy – something that could be described as 'democratic authoritarianism', or something similar.

China's next economic transition could be waiting in the wings. Measures that provide an impetus for growth rates will have to be accompanied by steps that ensure the consistency and stability of economic progress. This would herald a shift, or some would say a major adjustment, wherein the country's policies would have to broaden so that the priorities of accelerating growth do not impede or supersede initiatives that will facilitate putting in place the preconditions of sustainable growth. This would require the utilization of production processes that have a lowered energy intensity, which will be environment friendly, coupled with the adoption of measures that will help the conservation of water, soil and other scarce resources. Having achieved considerable economic progress, the impending considerations of sustainability require that China's governance and commercial establishment identify new drivers of growth, tap the unexploited potential of existing sources of growth and step up employment provision. This chapter and Chapter 12 will delve into the issues pertinent to the attainment of sustainable development.

## The underpinnings of China's present growth patterns: sustainability issues and imperatives

Perhaps we need a more microcosmic view of economic progress because, in the context of attaining sustainable growth in China, it is the underlying causes of productivity increases, particularly that of labour, which represent a vital aspect. During the post-1993 phase labour productivity was driven mainly by capital accumulation, most of which consisted of investment in physical capital. It must be noted that human capital formation was rather low. This is a significant point because, prior to 1993, labour productivity had been fuelled by a relocation of labour to more productive sectors than agriculture, such as industry and services, China would have fared better on three frontiers – employment provision, poverty reduction and reduction of income disparities – if this process had not lost its pace.

According to most growth-accounting estimates, over the period 1978– 2004 the contribution of capital accumulation to GDP growth has been over 50 per cent, that of employment growth has been less than 30 per cent and total factor productivity growth has contributed an annual increase of 2–4 per cent to China's rising levels of income. However, in order to understand the change in the sources of growth over the last 25 years it would be useful if the time span of over two decades is divided into two phases, the first one being 1978–93 and the second 1993–2004. Numerical estimates about the contribution of each factor of production, i.e. labour, capital and other inputs, differ but the conclusions that emanate from the studies are similar.

The sectoral transition that usually occurs in the initial stages of development, when there is a shift of surplus labour from the agricultural to the industrial sector, was underway in China by 1978. This trend continued for the first 15 years of the reform period but it petered out after the early 1990s. According to a study by the World Bank China office (2005) labour productivity rose by 7 per cent on average per annum over 1978–93 and employment increased by 2.5 per cent on average. However, even though the share of employment provided by agriculture declined during the time span mentioned, it stood at a fairly significant 50 per cent in 1996. During the post-1993 phase (1993–2004), the investment–GDP ratio also increased significantly, labour productivity rose by 7.8 per cent and unemployment declined by barely 1 per cent. Furthermore, increasing levels of productivity were also accompanied by rising capital–labour ratios. This trend reveals an important fact: during the initial stages of growth, the shift of labour from a less productive sector (agriculture) to a more productive one contributed significantly to the increases in labour productivity.

Subsequently, the relocation of labour into industry and to other more productive sectors, such as services reduced and, as a consequence, this contributed to an overall productivity increase of less than 1 per cent. After the early 1990s labour productivity increases were largely the result of infusions of capital and significant increases in industrial production over 1993–2004. Industrial value added output increased on average by 11 per cent per annum during 1993–2004. Estimates indicate that it was a rise in productivity in industry that contributed to overall productivity growth of over 5 per cent.

The slowdown in the capacity of the agricultural sector to absorb employment, coupled with the decline in the shift of surplus labour from the agricultural sector to the industrial or other productive sectors, are impediments to stepping up the pace of development in China. Be it the township and village enterprises or the services sector, both are more productive than the agricultural sector and more labour-intensive than large-scale manufacturing. Despite this fact, there has been little or no expansion in the TVEs and the growth of services is extremely limited. This restricts the scope of a shift of labour to more productive spheres and this in turn would limit growth prospects over the longer term.

According to the World Bank study the contribution of capital accumulation (depicted by the capital–labour ratio) increased over the period 1993–2004. Furthermore, the contribution of capital accumulation to GDP growth was 62 per cent over the period of 1993–2004, which was higher than the preceding period. Total factor productivity (TFP) contributed about 30 per cent to growth and total employment growth stood at a nominal 6 per cent. Studies also indicate that the capital–output ratio rose from 2.2 per cent in 1994 to 2.8 in 2004. Total factor productivity decreased from 3.7 per cent (1978–1993) to 2.7 per cent (1993–2004) according to the World Bank study mentioned.

Interestingly, a discussion about the sources of China's growth is a reminder of a frequent debate that was evoked when East Asia's phenomenal economic progress had taken the world by surprise. Extensive research on the subject revealed essentially two schools of thought – one that attributed the spectacular growth performance of East Asia's nations to a surge in productivity levels and the other that contended that it was massive investments in capital accumulation that drove the seemingly boundless prosperity of these nations for about two decades. A similar question is imminent in the context of China. The answer to this is important because it would help one determine and even forecast not just growth prospects but also the situation insofar as a wide range of developmental parameters are concerned.

Once again there are two fundamental explanations for China's buoyant economic performance and there is some argument about which of these reflects a more accurate understanding about what propelled the substantive increase in the country's growth rates. One elucidates that a greater proportion of China's growth was driven by physical capital accumulation and this was reflected by a fairly large investment–GDP ratio. A declining level of employment growth, particularly over the last decade, and rather modest contribution of labour growth indicates that China's economic progress was spurred by increasing levels of investment in physical capital.

The other explains that it is productivity increases that played a far more significant role than capital accumulation in providing an impetus to China's economy over the last two and a half decades. This is so despite the prevalence of moderate to low levels of investment inefficiency in China. Goldman Sachs, in its paper about China, states:

> After taking into account many of the controversies surrounding the TFP estimation for China we arrived at a similar conclusion: a sharp and

sustained increase in productivity was the driving force behind China's astonishing growth, although factor accumulation – the growth of physical human capital – was also important. During this period TFP gains average 3.3 per cent per annum and accounted for 36 per cent of China's growth, similar to the contribution by capital accumulation.

Ascertaining which explanation has more validity would be a digression because, taken together, both are two sides of the same coin. In the absence of either increasing levels of capital accumulation and an uptrend in both labour and total factor productivity it is likely that China's economic growth would not just have been lower and but it probably would have petered out way before 25 years had passed.

Notably, one of the reasons for productivity increases during the pre-1993 phase was the relocation of labour from agriculture to industry. Studies by the OECD indicate that productivity of non-agricultural labour is about four times that of agricultural labour. Thus, over the last decade and a half, although China has sustained its high growth rates, the potential for further increases in productivity and employment absorption has not been realized.

In its climb to higher levels of economic progress, as China carved out new growth centres it did this at the expense of the sectors that had driven the increase in GDP during the initial stages of economic progress and could have contributed towards further increments in growth and employment provision. When a developing country that is labour abundant has a process of growth that is driven mainly by investments in capital-intensive technology the result will not be employment provision of the magnitude that a country like China requires.

Another aspect of China's growth pattern is its rather high investment–GDP ratio. Estimates may differ but the fact remains that China's present ratios are not conducive to sustainable growth. The fact that the incremental capital–output ratio has not risen significantly (overall during the last decade or so) reflects the pile-up of excessive investment in some core sector industries. As a matter of fact, the People's Bank of China (2004) criticized what it described as, 'the blind expansion of seriously low quality, duplicate projects' in steel, aluminum and cement. A high investment–GDP ratio is an inevitability given the course that state-owned enterprise restructuring and financial-sector reform has taken. Estimates indicate that an investment–GDP ratio of 30–35 per cent would be considered sustainable; however, China's current investment share in GDP is much higher, some estimates indicate that it is over 40 per cent.

However, it is not merely the quantitative aspect of investment but the low levels of investment efficiency that characterize segments of the Chinese industrial sector; some spheres in its state-owned industry need to be viewed in particular. Although one aspect of investment inefficiency relates to the scope for increasing the productivity or the return per unit of investment, this problem has wider ramifications in China. Unequivocally, a skewed pattern of capital accumulation is an important reason for the prevalence of inequities in the distribution of income and in the access to social infrastructure. Understandably, the prevalence of low to moderate levels of investment inefficiency in China's industrial sector would have been less alarming if the sectoral allocation of investment was more equitable. This would have made for higher levels of allocative inefficiency.

Furthermore, China has a domestic saving of 46 per cent. (Domestic saving is the sum of household, public and enterprise saving. The savings of non-financial enterprises from their retained earnings have increased from 12.5 per cent of GDP in 1996 to almost 18 per cent in 2003. Government or public savings in China have remained at about 8 per cent of GDP.) It seems that a high level of savings is perceived by households as almost mandatory, given the absence of any social security, a process of pension reform that has yet to be completed and the negligible medical and education insurance cover for the lower income groups. One of the most important incentives to save arises from the allocation of funds that parents make towards the education of a child. Increasing job insecurity and intensifying competition will accentuate the need to provide not just for education but other contingencies that may arise over the short to medium term. Thus, inextricably linked to the process of identifying new sources of growth is the necessary orientation of China's patterns of public expenditure towards increasing the provision of social infrastructure provision, expediting pension reform and the utilization of household saving with more efficacy.

The economic, technological and institutional weaknesses with which China finds itself currently saddled do not arise from a deficiency of growth; rather they can be attributed to a lack of transmission of mechanisms that would have enabled the benefits of higher levels of growth to percolate to a large proportion of the population. The score card on poverty reduction during the 1990s, the increasing level of regional disparity and the rising levels of income and non-income inequalities are unmistakable indicators that this link between the three fundamental variables has weakened, and strengthening it entails ensuring the presence of effective transmission mechanisms. These are: i) poverty reduction; ii) human capital formation; and iii) technological advancement.

In the next section of this chapter I will examine one the most important transmission mechanisms of economic progress – poverty reduction. The other two transmission mechanisms of economic growth will be discussed in Chapter 12.

## Poverty reduction in China

Poverty reduction in China began during the 1950s and there were significant improvements on this front until the early 1990s.

China's first major economic transition began with the inception of Maoist rule. The decade following this may not have witnessed a remarkable growth performance but it achieved decreasing levels of poverty, infant mortality rates and rising levels of literacy. Human development indicators improved noticeably and China began to emerge from a scenario of abject poverty and deprivation after the early 1950s. The centrality of social welfare permeated through the various layers of the government administration to the grass-roots though the communes. It is the communes that had a crucial role to play in providing for the means of sustenance, health care and education.

Sadly, both the Great Leap Forward and Cultural Revolution had damaging consequences that led to reversals of a good proportion of the developmental gains that China had achieved during the earlier Maoist era. According to a study undertaken by the World Bank in 1978 there were approximately 260 million people living under the poverty line.

Having embarked on large-scale poverty reduction programmes since the early 1950s, China managed to reduce the number of poor from 200 million in 1981 to 34 million in 1999. Unequivocally, the country stands among the most successful instances of poverty reduction; notably, this was the result of measures that were implemented prior to liberalization and during the initial stages after it. The most significant reduction in abject poverty occurred during the 1980s as a result of the adoption of rural initiatives. The growth of rural industrialization, a sizable increase in the procurement prices of agricultural goods and an improvement in the rural–urban terms of trade led to an upswing in the rural economy. Incomes in rural regions rose by 15 per cent per annum and between 1981 and 1984 income poverty at $1 a day level declined from 49 to 24 per cent. There was a slowdown in the pace and magnitude of poverty reduction after the mid-1980s and it was not until the next round of procurement reforms, implemented over 1994–6, that the subsequent spell of significant poverty reduction occurred. Once again, this was the outcome of increases in agricultural prices and output and the launch of the 8–7 plan by the government in 1994.

Germane to any evaluation of poverty reduction in China is the link between increasing levels of prosperity in the rural regions and the quantum and expeditiousness with which the number of those below the poverty line has declined. At some point in time after the early 1990s, despite increasing growth rates, rural incomes were declining. The inability of all those who moved out of the agricultural sector to obtain employment, a contraction of the rural enterprise sector and declining prices of agricultural commodities are the factors that weakened the link with economic growth.

If one were to view the broad trends in poverty reduction after 1978 we can differentiate three phases.

i) Over the period 1978–85, total population living under the poverty line declined from 260 million to 97 million. The incidence of poverty declined from 33 per cent to 9.2 per cent. In terms of the standard $1 a day definition of the poverty line, there was a decline in poverty from 60 per cent in 1978 to 40 per cent in 1985.

ii) During the mid-1980s and through to 1992 there was a discernible increase in income poverty and non-income poverty. The incidence of rural poverty increased to 12.8 per cent in 1989 from 10.4 per cent in 1988. Urban poverty increased from 0.2 per cent in 1988 to 0.4 per cent in 1989.

iii) After 1992 some progress was made towards poverty reduction; however, it was evident that the extent of improvement made during the 1990s was less, in certain regions considerably so, than the poverty reduction that had been achieved by the early 1980s.

iv) A general observation that can be arrived at is that over the entire period of 1990–9 there was a reduction in the number of those people who lived under the poverty line (by all definitions of poverty line) according to the $1 a day definition of the poverty line, the headcount index reduced from 31.5 per cent to 17.4 per cent. In absolute terms, 14 million people were lifted out of poverty. Overall China achieved an impressive score in poverty reduction.

v) During the sub-phase of 1994–6 the most promising gains in terms of reducing poverty and improvements in the distribution of income occured.

As a matter of fact, over the last ten years, poverty-reducing growth in China has not been as remarkable as it was in the period prior to 1996. Inequalities of income did increase throughout almost the entire period of 1990–9, the exception being the years 1995–7. During the preceding decade, the rural Gini index rose by 4.04 and the urban Gini index by 6.06 points. Evidently, the poverty-reducing impact of growth had tapered off by the mid-1990s; this was partly due to the changing underpinnings of growth, which was discussed in the previous section. Besides this there were other reasons that relate to the manner and context in which poverty reduction programmes have been implemented.

A nuanced view of poverty reduction needs to be taken in order to understand the reasons for poverty not declining as substantially as it should have done. It is not that the objective of poverty reduction has not been accorded importance during the last decade; it has, but this was obviously not enough to offset the adverse consequences of changing patterns of sectoral importance that impacted a proportion of the population.

Growth strategies pursued during the 1990s did not embody measures that would provide an impetus to poverty reduction, in contrast to the rapid structural transformation that occurred at the inception of economic liberalization in China. It was the expansion and prosperity in the rural economy that drove economic progress until the mid-1980s, and the significant progress achieved in the ambit of poverty reduction was largely the result of an increase in output, not just in the agricultural sector but also in rural industry, including town and village enterprises.

The decollectivization of agriculture and other price-related reforms in the primary sector led to a rapid increase in output; it is estimated that the value of agricultural output increased by 7.4 per cent per annum over the period 1978–84. From 1978 to 1982 the number of planned product categories reduced from 21 to 13 and the procurement prices for a number of commodities were increased. For instance, by the beginning of 1979 the procurement price for grain increased by 20.9 per cent, by 23.9 per cent for oil crops, by 17 per cent for cotton, by 21.9 per cent for sugar crops and by 24.3 per cent for pork.

According to a UNDP report on poverty alleviation in China, the state procurement price contributed 16 per cent to output growth and 20 per cent to the increase in rural incomes during 1978–84. Furthermore, by 1984 output from TVEs constituted about 38.6 per cent of GNP and it provided employment for about 123.5 million people or 20.5 per cent of total employment. The result was a tripling of the per capita incomes of a sizable proportion of the rural population.

The subsequent shift towards export-oriented industrialization and the resultant expansion of the industrial sector, most of which was concentrated on the eastern coast, led to a change in the focus of growth strategy. The concomitant of this was declining levels of growth in the agricultural sector and as prosperity began to wane in a number of rural regions it dealt a rather severe blow to poverty reduction. There was an inherent bias towards urban development, despite the fact that it was economic progress in the rural economy that spurred growth during the 1980s. Although China exemplifies an instance of successful trade and investment liberalization, this did not have to obviate an expansion of rural infrastructure in areas where this was inadequate, neither did it have to exclude building other spheres of comparative advantage that would be able to absorb the excess labour, those who are currently unemployed.

Before proceeding further, a description of recent poverty reduction strategies that China has implemented follows.

(i) The Chinese leadership rolled out the new countryside agenda in April 2006. The fundamental objective of this programme is to provide an impetus (a much needed one at that) to rural expansion in the Chinese economy. The agenda dovetails an increase in educational and health expenditures with a reduction in taxes. The important provisions of the new countryside agenda are:

- Abolition of agricultural tax from 2006. The rural taxation burden has reduced by RMB100 billion annually and this means a per capita reduction of RMB120 in tax payments.
- The government expenditure on education will be increased by RMB42 billion per annum over the next five years. An investment of RMB100 million will be ploughed into road construction over the next few years.

- The introduction of a new co-operative medical scheme wherein a rural household will contribute RMB10 per person and this will be supplemented by a subsidy of RMB10 by the local government and RMB20 billion by the central government.

(ii) The 8–7 programme (8 for 80 million people and 7 for the number of years before the year 2000) called on central and local governments, mass organizations and enterprises directly under the central government to participate in poverty reduction. The 8–7 plan was basically a programme that provided tax reduction, financial grants and social-development projects for 592 designated poor counties.

(iii) The location of industry on the eastern coast led to a situation of regional disparity wherein the benefits of economic progress were clustered in the east and the western region lagged behind. In 1999, the average income gap between the eastern and western provinces was 1.4. In 1999 the central government decided to implement the Developing the Western Region strategy. In essence, the main objective of this measure was to reduce the disparity between the two regions by boosting development and creating new engines for economic growth in western provinces. The government plan was a fairly comprehensive one, which spanned five aspects, including infrastructure, construction (especially of water power, communications, transportation, tourism and broadcasting), ecological development and environmental protection, creating new propellants of growth in the industrial sector, development of technology and education and accelerating skills training and promotion of reforms and openness.

(iv) Enabling farmers to eliminate the shackles of poverty was one of the priorities of the tenth five-year plan. Measures related to improving the situation insofar as farmers, farming and farming areas were concerned were formulated. Under the aegis of this plan some of the initiatives taken in this direction included:

- Increasing income of farmers by removing unreasonable taxes and charges on their incomes.
- Changing the composition of agrarian production to such that it includes more commercial crops and fewer staples and, setting up of food-processing industries.
- Provision of better infrastructure and information and expanding the access of peasants to markets.
- Furthermore, in order to improve the prospects of employment for excess labour, restrictions on the mobility of rural residents were eased. As such, the urban residency regulation was modified so that all rural residents who had a stable job or source of livelihood could migrate (with their families) to small cities and towns and apply for permanent residency.

v) The Food for Work programme in 1984 was formulated to utilize surplus grain and cotton stocks to pay for infrastructure construction in depressed areas. The principle that defined this scheme was a prudent one because it linked the allocation of relief to increasing the income capacity of the poorer regions. It is this feature that differentiated the Food for Work programme from other methods of conventional poverty alleviation or reduction.

By the end of 2003, despite the poverty reducing programmes that were implemented, 6.2 per cent of the rural population lived at levels that were either slightly below or above the poverty line. A commonality that runs through poverty reduction strategies that have been implemented in China during the post-liberalization era is the rather lacklustre impact that these have had in preventing increasing levels of poverty over the medium or longer term. For instance, the appearance of the 'new poor' in the urban poverty profile, such as the marginalized sections, the elderly and sick, indicated that there were sections of the population (however small these may have been as a proportion of the population) that did not benefit either from liberalization or from poverty reduction. This was an ill that needed to be tackled, the exigency of which cannot be played down, particularly when one takes into account that the actual urban unemployment rate estimated to be 4.3 per cent in 2003 may be as high as 10 per cent.

Thus, the effectiveness of measures initiated to mitigate existent levels of poverty has been a mixed bag. The reason for this does not stem from conceptual limitations in the steps devised to tackle poverty and income inequalities because both the western region strategy and the measures that were set into motion to increase farmers' incomes had a multipronged focus. For instance, if one were to view the western region development strategy it becomes apparent that it placed great emphasis on the creation of conditions that would encourage a wide range of economic activities, including the establishment of industrial enterprises and many others. Even if one accepts that poverty alleviation measures did have some demerits, they were certainly as good as any other poverty reduction strategies.

As with poverty reduction initiatives in other developing countries so also in China (although to a much lesser extent) once allocations have been made toward poverty reducing programmes and projects, the assumption is that enough has been done in so far as tackling the problem of poverty in a particular region is concerned. However equally important is the design of an effective process of implementation that will ensure that funds allocated serve the objective for which it these are being deployment.

For instance if the 8–7 plan had been implemented with greater clarity and a more participatory approach at the local level its impact would have been larger.

A more recent measure of poverty alleviation is the new countryside agenda, which comprises a package of rural development measures and is among the most ambitious ones to be implemented over the last few years.

Its fairly comprehensive formulation does accord emphasis to increasing the per capita income and improving accessibility of poorer sections of the community to social infrastructure. The specified increment in government funding towards compulsory education reduces expenditure of rural households on junior, primary and secondary education by about 6 per cent. However, the plan to reduce taxes in rural regions will only increase per capita incomes by 1.4 per cent, which is clearly insufficient. The proposed expenditure and the scope that the new countryside agenda will certainly not be enough to tackle in entirety the problem of poverty, inequalities of income and other forms of socio-economic deprivation.

It is observable that China will need more than one such agenda if per capita incomes in the rural regions are to rise substantially to boost poverty alleviation and consumption. An assessment of this agenda is a reminder that any poverty alleviation strategy is not complete without measures that will increase employment opportunities. At this point in time China has surplus labour of about 200 million and this, coupled with the addition of 4 million graduates annually, underscores the fact that the significance of labour-intensive manufacturing in the country's economic progress has not waned, nor has its potential for further expansion been exhausted. China will continue to be a production hub for global manufacturing and it is well positioned and suitably endowed to take advantage of the numerous possibilities that continue to exist for increased participation and integration in the international product chain.

At the inception of liberalization inequalities between the rural and urban areas had declined and the income differential between the two continued to reduce until 1985. Thereafter, the disparity between rural and urban regions began to increase.

As indicated in Box 11.1 income distributions were even more skewed in the rural regions than in urban China. According to the China Statistics Yearbook of 2001, the average income of urban residents was nearly three times that of average rural income. Although there is polarization in the urban areas there is less inequality, particularly insofar as accessibility to infrastructural constraints and employment is concerned. This fact mirrors a crucial reality that pertains not just to China but veritably to the entire developing world – income disparities skew the accessibility to a wide range of social and public services. This in turn constrains access to employment and opportunity creation. Inevitably, this dampened the efficacy of poverty reducing schemes. Furthermore, given the reduction of public expenditure in the rural sector, as government expenditure allocations to agriculture (as a percentage of GDP) reduced from 13.6 per cent in 1978 to 8.3 per cent of GDP in 1985, it did contribute to a decline in rural incomes. However, the efficiency with which funds allocated were assigned also had a role in determining the outcomes of poverty reduction measures.

# Box 11.1  Increasing income and non-income inequality in China

During the early years of reform in China the Gini Coefficient was 0.30 and by 2002 it reached 0.46. This means that the national inequality has increased by more than 50 per cent over the last two decades.

According to a National Household Survey (2002) conducted in China the top 5 per cent controlled nearly 20 per cent of the total income while the top 10 per cent had nearly 32 per cent of the total income. The average income of the highest decile was 11 times that of the lowest.

In 2003 urban per capita disposable income in China was 3.23 times that of rural per capita net income. Furthermore studies point to the fact that if subsidies taken up by urban residents are accounted for in the calculation of urban incomes, the gap between urban and rural incomes would be much higher

The average urban maternal mortality rate in China is 33.1 percent per 100,000 births. The rural maternal mortality rate is almost double, it stands at 61.9 per cent per 100,000 births.

According to the Household survey conducted in 2002 by the Institute of Economics of the Chinese Academy of Sciences the richest one per cent of rural residents earned 6 per cent of the total rural income and the richest 5 per cent earned 18 per cent of the total rural income. Those who constitute the top ten per cent on the income hierarchy earn 28 per cent of the total income.

*Source: China Human Development Report* (2005), United Nations Development Programme.

Although central and provincial governments disbursed outlays in accordance to the requirement of the region concerned, county governments distributed it in consonance with the repayment ability of people. This was so because one measure of poverty reduction was the extension of subsidized loans and obviously those in dire need of financial support lacked the capacity to redeem the loan.

This initiative threw light on the vicious circle between accessibility and credit-worthiness wherein the extremely poor cannot afford to access some of the poverty alleviation programmes. In the light of this, poverty reduction would need to be employment-oriented and the access to health care and education would need to be subsidized. In a situation where employment provision is not possible, either because of a dearth of jobs or an inadequacy of training or skill, it would be necessary to have empowerment schemes that would enable individuals to obtain employment or become self-employed.

Furthermore, the inadequacy of investment outlays in public services such as health care and education also deterred the poverty alleviation programmes from being as effective as these could potentially have been.

## Conclusion

The fundamental success of poverty reduction hinges partly on the effectiveness of redistributive effort; even more important than this, however, is the inherent capability of growth strategy to result in a substantive alleviation of deprivation. Given the present scenario in the Chinese economy, it seems difficult to arrive at an accurate projection about whether poverty reduction efforts would be able to reduce the number of workers in its unorganized sector. A fact that one can be certain of is that enhanced access and expansion of social infrastructure would promote higher levels of well being among the workers in the unorganized segment. For instance, it cannot be denied that affordable health care facilities and medical insurance will improve the quality of life even among the poorest workers of the unorganized sector. Added to this, an increase in the per capita consumption of social goods will help reduce the non-income disparity. When China had the rather fortuitous combination of effective redistribution and a pro-poor growth strategy, the magnitude of poverty reduction that occurred as a consequence was about the largest that a developing country has had in the last few decades. The country's economic experience lucidly depicts that, however effectively implemented, redistribution measures are a supplement to and not a substitute for a pattern of growth that is inherently more balanced or embodies a pro-development approach.

This takes us to a further exploration of the economic imperatives that are linked to human capital formation in the next chapter.

# 12
## Human Capital Formation: Trends, Implications and Future Prospects in China

Empirical evidence tells us that the prospects of sustained economic progress are dimmed or dampened by the coexistence of accelerated economic growth and income inequalities. It is possible to have a scenario where, despite the prevalence of sharp inequalities in the distribution of income there are improvements in the access that lower income groups have to social infrastructure. Not that such a situation is ideal but it is certainly less alarming than having increasing disparities in both the income and non income dimensions. Over the previous decade or so, China's public services have been markedly inadequate and reduced accessibility to the poorer sections continues to be a problem. It was an irony that investments by local governments in production projects that would provide employment came at the expense of provisions in health care and education. Public expenditure on culture, education, science and health care declined from 3.8 per cent at the beginning of the 1980s to 2.8 per cent in 1994. Public expenditure on social services declined sharply from 31 per cent in 1978 to 13 per cent in 1994.

Human capital formation played a significant role in driving China's growth rates into the 1980s. Some estimates indicate that, keeping other factors constant, its contribution to economic growth was as much as 30 per cent during 1953–77 (the pre-liberalization phase). During 1978–99 human capital accumulation contributed much less to GDP growth; some studies indicate that it accounted for 13.8 per cent of growth.

In the context of human capital formation, a mention must be made of China's services sector. The country's most recent economic census states that previous reports had underestimated the size of China's service sector. The latest estimates indicate that the service sector contributes about 48 per cent to GDP and 50 per cent of non-farming labour is absorbed by this sector. As is the case with more than a few developing countries, the informal or unorganized sector comprises a large constituent in China's service sector and it is becoming a significant avenue of employment provision.

This illustrates the vital part that human capital formation can play in enhancing and increasing opportunities in this realm because value added in the services sector depends on the levels of skill and educational attainment. At the higher end of the service sector an increasing degree of specialization and the unrelenting pressures of raising competitiveness will increase the demand for skilled and technically qualified individuals of which, in any case, there is a shortage. However, even at the lower and medium end, moderate levels of educational attainment will enable the expansion of opportunities in services. It is likely that the informal segment of the service sector in China will continue to exist, even if there is a significant rise (in per capita terms) in the extent of educational attainment.

The reduced role of human capital formation in the growth process can be partly explained by the increasing numbers of those who obtained schooling and higher levels of educational attainment. However, a discermble proportion of the slowdown in human capital formation is avoidable and constitutes an unfavourable feature of China's current patterns of economic progress. It is not as if the nation had exhausted its potential for human capital formation; on the contrary there exist some regions in the country that are confronted with a deficiency of health care and educational inputs as a result of poverty-constrained access or lack of availability or both

Poverty limits the access to health care and education, despite the availability of social infrastructure, and this will deter sustainable development, an unequivocal fact that is often overlooked.

This takes us on to a concise description of the two pillars on which human capital formation rests – health care reform and education.

## Health care reform in China: was it an instrument of inequity?

Consistent improvements in per capita income would not be possible without an expansion in human capital formation, on which the employability of individuals depend. It is not uncommon to find, in developing countries, situations where the presence of employment opportunities in certain sector coexists with stark unemployment because of a lack of training or skill formation. This is an anomaly that dilutes the impact of poverty reduction efforts and can be remedied by the design and effective implementation of policies that would increase human capital formation.

Unlike in most developing countries, a slowdown in the expansion of public services in the Chinese context is not impeded by a paucity of resources. Health care reform in the country provides us with a vivid corroboration of this fact. At the WHO's Alma Alta conference in 1978, China's health care system was cited as a model for countries to pursue by 2000. The sad irony is that, by the year 2000, the nation ranked 188th out of 191 countries in terms of fairness in financial contributions to the health sector.

When we review the changes that have occurred in the Chinese health care sector it is an eye opener. It tells us that the lack of access is a direct outcome of the weaknesses in the delivery systems of public health mechanism. This, in itself, is a pointer to the limitations that privatization can have on enhancing the provision of public services if it is not accompanied by other effective measures to increase accessibility.

Inevitably, privatizing led to rapid cost escalations in the health care sector, with inpatient and outpatient costs increasing at an annual average rate of about 16 per cent during the 1990s. This apart, the breakdown of the health care infrastructure that existed in the rural economy during the pre-liberalization phase resulted in sharp inequities in the distribution of health care facilities. Moreover, preventive health services and outreach programmes have been considerably weakened by 20 years of health reform.

Dismantling the communes brought with it a number of advantages; however, it also resulted in a contraction of health care facilities that the lower income groups could afford. Over the period of 1949 to the late 1970s, investments in the health sector were prioritized. Expenditures in this sphere were directed towards the construction of an equity-oriented public health system. Basic services were provided by the 'barefoot doctors' and community health workers, added to which there was a three-tiered network of clinics, health facilities and hospitals at the township and country levels. Furthermore, community-level curative health systems were supported by investments in preventive health care measures, which included, for instance, mosquito control and clean water projects. Added to this, 90 per cent of the rural citizens were covered by medical insurance by the late 1970s.

The reduction of public finances may have been inevitable when China began its transition towards becoming a market-oriented economy and, thus, the initial blow that this dealt to health infrastructure may not have been avoidable but the continued decline in the provision of even basic health care and medical facilities could have been reversed amid rising levels of economic progress. The glaring inadequacy of health infrastructure in the country's rural economy could have been avoided, but the fact that it wasn't represents an unequivocal lapse and this constitutes an important aspect of reform. The State Council, in one of its documents (Document no. 4, 1991 of the State Council), stated in the foreword, 'During health reform we ignored the support of rural health work. Investment for health care was reduced, the lower levels of the health care system in the towns and villages were severely hit.'

Over a decade later, according to the *China Daily* (2005), the health minister of China, Gao Qiang spoke of the inequity and weaknesses of the rural health system as a factor that contributed to the SARS epidemic in 2003. The minister cited an official national survey in 2003, which indicated that nearly 49 per cent of patients that required treatment did not visit a doctor and 30 per cent of patients that needed hospitalization did not receive it because they could not afford the costs involved. Furthermore, the government contribution to hospital costs had declined from 30 per cent to 8 per cent of total government spending in 2000.

The country spends about 5 per cent of its GDP on the health sector and, thus, low allocations to this sector do not explain either the deterioration of the rural health care infrastructure or the breakdown of preventive public health measures. The present insufficiency of affordable health care for the poorer sections of China's society is largely the outcome of the prevalent structure of health expenditure that has not assigned much emphasis to increasing the access of affordable case in small towns and villages. An indicator of this is the allocation of 25 per cent of total government health spending (2005–6) to four of China's wealthiest cities – Shanghai, Beijing, Zhejiang and Jiangsu.

Although the level of curative care and the availability of essential drugs have improved, even in the most remote areas, the accessibility to poorer sections of society continues to be impeded by a lack of purchasing power or affordability. By 1992 only 10 per cent of rural residents were covered by medical health insurance. The commercialization of health care, which emphasizes fee-based financing of curative care, reflected the fact that the priority that had earlier been accorded to the programmes of public health care (which included public health education and infectious disease prevention) did not seem to prevail in present times.

Subsequent to the outbreak of SARS, in 2003, the government made some commitments to improve the public health infrastructure; however, it will take some time and a concerted effort in expanding both availability of and access to health care facilities, particularly in the rural regions. In a New Year message to China on 1 January 2007 Gao Qiang stated that the medical care reform scheme will consist of increased government investment, stricter professional supervision and reduced medical costs for citizens in urban and rural communities.

## The link between human capital formation and technological advancement

Studies about the distribution of education indicate that China has a Gini index that ranges from very equal 0.15 to less than 0.45. It must be noted that after 1995 this inequity in the realm of education has continued to widen. The negative consequences of this are not difficult to gauge. First, it represents in certain provinces of the country a huge loss of social welfare. Second, it is worth remembering that if human capital formation had not taken place on the scale that it did during the era that preceded liberalization, despite the inherent disadvantages that beset the policy context of the time, it is very improbable that China would have taken the rapid strides that it did towards economic betterment.

There exists a link between the sustainability of reasonably high levels of economic growth and human capital formation, and this becomes rather pronounced in a scenario where China is carving out new sources of comparative advantage in the production of technologically intensive goods.

When one juxtaposes China's rather sluggish performance over the last decade in the ambit of human capital accumulation with its stated objective of etching for itself core competences in the sector of hi-tech manufacturing it throws light on a blatant contradiction between policy formulation and the prevalent realities on the ground.

At this point I will discuss the link between technical upgrading, the creation of domestic industrial capabilities and human capital formation in China. Chapter 13 will also present a discussion about the impact that foreign direct investment-linked technological transfer has had on technical progress in China.

In 1985, a report by the Communist Party Central Committee on 'The Reform of the Science and Technology Management System' stated that the ultimate goal of China's science and technology (S&T) policies was the establishment and support of an entirely new S&T structure.

At the apex, China has an institutional structure that has enabled a fairly effective process of technological transfer mainly from TNCs and MNCs. China has a well-defined and centralized S&T strategy, which it executes mainly through three sectors. These comprise R&D institutions, government-owned and private enterprises and the universities. Understandably, a fair degree of co-ordination exists between its industrial policy, S&T programmes and its R&D.

Relative to the developed world (as indicated in Table 12.1), despite growth in China's gross expenditures on research and development (GERD), China does lag far behind in R&D funding. According to the OECD, in 1998 some 85 per cent of world R&D expenditures were accounted by only seven countries (all members of OECD). (The United States accounted for about 44 per cent of all OECD R&D investment.) Most developed countries spend between 2 and 2.5 per cent of their annual GDP on R&D.

However, as indicated in Table 12.2 among the non-OECD nations, China has the largest R&D expenditure. China's R&D expenditure relative to GDP

*Table 12.1*   National R&D statistics

|  | 1995 | 1996 | 1997 | 1998 | 1999 | 2000 |
|---|---|---|---|---|---|---|
| Gross expenditure on R&D (GERD) (billions of RMB) | 34.90 | 40.50 | 50.90 | 55.10 | 67.90 | 89.60 |
| Annual growth of GERD (%) | −0.60 | 9.50 | 24.90 | 10.90 | 26.00 | 17.90 |
| GERD/GDP (%) | 0.60 | 0.60 | 0.64 | 0.69 | 0.83 | 1.01 |

*Source*: A Special Report for the Environment, Science and Technology Section, US Embassy, Beijing, China (2002), *Data Books for 2000 and 2001*, Ministry of Science and Technology.

*Table 12.2*　R&D as a percentage of GDP by country

| Country | 1995 | 1996 | 1997 | 1998 | 1999 | 2000 |
|---|---|---|---|---|---|---|
| China | 0.60 | 0.60 | 0.64 | 0.69 | 0.83 | 1.01 |
| Mexico | 0.31 | 0.31 | 0.34 | 0.46 | 0.40 | N/A |
| India | 0.81 | N/A | N/A | N/A | 0.86 | N/A |
| Russia | 0.84 | 0.79 | 0.90 | 0.97 | 1.01 | 1.09 |
| Japan | 2.89 | 2.77 | 2.83 | 2.94 | 2.93 | N/A |
| United States | 2.51 | 2.55 | 2.58 | 2.60 | 2.65 | 2.76 |

*Source:* A Special Report for the Environment, Science and Technology Section, US Embassy Beijing, China (2002), Ministry of Science and Technology China.

was in the range of 0.6–0.7 per cent for a decade, before increasing sharply in 1999 and 2000. According to the S&T indicators report by China's Ministry of Science and Technology (2000) the ratio of Chinese enterprises' R&D expenditures to sales revenues or 'R&D intensity' remained rather low at around 0.5 per cent throughout the 1990s. In comparison, R&D intensity of US firms was over 2 per cent for the similar time period. Furthermore, 75 per cent of the work conducted by China's S&T community has focused on product or process development. Basic research constituted only about 5 per cent of S&T work and applied research only about 20 per cent of S&T work.

Thus, the upgrading of domestic absorptive capacity (the efficiency with which a sector or industry utilizes and assimilates a particularly technology or a set of technologies) depends on the expansion in other sectors, as it does on the availability of the required skills and training. Creating core competences in the segments of manufacturing that are technology-intensive needs to be matched by that presence of specialized and professional personnel if technology obtained is to be utilized effectively. Creating channels of technological transfer through FDI and other forms of co-operation with multinational and transnational corporations represents one of a number of constituents that would be required for technological transfer to fructify into rising levels of technical advancement in any region or country.

As indicated in Table 12.3, by the standards of the developing world, China has a considerable number of scientists, engineers and other professionals; the percolation of technical progress to a larger proportion of the local population entails the availability of technical and managerial skills. Vital though these inputs are there are also other prerequisites.

Human capital formation requires increasing levels of educational attainment and training across a wide gamut of spheres so that individuals will have more options of skill development. Importantly, the expansion of indigenous domestic industry also means fostering entrepreneurship. There appears to be some truth in the notion that entrepreneurs are not born out

*Table 12.3* National Science and technology personnel, 1991–9 (in millions)

|  | 1991 | 1992 | 1993 | 1994 | 1995 | 1996 | 1997 | 1998 | 1999 |
|---|---|---|---|---|---|---|---|---|---|
| Total | 2.29 | 2.27 | 2.45 | 2.58 | 2.63 | 2.90 | 2.87 | 2.81 | 2.91 |
| 'Scientists and engineers' | 1.32 | 1.37 | 1.37 | 1.54 | 1.55 | 1.69 | 1.67 | 1.49 | 1.60 |
| Percentage of total | 57.80 | 60.40 | 56.00 | 59.70 | 59.20 | 58.10 | 57.80 | 52.90 | 54.90 |

*Source:* A Special Report for the Environment Science and Technology Section, US Embassy, Beijing, China (2002).

of an educational process; however, it is also valid that it is education or training or both that hones entrepreneurial talent in a number of instances.

Although an engineer would able to present a graphic and detailed analysis of the other requisites needed for the optimum utilization of advanced technology, from an economic perspective there are some vital issues that need to be highlighted.

(i) The assimilation of sophisticated technology needs much more than the utilization of the same by a few industries, it involves a policy and non-policy context that supports and fosters innovation. Furthermore, it must be noted that innovation includes both technical and non-technical innovative endeavour and this is an important point, particularly in the context of spurring employment provision. (This may not be the most exhaustive definition of the term; however, it tells us that innovation includes a wide range of product and service-related applications, which include both inventions and improvised applications.) It is not the advent of new technology alone but also the adaptation of technology acquired in accordance to specific features and requirements of local markets that comprises technical innovation. The East Asian industrial policy is a reminder that the assimilation and localized adaptation of technology obtained was an integral medium of rapid technical progress.

(ii) Non-technical innovation, which maybe undertaken in any realm, industry or non-industry, could be related to marketing, finance, management or any other sphere; it includes the introduction of new techniques, services and improvements on existent organizational practices.

(iii) Innovation is also a conduit through which opportunity creation and consequently income can increase. When there is a rise in per capita income if a significant proportion of this increment occurs in the lower income groups it has a discernible impact on the diffusion of technical progress. This is so particularly given the commercialization of some segments of the R&D apparatus in China. The country's highly centralized technological strategy, which embodies the crucial link between R&D, industrial policy and the market, has been the main driver of technical progress in the country.

However, in the recent past the industrial economy of China has begun to witness the emergence of other avenues of technical progress that are supplements to its core central strategy. One instance of such a medium is the emergence of small high-technology firms that originated from the traditional R&D institutions. These are endowed with scientific and professional excellence, added to which these firms have distinctly focused market orientation.

(iv) An important implication of this trend relates to the role that the distribution of income has in the market for technology. A skewed distribution of income increases the demand for technology that pertains to the industrial sector and is likely to be capital-intensive. Sectors and regions that have a higher number of lower income groups will not have the bargaining position to be able to access markets that have the technology that is more appropriate, in that it is compatible with smaller scales of production or those that are more labour-intensive (preferably both).

Rising levels of income in the poorer sections would increase the likelihood of the adoption of technology that can be utilized effectively in agriculture, small-scale industry, the service sector and other such segments. The predominance that a specific sector and a certain strata have in the determination and access to technology, without any other sectors having more than a negligible role in the markets for technology, will limit the dissemination of technical progress. Thus, in an environment where significant income and non-income disparity exists, it is inevitable that the percolation of technical progress will be confined mainly to the higher income groups and this includes those who are equipped with higher levels of education.

(v) Thus, demonstrably, there is a link between a skewed income distribution and a discernibly uneven dissemination of technology. The feature of enclaved technological advancement characterizes a number of modern industrial developing countries and it needs to be differentiated from a systematic process of technological diffusion.

A faster pace and a higher degree of product innovation are inevitable in a country of 1.3 billion individuals that have as differentiated a consumption profile as one could imagine. At one end of the consumer spectrum, it has the poor rural farmer and at the other end the multi-billionaires most of whom are as brand conscious as they can get. Understandably between these two ends is an entire range of buyer's preferences and catering to what will become an increasing heterogeneous demand profile will encourage innovation. Over a certain period the important point is whether this will result in a discernibly higher proportion of home grown innovative endeavour or not remains to be seen.

## Conclusion

Undoubtedly China has made considerable progress in the ambit of economic development. However, there seems be a disconnect between steps taken towards reducing levels of poverty and the measures taken to increase human capital formation. The coexistence of high levels of economic growth rates and a slowdown in the improvements in social indicators such as a reduction in the number of people living below the poverty line, infant mortality rates, maternal mortality rates, the proportion of the population that have access to basic health care sheds light on a crucial distinction in the context not just of China but other developing countries where growth rates have begun to increase. At any point in time the formulation of social policies that will support economic growth is a necessary but not a sufficient condition for sustainable economic growth or continuous economic development.

Thus, sustained growth entails that the country needs to make faster and longer strides in the realm of improving the prevalent situation of social development. One of the most critical preconditions for this is to have growth strategies that are more broad-based, such that these encompass measures that are directed towards reducing not just existent levels of poverty, income and non-income inequalities, but also mitigate the causes that have led to this. This is a crucial aspect that has not characterized China's economic policy, particularly after the 1990s. It can be said that China's social policy functioned more or less as an adjunct or appendage to its centres of growth. Those spheres that were outside the purview of this were not prioritized, even if these were assigned importance in principle, resource disbursement towards infrastructure provision indicates the rather skewed approach underlying social policy.

Second, the prevalence of high and even rising levels of capital intensity, coupled with a situation of low or negligible expansion in sectors that are more employment-intensive, will reduce the impact of growth on poverty reduction. The imperatives of sustaining even its present levels of economic progress mean that China will have to induce an increase in the levels of investment in sectors that demonstrably have the potential to make a greater contribution to growth. It is this rather crucial objective that will strengthen the link that economic growth has with poverty reduction.

## Appendix

Although the Chinese government has attempted serious educational reform, studies by the World Bank and Chinese educators cite certain problems in the present system. These are:

- Universities have little autonomy from the government.
- High school education is exam-oriented and does not focus enough on cognitive development.

- Universities are slow in adapting to new technologies.
- Despite government support of higher education and tuition limits, attending university is still not affordable for most Chinese.
- Government encouragement for private universities is lacking and most private universities can only confer the equivalent of an Associate's degree.

# 13
# China's Foreign Direct Investment Story: An Evaluation

China's ascent towards becoming the leading foreign investment destination of the global economy was unequivocal by the mid-1990s. It has since elicited innumerable discussions, research and, of course, international media reportage. The fact that a communist country would manage to get massive inflows of foreign investment was hailed by many, in academia and outside, as spectacular. When the discernibly positive outcomes of trade and investment liberalization in China became manifest it was described by most who analyzed it as nothing short of impressive. As is invariably the case, hype is followed by a critical examination and this chapter presents important insights that emerge from China's FDI–export-led model.

When one views China's surge of foreign investment inflows over the last decade or so it tells us the story of a country whose tremendous growth potential reverberated globally and whose pursuit of the one country–two systems model garnered impressive outcomes. The simultaneous expansion of foreign investment and trade underpinned the country's FDI–export model, the centrality of which was an integral feature of the economic liberalization in China. Trade and foreign investment liberalization in China was not simply about pulling down tariff barriers on trade and removing entry restrictions on foreign investment. It was much more; even the freeing of markets was regulated and controlled by the political establishment. This meant that incentives and concessions granted to foreign enterprises were constituents of its industrial and trade policy.

Before proceeding it would be useful to begin with a concise description of the impact that China's accession to WTO has had and is likely to have on the Chinese economy. This chapter will enumerate trends of foreign investment and trade in the Chinese economy. It will then proceed with an evaluation of the FDI–export model.

## China's accession to the WTO

The accession of China to the WTO during 2001 was a momentous step. The impact that this will have on the Chinese economy has been discussed at length and, either way, inferences arrived at are inclined to exaggerate the impact of WTO. Some hail the monumental gains that China would be able to reap from having a greater degree of openness as a result of its entry into WTO. The other view is rather pessimistic, with assessments decrying the extremely negative fall-out of this decisive step.

It must be noted that the economic imperatives and problems that confront China existed even before 2001. For instance, the pre-eminent task of job creation and expansion of its rural economy, coupled with reducing the costs of state-owned enterprise reform required resolving prior to 2000. One of the compulsions underlying WTO entry were the mounting debts that the country's state-owned sector found itself reeling under, this despite the precedent initiatives of reform and the diversion of large amounts of investment capital.

For purposes of analysis, visualize for a moment that China had not entered the WTO. It would still not have changed the basic realities, which pervade the Chinese economy, in that it would not have reduced the imperatives of sustainable growth, nor would it have it have taken away the importance of enhancing levels of efficiency, particularly in the state-owned sector. It would not have exempted China's financial and banking sector from continuing reform. Thus, undeniably, WTO entry will entail an adjustment for the Chinese economy and this will fundamentally expedite surmounting the challenges that confront the country.

If one were take a more realistic standpoint of the economic implications of joining the World Trade Organization for China it is important to set aside both extremely positive and negative anticipations about the issue. Two important points emerge about the probable impact.

(i) The usual outcome of a reduction of tariffs across a wide range of imports is intensifying competition in the domestic markets. There may be an adverse repercussion of this on small and mid-sized companies; however, it must be noted that the pressures of gearing to higher levels of competitiveness are something that non-pillar industries in the private sector have had to contend with for some time. This has been the case because the high import content or intensity of its exports has enabled the entry of a fair share of imports at tariff rates even lower than the average tariff level in developed countries. The tariff reduction will bring some unfavourable effects for the automobiles, agriculture and telecommunication sectors. Other sectors will be impacted by the removal of non-tariff barriers that will decree a reduction of subsidies and other concessions granted by the government. Notably, the possibly negative implications of certain WTO provisions will be countervailed significantly by the prevalent high import intensity of China's exports. This means that the gains and losses that will arise from joining the WTO will be shared by both the domestic (in terms of origin) and the foreign-funded enterprises.

(ii) There is a surfeit of empirical evidence that tells us that the eventual impact of WTO provisions on any economy is significantly shaped by the bargaining strength of a country. China has a bargaining position that is nothing less than strong, given its importance in the global economy. Furthermore, it has successfully functioned within rather binding constraints and, in doing so, combined quite effectively the embodiments of liberalization within its communist political system. Thus, at the very least, it would be realistic to expect that it would be able to obtain for itself a rather advantageous position vis-à-vis WTO negotiations.

According to a UNCTAD report (2002) about the impact of China's accession to the WTO the country's entry does bring with it challenges to Chinese companies particularly in the agriculture and financial sector. The general view is that the adjustments that it brings in its wake will be effectively tackled, a belief that is substantiated by China's present economic strength and its previous experience at being able to address and even turn to its advantage difficult and even contentious issues and problems that arose especially during the initial liberalization period.

Importantly, however there is not much agreement on the impact of the accession on employment growth.

The United States Trade Representative issued its third annual WTO compliance report in December 2004. This stated, 'While China's efforts to implement its WTO commitments have been impressive they remain far from complete.'

Plausibly, and there are unmistakable signs of this already happening, China's leadership will manoeuvre into a position where it can adhere to WTO provisions in a manner that will infringe minimally on its domestic interests. According to the US Security Review Commission (2005), while China has made progress towards meeting some of its commitments in a number of important areas, firms continue to face market access barriers in China and unfair trade practices in US and third-country markets. It enumerates that although the US and WTO provide remedies and safeguards for firms facing unfair trade practices and import surges from China, these trade tools have remained underutilized and ineffective. The anti-dumping duties have gone uncollected, countervailing duties are presently inapplicable to China. The US government has been slow to implement the China-specific textile safeguard and then this was immobilized at a crucial time. Relief under the China product-specific safeguards has never been granted by the President despite three international trade commission decisions authorizing relief for the parties concerned. Some US firms have complained that they have not been given the market access that had been promised by under WTO.

Undoubtedly, China's strategic importance to the US economy has also conferred on it an uncontended edge regarding whether or not it will conform to the provisions of WTO. According to a US Department of Commerce report that was cited in the CRS Issue Brief for the Congress (2000):

China's unmet infrastructure needs are staggering. Foreign capital, expertise and equipment will have to be brought in if China is to build all the ports, roads, bridges, airports, power plants, telecommunications networks and rail line that it needs. Finally economic growth has substantially improved the purchasing power of Chinese citizens especially those living in urban areas along the East Coast of China. China's growing economy and large population make it a potentially enormous market.

Furthermore, this fact makes any stringent action in the event of non-compliance to any provision of the WTO extremely unlikely. It is naive to expect the Chinese government to relinquish every barrier to its markets, where either greater liberalization of its services or the agricultural sector is concerned.

## Broad trends in foreign investment

(i) A consistent expansion of foreign investment actually began after the mid-1990s. (The increasing significance of FDI in total investment in China is indicated in Table 13.1). This process was set into motion with Deng's famous tour of the South, subsequent to which there were improvements in the country's investment climate. From 1979–2004 China utilized a total of US$560.4 billion; interestingly, most of this comprised of investment inflows that came in after 1992. Over the period 1993–7, FDI accounted for over 30 per cent of the fixed asset investment of non-state firms. By the mid 1990s, when restrictions that existed earlier were eased, the increase in foreign investment was not just sizable but also more rapid. Since 1993

*Table 13.1*   Share of foreign direct investment in total fixed investment (%)

| Year | FDI/total fixed investment |
|------|----------------------------|
| 1991 | 4.36 |
| 1992 | 7.51 |
| 1993 | 12.13 |
| 1994 | 17.08 |
| 1995 | 15.65 |
| 1996 | 15.10 |
| 1997 | 14.79 |
| 1998 | 13.23 |
| 1999 | 11.17 |
| 2000 | 10.32 |
| 2001 | 10.42 |
| 2002 | 10.10 |

*Source: Chinese Statistical Yearbooks.*

China has managed to obtain the highest inflows of FDI in the developing world.

(ii) Small companies in Hong Kong, Taiwan and Macau, which invested in the mainland to avail of the low labour costs, comprised an important source of FDI in China during the initial phase of liberalization. In 1995, the manufacturing sector consisted of 1504 foreign-invested enterprises and about one-third of these were set up with capital from the overseas Chinese diaspora in these regions.

Undoubtedly, a facet that strikingly differentiates economic liberalization in China from the course that it took in number of other developing countries is that its initial phase was not spearheaded by the TNC-led FDI expansion. Instead, the impetus to growth during the 1980s and the expansion of the private sector came from small and medium-sized firms wherein the investment outlays were moderate by international standards. As a matter of fact, it is interesting to note that TVEs constituted 36 per cent of joint ventures and over 25 per cent of China's total export earnings.

(iii) Domestic entrepreneurs were encouraged as a consequence of liberalization; once again this was unlike the crowding out of indigenous home-grown private-sector players that occurs in a number of countries. The takeover of domestic and locally-owned companies through mergers and acquisitions and complete buy-outs is one outcome of investment liberalization that China's private sector was not impacted by. Foreign investment bridged the gap insofar as the shortfall in capital was concerned for a number of private entrepreneurs in China throughout the 1980s and early 1990s.

Furthermore, small and mid-sized businesses outside the realm of the state owned sector had minimal access to bank finance until 2001. It is therefore plausible that FDI may have played a significant role in enabling a sizable number of private companies in China to keep afloat.

(iv) In this context it must be noted that actual FDI inflow from Hong Kong was US$170 billion over the period 1983–2000 and this accounted for about half of the FDI that came into the country during this time. FDI inflow from the US, Japan and Taiwan constituted about a quarter of total foreign investment during the same phase.

(v) The share of investment from Hong Kong in China's total FDI decreased from 68 per cent in 1992 to 48 per cent in 2000. In quantitative terms, the importance of the US as a foreign investor had become rather significant by the same year, when it contributed 10.8 per cent of total foreign investment. The proportion of FDI originating from the UK, Germany, France, the Netherlands and Canada constituted over 10 per cent of total FDI in 2000.

(vi) The present scenario in China is one where investments made by European and American corporations are focused on tapping China's market size and, in this context, export promotion may not always be the primary objective. Foreign affiliates in China use it as a manufacturing platform, not just for sales in the global market, but 60 per cent of the output of joint ventures and wholly foreign-owned firms is sold in the domestic markets. As far as local firms (i.e. those without an element or stake of foreign ownership) are concerned, the products of foreign affiliates is similar to imports and in 2002 and the sum of imports and domestic sales of foreign enterprises constituted about 40 per cent of GDP.

## Broad trends in China's trade

(i) China's phenomenal expansion in trade (as indicated in Table 13.2) has been one of trailblazing stories of economic liberalization over the last decade. From a general standpoint, it exemplifies the promise of the gains that can emanate from liberalizing but, on further analysis, it becomes evident that the monumental increases in exports that the country achieved was the result of managed or controlled liberalization.

(ii) Although the country had begun to move away from the system of physical planning of foreign trade that it adhered to until the 1980s, it was not as if the Chinese government dismantled all controls in one sweep. Even if it had done so, the impact would have been negative, as the rather chaotic effects of Big Bang liberalization in Eastern Europe underscored a decade after China's markets had begun to open.

(iii) Thus, all restrictions on trade were not relinquished in one go; these were reduced gradually over a period of time and the controls that existed worked effectively to ensure that the composition of exports and imports were in line with the predetermined economic priorities.

(iv) Three important measures related to the pricing of traded goods and the devaluation of an overvalued currency propelled China's trade expansion. These included:

*Table 13.2*   China: increasing trade/GDP ratio

| Year | Total trade | Trade/GDP |
| --- | --- | --- |
| 1978 | 3.55 | 9.80 |
| 1985 | 20.66 | 23.10 |
| 1991 | 72.25 | 33.40 |
| 1994 | 203.80 | 43.60 |
| 1995 | 234.99 | 40.20 |
| 1999 | 298.96 | 36.40 |
| 2001 | 421.93 | 44.00 |
| 2003 | 851.20 | 57.80 |
| 2004 | 1154.80 | 70.70 |

*Sources*: *China Statistical Yearbook* (2004) and State Statistics Bureau.

(a) The phased devaluation of the renminbi over 1980–95. Observably, overvaluation of the currency required maintaining a rigid system of exchange control and, thus, devaluing the currency meant that exporters who, during the pre-reform phase, had to surrender 100 per cent of their foreign exchange earnings to the government were allowed to retain part of their foreign exchange earnings. Importers too could finance their imports without seeking permission to purchase foreign exchange.

(b) In 1984 the State Council decided to rebate the indirect taxes, the deduction of which had dampened the profitability of exporters.

(c) The duty drawback policy that was implemented after the mid 1980s facilitated the rebate of import duties on raw materials, components and parts used for export processing. Undeniably, this initiative, in conjunction with the other two, was an important contributory step towards the expansion of the country's trade wherein, by 2002, processed exports amounted to US$180 billion or 55 per cent of China's exports.

(v) The increasing proportion of labour-intensive manufactured goods in the composition of China's exports reflected a domain in which the country's comparative advantage had evolved over the last two decades. However, a noteworthy fact is that, although China's endowments may have conferred on it an inherent edge to become one of the leading exporters of a certain category of manufactured goods, it was not until certain policies were initiated and an investor-friendly macro-business environment was put into place that the nation could build upon its intrinsic strengths.

## Evaluating China's FDI–export model

The emergence of China's FDI–export model spans two distinct phases. During the initial stages of its emergence during the early 1980s, the country's export-processing industries were set up predominantly by investment from Hong Kong, Taiwan and South–East Asia. At this point, the FDI–export linkage did result in employment provision. However, the accrual of other gains, such as the dissemination of technological progress and skill building, was limited. Increasing levels of investments in the production of light goods, such as electrical goods, toys, footwear, clothing and leather goods, entailed processes that would transform imported intermediate goods into finished or semi-finished goods. Consequently, in terms of facilitating technology transfer or enabling the integration of domestic Chinese enterprises into the global production structures, the first stage of China's FDI–export model was rather limited As FDI in labour-intensive industries increased it led to the rapid rise in exports. The patterns of trade liberalization that were beginning to appear in China were apparently similar to the foreign investment–trade linkage in East Asia; however, there was markedly a point of difference between the basis of trade expansion in China and East Asia. Unlike Hong Kong, Macau and Taiwan, where domestic companies controlled a large part of the production in export-oriented industry and foreign companies were purchasing agents, it is foreign enterprises that were involved in the setting up and expansion of export-oriented industries in the Chinese economy. The reason for this was not ambiguous, home-grown or indigenous private-sector companies lacked both the access and the some of the organizational inputs required to be able to drive export expansion independently in the absence of collaborative agreements with foreign companies. This was evidently the fall-out of the overarching slant that bank lending had or was compelled to have towards SOEs.

Studies that evaluate the impact of FDI in China cite the extensive application of rather rudimentary labour-intensive assembly operations. If this phase had not taken place it would have been unrealistic to expect that China would have begun to climb the value chain. Furthermore, given the country's prevalent political and economic context at the time that liberalization was initiated, the possibility of having an FDI strategy that would enable China to leapfrog into the production of capital and technologically intensive goods seemed far-fetched. Not for long though. During the subsequent phase, the onset of which began by the mid 1990s, investment inflows into China came from the US and advanced countries of the OECD region; East Asia was no longer the main source of foreign investment in the country. Importantly, it was not just the increasing quantum of investment but the increasing inflows into the skill-intensive and capital-intensive sectors, such as automobiles and semi-conductors, that signalled that the composition of foreign investment would be different from what had occurred in the preceding phase.

In descriptive terms, thus, the quality of FDI improved significantly after the mid-1990s, with the inflows of foreign investment into sectors that required the use of advanced technology and human capital formation. However, this positive aspect cannot be separated from the precedent phase or from the qualitative aspect of the reform measures. Notably, the qualitative aspect of FDI bears correspondence to the nature of China's reform. When the impact of initiatives was rendered weak by inadequate or staggered implementation, FDI did not do much, either in the ambit of advanced technology transfer or expanding skill-intensive activity. As measures to restructure China's SOEs and its banking sector begun to gain ground it influenced the nature of FDI inflows. One important factor is that, by this time, it had become evident to the global community that liberalization in China was distinct constituent of its policy stance, from which it could not retract (this regardless of the communist political establishment).

China has become a location for the assembly of consumer electronics and information technology goods such as computers and exports of high technology products have risen significantly from US$26 billion in 2000 to US$35billion in 2002. Tables 13.3 and 13.4 indicate the changing composition of imports and exports to the US. Table 13.5 intimates other important trading partners.

Interestingly, China did not wait for its comparative advantage in labour intensive manufacturing to peter out before it embarked on measures to diversify into the production of technologically intensive products in the early 1990s. Undoubtedly, this can be viewed as a prudent initiative because labour cost accounts for a rather small proportion of the unit price of most manufactured (including assembled) goods. The cost of other inputs (parts and material) and procurement of the same constitutes a larger share of the price and, thus, tapping into and creating other sources of comparative advantage was a well–timed initiative.

At this point it is important to note that most of the components and parts that embody a high technical content are sourced off-shore. Having begun its foray into hi-tech manufactured goods, China's industrial sector needs to scale up the value chain so that it can produce cost-effectively an increasing

*Table 13.3*  Top five US imports from China (in billions and % change)

| Item | 2000 | 2001 | 2002 | 2003 | 2004 | 2000–4% change |
|------|------|------|------|------|------|----------------|
| Computer equipment | 8.3 | 8.2 | 12.0 | 18.7 | 29.5 | 255.4 |
| Miscellaneous manufactured goods* | 16.3 | 16.5 | 19.5 | 21.8 | 23.7 | 45.4 |
| Audio and video | 6.3 | 6.3 | 8.9 | 10.0 | 11.2 | 77.8 |
| Footwear | 9.1 | 9.6 | 10.1 | 10.4 | 11.2 | 23.1 |
| Clothing | 7.0 | 7.2 | 7.7 | 9.0 | 10.5 | 50.0 |

* Toys and games.
*Source*: CRS Issue Brief for Congress, China US Trade Issues, August 2004.

*Table 13.4*  Top five US exports to China (in billions and % change)

| Item | 2000 | 2001 | 2002 | 2003 | 2004 | 2000–4% change |
|------|------|------|------|------|------|----------------|
| Semi-conductors and other electronic components | 1.3 | 1.7 | 2.2 | 3.0 | 3.6 | 176.9 |
| Oil seeds and grains | 1.0 | 1.0 | 0.9 | 2.9 | −2.8 | 180.0 |
| Waste and scrap | 0.7 | 1.1 | 1.2 | 1.9 | 2.5 | 257.1 |
| Aerospace | 1.8 | 2.6 | 3.6 | 2.7 | 2.1 | 16.7 |
| Basic chemicals | 0.7 | 0.6 | 0.8 | 1.4 | 2.0 | 187.4 |

*Source*: CRS Issue Brief for Congress, China US Trade Issues, August 2004.

*Table 13.5*   China's top five trading partners during 2004 (in billions)

| Country | Total trade | China's exports | China's imports | China's trade balance | Trade balance as reported by partner |
|---------|-------------|-----------------|-----------------|-----------------------|--------------------------------------|
| EU | 177.3 | 95.9 | 63.4 | 32.5 | −90.7 |
| US | 169.7 | 125.0 | 44.7 | 80.3 | −162.0 |
| Japan | 167.9 | 73.5 | 94.4 | −20.9 | −20.5 |
| Hong Kong | 112.7 | 100.9 | 11.8 | 89.1 | −3.9 |
| ASEAN | 105.9 | 42.9 | 63.0 | −20.1 | N/A |

*Note*: As indicated, estimates provided by Chinese trade data about bilateral trade differ significantly from the official trade data of other countries about their trade with China. *Source*: Official Chinese trade data.

proportion of technologically intensive products. Undeniably, the industrial sector has extended the purview of its manufacturing beyond the assembly stages of the production in product categories that include machinery, semi-conductors and IT-related goods. In 1999, foreign-invested enterprises in the machinery sector accounted for 24 per cent of the total number of firms.

However, it still has a distance to cover before it can achieve a comparative advantage in the manufacture of hi-tech goods as well-defined as the one that it has in the realm of labour-intensive manufactured goods. In this context, the question that arises is whether China is likely to be able to do so. This takes us on to a discussion about some of the issues that will help us answer this.

Policy thrust has a vital role to play in the fructification of economic objectives. However, the intended shift towards becoming a manufacturer of hi-tech production entails much more than government-directed measures. It requires a process of transformation that would enable it to define new sources of competitive advantage and, in doing so, confer on it increasing levels of value addition. This defines a compelling need for measures that go beyond the purview of ensuring low costs to those that would enable industry to gain a competitive edge in the manufacture of knowledge-intensive products. There are 2 major determinants that will decide the extent of China's proficiency in this sector.

First, the technology that is acquired, a prerequisite that one cannot make categorical assumptions about. Second given the access that it has to the technical inputs required for the production of hi-tech goods, another determinant would be the levels of efficiency and competitiveness that characterize the companies in this sector. The government has said that it hopes the US will ease its controls on exports of hi-tech products to China, responding to reports Washington is planning to tighten such curbs. 'We hope the United States will adopt concrete measures to relax restrictions on high-tech exports to China, so as to better resolve the issue of the Sino-US trade imbalance', Foreign Ministry spokeswoman Jiang Yu told a regular news conference (*Shenzhen Daily*).

Foreign capital and the imports of hi-tech products are an important medium through which China will increase the pace of technological upgrading in its industrial sector. As in the earlier phase of its liberalization, present FDI policies stipulate certain conditions that would boost technological transfer from foreign corporations to local companies. For instance, specifying the use of local suppliers that have been designated by the government is one route through which dissemination of technical knowledge can occur.

Attaining this objective does not merely involve the deployment of investment towards the acquisition of advanced technologies. Undoubtedly, it necessitates a larger context that consists of initiatives directed towards creation of mechanisms and channels through which the industrial sector will be able to step up its evolution of core competences in the realm of hi-tech manufacturing. Some of the measures that would facilitate this would be an expansion and enhancement of education, research and innovative development facilities.

Despite attempts to restrict China's access to obtaining advanced technologies, the country's foreign investment policies have been rather successful in overcoming most deterrents to procurement of advanced technology. The imminent question is whether the existent policy structure will be able to diffuse technology acquired sufficiently through the various tiers of China's industrial sector, including the small and mid-sized locally owned companies. This takes us on to examining whether the dissemination of technical progress in China will be pervasive or not. The answer to this entails an enumeration of important aspects of technological upgrading that we see emerging in China's industrial economy.

## Protectionism: its impact on technological upgrading

First, in the absence of adequate reform that would enable China's companies to be competitive or without policies that support it directly or indirectly, it would not be possible to establish a clearly defined link between the predominance of foreign enterprise across veritably every sphere of its industry and its scaling up the value chain. Thus, restrictions pertaining to a fairly wide range of matters, such as the marketing of products, the use of certain inputs from local suppliers and the determination of product composition can be viewed as uncompetitive from a conventional standpoint. The irony that arises in China's case is that its competitive edge stands very much on the basis of policy-led measures and this includes even the role that market forces have had. It is very unlikely that China would have been able achieve the modernization and the sizable expansion of its industrial sector without these potentially constricting policy stipulations.

Another aspect of China's industrial policies relates to the protectionism that it extends to foreign enterprises. This may have served some useful purpose; however, it can impede a pervasive process of technological advancement in its industrial sector. Thus, limiting or preventing rival foreign firms from entering its markets or restricting the imports of certain inputs will certainly not be conducive to increasing the levels of efficiency. If the efficiency or productivity differential between the local or domestic enterprise and the foreign firm reduces, as it can as a consequence of protectionist policies, it would mean that domestically owned enterprises can catch up in terms of being able to operate as efficiently as their foreign counterparts. Be this as it may, there is a possibility that the domestic or local enterprise may still not be competitive enough by global standards.

Theoretically, protectionism is not a positive feature; it inhibits competition and prevents significant improvements in the economic performance of a firm, corporation or even a country. It would be easy to remedy the problem of protectionism if its existence was confined to a handful of countries. However, the reality is that there are hardly any nations that are without their protectionist barriers, a fact that every WTO proceeding corroborates. Getting back to the specifics of China's context, higher levels of technical progress would not simply be facilitated by dismantling protectionism. It would, however, necessitate a shift from anti-competitive protectionism to a structure of protectionism that is more conducive to competitiveness. Some of the inefficiencies that have crept into China's automobile sector are reminiscent of Mexico's auto sector, where the application of NAFTA (North American Free Trade Agreement) restricts the entry of new foreign enterprise.

Undoubtedly, there are numerous instances of protectionist policies that lower levels of efficiency and encourage obsolescence. Equally true, as empirical evidence demonstrates, is the inextricable link that protectionism and the creation of industrial capabilities have had in a number of countries, including those in East Asia and the United States.

Although patterns of industrialization and the processes that have driven them vary across countries it is fairly common to find that during certain stages of a country's industrial advancement protectionist policies have played a role in enabling not just the expansion and consolidation of important sectors in industry but also the creation of certain core competences. Thus, denouncing or defending protectionist policies skirts the main question, which, in essence, is about whether or not the nature of protectionism that exists in any country can be an effective tool or transmission mechanism of industrial progress.

Automotive manufacturing in the United States during the 1980s provides a rather useful example of how protectionism worked as an instrument of upgrading in the automobile industry. By 1980, US automobile manufacturers were lagging behind their competitors in Europe and Japan, with the sector riddled with inefficient plants and beset by low standards of product quality and design. The consequence of this was the increasing demand for Japanese automobiles, which were not just more energy efficient but also had lower price tags. In 1980 one of out of every four cars sold in the United States was an import. By 1980, almost 2 million Japanese cars and trucks were sold in the US. At that point in time it almost seemed inevitable that leading carmakers of the US, namely Ford, Chrysler and General Motors, would find themselves in a slump (so much so that Ford and Chrysler suspended production at two major plants in November 1980). It was inevitable that the pressures to curb car imports would begin to mount on the Reagan administration.

A cutback in car exports from Japan was predictable and, when President Reagan met the Japanese Prime Minister Zenko Suzuki in 1981 to find a satisfactory solution to the problem, American trade representatives hinted that protectionist legislation was probably just around the corner. True enough, export ceilings were imposed under the Voluntary Export Restraints system in 1981 and this limited the number of Japanese car exports to the United States between 1981 and 1991.

Make no mistake, this was only one aspect of protectionist policy because it was not merely curtailing the auto imports from Japan that revitalized the US auto industry. Through direct investment, Japanese manufacturers set up plant facilities and engaged in American parts procurement to further promote American production initiatives. Over the period 1978–89, seven Japanese manufacturers (Honda, Nissan, Toyota, Mazda, Mitsubishi, Fuji Heavy Industries and Isuzu) established production operations in the United States. These operations were established either independently, jointly with other Japanese manufacturers, or with American manufacturers.

Furthermore, in February 1985, the Market-Oriented Sector Selective (MOSS) talks were launched between Japan and the United States on the opening of the Japanese market. Following these negotiations, procurement of parts from American suppliers by Japanese manufacturers increased at a rapid rate. Purchases of US parts by Japanese manufacturers were worth $2.5 billion in 1986. By 1994, this had increased to $19.9 billion. Notably, during from 1986–94, the output of Japanese manufacturers' local production operations in the US had grown from 620,000 units in 1986 to 2.15 million units in 1994. At the same time, the number of American parts suppliers doing business with Japanese automobile manufacturers increased considerably, from 800 companies in 1987 to a total of 2726 companies in 1994.

Reducing imports in the absence of any other measures directed towards retaining a certain degree of competitiveness would have had a rather unfavourable consequence. However, this was not the case in the US automobile industry. By not imposing curbs on manufacturing by Japanese auto majors, the door to competition was not shut, not completely at least. Automotive manufacturing in the United States was able to upgrade and improve its standards of performance, efficiency and quality. In a sense one could say that Japanese investors in this sector were accorded preferential treatment because the curbs that applied to others were not stringently imposed on them.

The instance cited demonstrates a variant of protectionism that has worked as a medium of upgrading in the automobile sector in the United States. By no means does the example categorically suggest that China can achieve similar results in its industries by adopting protectionist policies resembling those pursued in the United States. However, it elucidates that protectionism does not have to exclude competition and it is necessary for industrial strategy in China and other countries to formulate mechanisms that ensure the coexistence of protectionism and competition. Observably, extending protectionism to a sector for a prolonged period of time makes it a breeding ground for a plethora of inefficiencies.

Foreign investment compensated for the deficiency of investment in China's private sector. This could be viewed as a strength insofar as it facilitated resource mobilization. However, the undue dependence of industrial expansion in China on foreign investment has its obvious downside. Although the constitution was revised in 1999 to extend private property rights that had been availed by foreign enterprises to domestic entrepreneurs and local companies (locally owned), the observable link between foreign investment and the proliferation of industry in China continues to persist. Moreover, increasing foreign investment inflows into hi-tech activities would reinforce this fundamental aspect of China's economy. This takes us on to a review of another integral determinant of technical upgrading in China – the impact that technology transfer has had and is having on the dissemination of technological progress China.

## The trickle-down effect of technology transfer

According to an extract of the report of the US Security Review Commission (2005), the execution of China's technology transfer programme has enabled it to accelerate the pace of its technical progress. The report by the commission states:

> The technology that China is developing and producing is increasing in sophistication at an unexpectedly fast pace has been able to leapfrog in its technological development using technology and know-how obtained from foreign enterprises in ways that other developing nations have not been able to replicate.
>
> The rapid advancement is evident in the level of technology that makes up China's trade surplus with the US in advanced technology products ... Advances in China's technology infrastructure and

industry along with other similar advances in other developing countries pose a significant competitive challenge that is eroding US technology leadership.

The report also evidences the US establishment's apprehensions about China's entry into certain spheres of high-technology sectors. In this context it states:

China's incentives for technology industries are part of a coordinated strategic effort to obtain dual-use technology. This strategy is focused on the software and integrated circuit industry. The two industries the US defense establishment identifies as vital to today's information based network centric warfare ... While the US defense industry is not dependent on Chinese imports at the present time, the Chinese government coordinated strategy of utilizing incentives to spur the development of domestic capacity in the dual-use technology industry is weakening the health of the key US commercial sectors on which the US defense establishment relies ... The increasing reliance of the US military on the private sector for certain technological development coupled with the movement offshore of much of the private sector's industrial and technological production and some of its design work and R&D activities in which China is increasingly engaging raises the prospect of future US dependence for certain items critical to US defense industry as well as to continued economic leadership.

China's systematically designed and effectively implemented strategies of technology transfer which have been successful given that the purpose they serve for the nation, are crucial, with the potential to become even more important in subsequent years. Equally true, is the fact that besides the geopolitical dimension there is another equally vital facet of technology transfer which pertains to the impact that it has had on creating and fostering domestic industrial and technical capabilities.

China has the basic structural requisites such as a policy framework and the institutional mechanisms that are prerequisite for technical advancement. At a fairly early stage of its liberalization it enforced policy stipulations that would increase its access to relatively advanced technology. Despite this, technical progress is not as rapid and certainly not as deep-seated or entrenched as it should be. The reality is that a process of effective technology transfer has not been able to propel the creation of domestic and technical capabilities in China on a scale that can be considered extensive.

Prior to liberalization and even after it until the early 1990s, it is the large and medium-scale enterprises that have been the most important medium of technical change in the Chinese economy. Besides this, the country also had its research and academic institutes, which were less important but also significant facilitators of technical progress in China. Before 1978 the Soviet

model of industrialization and modernization conditioned China's industrial strategy. At the time this seemed the most suitable direction for industrial policy to take, given that centralized planning was also the defining
feature the Chinese economy. The corollary of this was the narrow focus of its
technical development programmes on the military sector and space launch
vehicles; the achievements of its R&D programmes have mainly stenimed
from these spheres.

In essence, until the early 1990s, the industrial sector was at best on the
periphery of the country's R&D programmes and technical upgrading and
modernization that occurred in industry was enabled by policies that linked
FDI with the procurement of technology and imports of technology. In
consonance with this, the SOEs were the main beneficiaries of science and
technology programmes and, by 1993, more than one-third of enterprises in
China's state-owned sector had established technical development centres.
The purpose of these centres was to improve the efficiency and quality of
production capabilities. This has happened but in rather moderate measure;
the attempts to use imported technology as a springboard that will drive
the creation of domestic technical capabilities in China have been partly
but not entirely successful. The reason for this is that the indigenization or
localization of foreign technology didn't quite fructify, certainly not by the
extent required.

Instead, the general trend in industry can be described as the adoption
of follow-up strategy wherein most large Chinese enterprises emphasize
product imitation so that when new products enter the markets local
companies will be able to produce an identical substitute for domestic sale.
An impediment to the indigenization of technology in the Chinese context
arises from the lack of cogent markets for technology in China; some would
describe these as fragmented. This, coupled with a lack of co-ordination
between industry, academia and research institutes, perpetuates the undue
reliance on technology imports.

The Chinese government has been cognizant about the deterrents to
having a faster and wider diffusion of technical progress. Interestingly, a
decade ago Premier Li Peng (1988–98), in the report on the outline of the
ninth five-year plan, stated:

In developing pillar industries, the initial technology must be relatively
advanced. While importing advanced technologies we should boost our
own technological development and renovation capabilities, build up the
scale of economies and pay attention to economic returns.

Consistent with the objective of increasing the pace of technical progress,
the Chinese government identified certain sectors, most of these technology intensive, that were designated as pillar industries. These included
machinery, electronics, petrochemicals and construction materials and

China's State Development Commission introduced industrial policies that were designed to develop and protect domestic markets in these pillar industries.

Consequent to the incentives provided by the government, although there has been some progress in the levels of indigenization it remains far below the extent required to spur the expansion of domestic technical capabilities. According to a report in *Foreign Affairs* by George Gilboy (2004), over the last decade large and medium-sized firms have spent less than 10 per cent of the cost of importing equipment on indigenizing technology. Surprisingly, even state-owned companies in the sectors of telecom, equipment, electronics and industrial machinery spend less than 10 per cent on indigenization of imported technology.

Throughout the 1980s and 1990s, China's imports of technology comprised the purchase of manufacturing equipment; sometimes this took the form of complete assembly lines. Hardware accounted for 80 per cent of its technology imports and licensing, knowledge-related services and consulting or soft technology constituted 20 per cent. It must be noted that it is soft technology that provides the route to acquiring the knowledge embodied in the equipment imported. Although there has been an increase in the imports of soft technology, mainly in the form of licences obtained for the use of imported equipment, expenditures towards the indigenization of technology by the industrial sector in China is much lower than the required level.

Availability of technology did not result in either an expeditious or an adequate diffusion of technology. Those industries that needed a particular technology obtained it by importing the same, this was perhaps a pointer that the incentives for absorbing, assimilating and indigenizing foreign technology have not been sufficient. This feature stands apart from what existed in East Asia, where import substitution and the acquisition of foreign technology were used rather effectively as levers in the evolution of domestic technical capabilities.

The provision of incentives and other policy measures has not been able to raise the demand for locally developed technology in China. During 2002, Chinese firms allocated less than 1 per cent of their total science and technology budgets to purchase domestic technology. Added to this, according to the national R&D census in 2000, Chinese industrial firms allocate 93 per cent of their R&D outlays in house, about 2 per cent is disbursed on collaborative activities with universities and only a minuscule 1 per cent is spent on projects undertaken in collaboration with other domestic firms.

Plausibly, larger enterprises find it easier to acquire advanced technology through imports and it is the smaller firms in the state-owned and non-state sector that have contributed significantly more to the diffusion of technical progress in China. Most of these firms cannot avail of the government

sponsored science and technology development programmes; the beneficiaries of these are large-scale enterprises. Thus, most smaller firms would
find it more expensive to import advanced technology and it is this neces-
sity to adapt and assimilate existent technology that has made this sector
unexpectedly important as a propellant of technical development.

The potential significance of smaller enterprises in the process of indigenization has not been grasped and, until very recently, the policies initiated
do not reflect an understanding of this fact. The impetus to demand for
indigenous technology could come from the smaller enterprises; however,
the constraints that these firms encounter constrict the expansion of this
sector.

## Conclusion

Quantitative estimates that attempt to evaluate the role of FDI in China
may differ in their observations and inferences about the precise contribution that trade and investment liberalization made to China's impressive
economic performance. Regardless, liberalization was an important instrument that helped to surmount the constraint of financial capital and much
else. In a broader context it is the interplay between policy instruments,
institutional mechanisms, China's economic and political circumstance and
its ideological underpinnings that shaped the impact of foreign investment.

# 14
# China's Economic Experience: Insights, Lessons and a Perspective

China's economic resonance is an amazing story; some would describe as it as a stupendous saga of transformation of a developing country that had more than a few odds stacked against her to one of the most important nations in the global economy. Illustratively speaking, China's impressive economic performance was the result of a unique blend of rather disparate elements, such as communism, a market-based economy, foreign investment, capital controls, liberalism and political conservatism, that that worked well enough to result in an impressive economic performance for over a decade. Managing the coexistence of all these apparently mutually exclusive features was a balancing act that was not easy. However, it demonstrated that it is the context and circumstance prevalent in any nation that should determine its policies and strategies of growth.

China's rather dramatic ascent in the global economy made it a nation to be reckoned with, and the path that it traversed and the approach that its leadership had towards a wide range of issues, such as neo-liberalism and democracy, differentiated it from other nations. Another striking fact is that the country is emerging as a superpower at a time when it continues to be a developing country (by certain measures of development). Its prevalent per capita incomes and standards of living are not as high as those that existed in Great Britain and the United States when these were becoming (at different points in time) frontrunners of the developed world.

The discernible influence that China has begun to wield in geopolitics coexists with the developmental challenges that it needs to surmount; undeniably this is a unique combination. Thus, China has two distinct facets; one relates to its achievements and the other to the constraints and the issues of sustainability that it needs to grapple with. Taken together, important lessons can be drawn from both these aspects in the context of developing nations.

Delving into China's economic experience lends us a distinctly new perspective, perhaps even another dimension to the meaning and interpretation of liberalization, economic transition and modernism.

The question is: does China embody a model of growth that can be pursued by other developing countries? Replicating a model of growth seems convenient; however, it is not actually feasible because the economic experience of every country is a unique one. Having said this, it is undeniable that China's economic strategy as it has evolved does consist of certain important principles that can be useful in guiding development strategy. An elucidation of each insight that can be drawn from China's economic experience is as follows.

## Reinventing neo-liberalism

China's pursuit of liberalization and the outcomes that this ushered in its wake questioned a number of assumptions that had been rigidly upheld up to about two decades ago. First, the presumed correlation between economic liberalization and political reforms wasn't exactly validated by the course that political adjustment took in China. Second, liberalization in China was not an instantaneous process, nor was its consequence the imposition of democratic systems in one sweep of policy change. China's pursuit of economic liberalization was accompanied by subtle, almost subterranean, political change, the nature of which was more muted and its extent much less than the outcomes that economic liberalization was expected to bring with it.

In other words, China managed to achieve considerable economic progress in the absence of a full-fledged democracy and this fact questioned generalized assumptions about the consequences of liberalization and the preconditions that it would entail in due course. Debunking this, as a weakness that characterizes the underlying basis of the country's policy framework, is hardly an insight; it is more relevant to understand that having a democratic system (in the Chinese context) would entail much more than a one-off political adjustment. Eastern Europe's rather dramatic transition to free-market policies corroborated that if China had pursued Big Bang liberalization it is very likely that the result would have been a situation of chaos and confusion, perhaps even anarchy.

Anticipating that a democracy would function in a backdrop wrought with tumult and uncertainty is unrealistic. Empirical evidence about the economics of transition underscores that democracy is not an ad hoc feature that falls into place merely by relinquishing totalitarian or authoritarian control. Undoubtedly, this is an important prerequisite but certainly not the only one. The aftermath of ending communism in Eastern Europe tells us the story of a rather chaotic and tumultuous low growth phase of transition, which was, by all accounts, not a short term phase of structural adjustment. Admittedly, if China had to pass through such a phase it is probable that it would not have scaled the heights of economic progress that it did and it is unlikely that it would have found itself with a vibrant democracy.

From a standpoint of applicability, China's model of economic liberalization is more suitable for contemporary developing countries than the route of 'quick-fix liberalism', which was pursued by Eastern Europe and some of the Latin American countries. It is not that the lack of democracy in China is a positive feature but the fact that it did not attempt to transplant, with instantaneous policy change, a system that worked in an almost divergent macroeconomic environment in its own economy proved advantageous.

Interestingly, economic reform in China did not pave the way for a political upsurge; it has resulted in a process of subtle political transition. On deeper scrutiny, it is China's gradualist approach to transition that invalidated the widely held assumption that market forces would threaten the survival of China's socialist market economy. Notably, it was a gradual and controlled process of decentralization throughout the various tiers of China's governance that staved off a turbulent political upheaval. If this had not been the case and the Chinese economy had been thrown into the midst of a flurry of sudden systemic changes such that the country did not have time to attune itself to, the actual consequences of economic liberalization would not have been as anticipated.

To the world at large, China's emergence from communism and its foray towards liberalism and capitalist forces may have seemed a fast-paced one, particularly when the country began to garner huge amounts of foreign investment and its attractiveness as a production hub for a wide gamut of industries and companies was a subject of many a headlines in the international media. However, the not so visible precursor to its rapid ascent was a relatively subtle process of economic reform, which began during the late 1970s and proceeded in fits and starts until the early 1990s, after which it began to gather momentum.

*Lessons*: The empirics of China's tremendous progress shows developing countries that it is not a single constituent of change, however forceful an impetus this may provide, that is sufficient to set into motion a continuous period of increasing growth. The precedent measures that have been implemented before increasing levels of economic prosperity become manifest have a crucial role to play in the economic growth of any country. Equally important are the subsequent steps initiated to ensure sustainability of progress once attained. Thus, the measures taken to unleash economic growth and the initiatives adopted to manage rising levels of affluence are integral components of economic development.

China's ability to make the transition to a market-oriented economy did not stem merely from a sudden spurt of ideological or economic transformation. It exemplifies that structural transformation is a tenuous process that encompasses much more than the implementation of certain policy measures. Effectiveness of policies entails an appropriate context to work within and, despite the problems it encountered, China had, by the early 1990s, a strategy that could herald decisively positive outcomes within the macroeconomic environment of the country at the time. This is also one of the reasons that enabled China to avoid sharp reversals in its progress after the 1990s, despite the rather imminent concerns that have arisen about the sustainability of its economic growth.

The impact of economic liberalization in China has been discussed in earlier chapters and it is obvious that, unlike a number of developing countries, China was able to use foreign investment and trade liberalization as an instrument of growth. This is certainly not because liberalism came in a specifically customized package for China; rather it was through the formulation of targeted incentives, concessions and even restrictive stipulations that liberalization became an important facilitator of increasing growth rates.

*Lesson*: Importantly for developing countries, the role that liberalization has played in the Chinese economy vividly demonstrates that the extent of influence that FDI exerts on the growth process will be determined largely by a fairly extensive range of variables, which span the economic, political and institutional realms.

Notably, FDI policies adopted by China were not the result of relegating centralized systems to the periphery of decision-making; as a matter of fact, they were an outcome of calculated political deliberation. China's transition was steered by political forces, as it was by economic circumstance; the consequence was an adaptation of neo-liberalism in accordance to the larger realities that prevailed in China at the time. Perhaps this is the reason that economic liberalization became a pivotal element and consideration in the policies that the country has initiated over the last two decades, despite the marked ideological divide that existed within the precincts of the country's political establishment about liberalism and its implications, particularly until the beginning of the 1990s.

Adherence to the conventional prescriptions of neo-liberalism would, in all probability, not have conferred on China an external macroeconomic position that was as favourable as the one that it has currently; nor would its manufacturing sector have expanded on the scale that it has.

*Lesson*: Despite some inherent limitations that beset economic strategy pursued in China, it has had an overriding strength in that it was closely correlated to the innate features of the country's economy, the specificities of its political structure and ideological conditionings.

This insight is a pointer to the rather half-baked approach that a number of developing countries had towards liberalization. Somehow, this process was whittled down to easing trade and investment barriers, which became disembodied from the other vital changes that were required in the macroeconomic environment and the policy framework so that it had a more positive and a greater developmental impact. Predictably, as it turned out for a number of countries, the outcome was certainly not one where either foreign investment or increased levels of trade had a significant role to play in stepping up the pace of development or, for that matter, growth over the medium term. Furthermore, even the gains that arose from pursuing liberalization across a number of developing countries in Latin America and Africa were short-lived and accrued to an extremely small proportion of the population.

Perhaps it is necessary to reiterate that it is not liberalization that is being criticized but the narrow interpretation of the preconditions entailed if it is to have a contributory role in economic progress. Thus, the role or the function that FDI will take on, besides the rather normative one of bridging the investment gap, varies in accordance to the prevalent industrial and institutional structures that exist in a country at any point in time. The empirics of liberalization in China underscored this fact.

In drawing out lessons about whether the critical role of FDI in China can be made to apply in other developing countries it is important to note that it is both the quantitative and the qualitative aspects of FDI that denote the success of economic liberalization. Viewing the impact of economic liberalization merely in terms of the quantum of investment inflows that the country was able to obtain would lend itself to shallow inferences. This is so because foreign investment also a medium of technological transfer, skill upgrading and a facilitator of economic integration.

In interpreting what may have seemed at the outset as China's astonishing success at pursuing the FDI led export model it is important to note that it is the country's bargaining position that has played a key role in making foreign investment a rather critical input of its economic progress. At a rather early stage of its economic progress China demonstrated that it could negotiate a strategy of investment and trade with the MNCs that would work to its advantage.

There are economists who cite, and correctly so, that its large size, a centralized government and the existence of a wealthy non-resident Chinese community enabled it to have a certain bargaining position. Equally true is that its governance used the strengths that it had in a deft and constructive manner to give the economy a leverage that was enough for it to become among the most important nations in the global economy.

Furthermore a severe resource crunch during the early seventies and the deterrents that the country was confronted with could certainly have taken the spotlight of the country's unbridled economic potential. It did not and this is the moot point for developing nations that may not have the size and scale of China's economy, but they have positive endowments that can confer on them a bargaining position that would help them in the design of a trade and foreign investment strategy that is more appropriate for the socio-economic contexts that they have.

A number of African countries are resource abundant and yet the prevalence of abject poverty indicates that they have not been able to muster a bargaining clout that would enable them to devise better-suited and, consequently, a beneficial agenda of liberalization.

Another crucial point of relevance to other developing countries pertains to the undeniable significance of gradualism in enhancing and increasing gains that have accrued from liberalization. An apt examples to depict this point is the approach that China's monetary authority has had to currency convertibility.

As discussed earlier, export-oriented manufacturing has been one the most successful aspects of the nation's liberalization process. By 1990 the country's foreign exchange reserves had begun to increase almost exponentially. Plausibly, this may have set the tone for expediting the 'marketization' or the full convertibility of the renminbi. However, the Asian crisis applied brakes on any possibility of this happening over the short term. It is possible that if the currency liberalization in some countries of South-East Asia such as Thailand, Indonesia and, to a lesser extent, Malaysia had not triggered a spate of bank runs and financial instability the stance towards full capital account convertibly in China would have been a less conservative one.

Understandably, when countries with stronger financial and banking fundamentals had been adversely impacted, the message rang loud and clear – China could very well have found itself in throes of a financial crisis if it had liberalized its currency. Although China's capital controls are porous and there is a leakage in terms of money that leaves its shores through channels such as black-market lending, the magnitude of capital flight that could have occurred if the People's Republic Bank of China had opted for full convertibility of renminbi could have been huge.

In a sense, the Asian crisis corroborated that the cautions and some would say even guarded approach the government had towards certain aspects of neo-liberalism was a prudent one, and it certainly drove home the point that developing countries need to consider issues related to capital account convertibility of their respective currencies.

The renminbi was de-pegged from the US dollar in July 2005, which is when China moved to a managed floating exchange rate regime. (Instead, the RMB exchange rate is now determined based on a basket of certain major currencies, with assigned weights selected in line with the real situation of China's external sector development. Proper measures can be taken to manage and adjust the RMB exchange rate based on market supply and demand, while considering the changes of the basket of currencies, so as to maintain the stability of the RMB exchange rate at an adaptive and equilibrium level.) According to Zhou Xiaochuan, Governor of the People's Republic Bank of China, this was a measure that would reflect the competitiveness of the RMB against major currencies. Furthermore, it would make it easier for it to absorb the impact generated by an unstable US dollar and moderate the fluctuations of RMB exchange rates at the multilateral level, thus safeguarding the overall stability of China's economy.

On the basis of recent reports one can anticipate a gradualist stance, towards exchange rate liberalization. According to a report by Hongkong and Shanghai Banking Corporation (April 2006) the Governor of the People's Republic Bank of China, Zhou Xiaochuan, stated:

> A market oriented exchange regime is a policy goal, but the process will be only gradual and in a controllable manner. The policy analysis and forecasts conducted before the reform have produced different views about the impact of reform . . . Six months after the reform most Chinese enterprises have adapted smoothly to the reform after undertaking painful restructuring. However, a few sectors suffered severely from exchange rate adjustment. On such a count we may conclude that market forces could be allowed gradually to play a greater role in the floating exchange rate.

## Economic transformation and turnaround: beyond structural adjustment

Structural transformation is not a matter of sporadic adjustments; an illustrative endorsement of this fact is provided by China. Unlike its counterparts in Eastern Europe, transition has occurred over the much longer time horizon of two decades in China. The process has certainly not reached finality yet and it is from this fact that a cue can be taken. Having attained impressive reductions in abject poverty, China has a distance to cover; despite the existence of its predominantly communist underpinnings, the country has witnessed rising inequalities of income over the last decade. Almost 30 years (after 1978) and tremendous progress later, China needs to identify new sources of growth to continue and extend the purview of reform measures. Thus, it cannot allow the pace of structural transformation to slacken.

*Lesson*: A transformation from 'developing' to 'developed' involves a major transition that can be quite long winded and could continue even after a prolonged period of economic advancement. The Chinese economic experience corroborates this. Conversely, spurts of growth and a dash of smart policy thinking would result in a short spell of economic progress and not much more.

Although China finds itself positioned on a trajectory of fairly high growth rates it needs to continue the process of reform and structural transformation. Sustained progress has reduced the developmental challenges that China has had to surmount but it hasn't taken away from it the momentous task of grappling with developmental imperatives. In the context of the developing world this is an important fact because it underscores that it is absolutely exigent to differentiate between measures that will provide a temporary impetus to growth and those that are less transient and more comprehensively formulated.

The empirics of China's economic progress is reminiscent of a cliché: all goods things take time. It entails more than a span of increasing growth rates for over a decade and a half for a country to continue its ascent towards higher levels of development.

It is not as though China has run out of the compelling need for reform in certain realms, for instance, in the institutional sphere. However, when one investigates its economic experience over the last few decades it becomes evident that, at different points of its transition, the nature and magnitude of adjustment required to propel its progress will vary. Unleashing economic growth was facilitated by the implementation of certain measures that enabled its industrial sector to have a distinct comparative advantage in manufacturing across a spectrum of industries, particularly in the ambit of light consumer goods manufacturing. The thrust was on export-oriented production and most policies enacted reflected this. The extent of political adjustment made was determined not by the totality of what was required but by what was needed to ensure the continuity of liberalization. Added to this, the bounties of increasing economic growth could have even diverted the focus from the exigency of having more concerted institutional, legal and other politically linked reform.

Undeniably, sustaining growth in contemporary China will be contingent on tackling problems that have not been addressed at all or have not been resolved adequately. Issues related to state-owned and financial sector reform along with other concerns, which may have distinct political connotations, cannot be procrastinated over for long. It is the approach and efficacy with which these matters are dealt with that will have a determinate role in shaping the magnitude and pace of progress in the country.

Interestingly, one can draw a parallel between the nature of reform required and the new sources of comparative advantage that China will have to evolve in technology-intensive spheres, labour-intensive manufacturing and in the realm of the service sector. Fundamentally, it was a single major core competence, that of low-cost manufacturing, that underpinned the increase in China's growth rates from the early 1980s to the late 1990s. However, at the stage of development that the country finds itself it needs to create more than one sphere of competitive or comparative advantage if it is to ensure a consistent rise in its per capita incomes. China has begun to focus on not only production of technology-intensive goods but also on the building of skill-intensive capabilities. However, it is important that the endeavour to carve out areas of specialization in skill and technologically oriented sectors should not be at the expense of existent sources of comparative advantage. Thus, creating new sources of growth should not undermine those that currently exist.

As discussed at various points in the preceding chapters, the rather profound role that policy parameters have had in determining the course that economic transition has taken in China has been an irrefutable characteristic of its transformation. This is an aspect that continues to apply to the present context – indisputably, the political economy of reform of present-day China is as much a reality as the political economy of liberalization that was a key variable during the preceding phase.

*Insight*: We can draw from China's precedent experience that well-timed adjustment and policy-induced change enabled it to avert the tumult and trauma of a dramatic transition to a market-based economy. Present circumstances in China contrast sharply with what existed three decades ago, its strength and resilience gives to it an importance that resounds globally. However, an evocation of one of the underlying principles of its success tells us that if China is to prevent its track record of progress from becoming erratic and less consistent it cannot avoid stepping up the pace, widening the scope and enhancing the depth of institutional reform. Furthermore, excluding the changes that this would entail would simply reduce the efficacy of reform.

Even if one were to narrow the scope of reform process it does not take away the fact that institutional reform is an inextricable facet of political adjustments and it would encompass changes that have been kept at bay so far. The lesson herein is: the creation of a wider range of core competences needs to be supported by a reform process that is broader-based.

In addition, China's economic transformation demonstrates that much more than a single turnaround decision, adjustment or fortuitous event is required for sustained economic progress. In the course of its economic transition, the Chinese leadership has found itself at critical junctures amidst situations that teetered on the verge of precariousness. There have been three such instances that could be described as turning points for the Chinese economy over the last three decades: the first of these appeared in 1978 when Deng Xiaoping announced the opening up of the economy, the second in 1985 and the third was the post-Tiananmen phase (1989–92).

As explained in the previous chapters, it is understandable that the initial steps taken towards easing the stringent restrictions within which the economy functioned and the setting up of special economic zones subsequently would usher in a whirlwind of change. However, even after about a decade of liberalization there could have been a dramatic reversal in 1989 after the Tiananmen Square massacre. This could very well have steered the Chinese economy off the path that led to liberalization, even though this had been initiated a decade earlier.

In 1989, when the Chinese Army was mobilized to repress student demonstrators who were asking for democracy, the means used to quell this shocked the world. Perceptibly, the fact that Deng, with the help of some others in governance at the time, was largely responsible for the Tiananmen Square crackdown reflected that the leadership had its own views about the content, extent and magnitude of liberalism that the reform process would embody. At the time it seemed that the upper echelons of China's political realm had an irrevocable stand on democracy and this expressed itself vividly when Zhao Ziyang was arrested.

Zhao Ziyang, who had been a protégé of Deng, was a liberal voice in the country's political establishment; he played a crucial role in setting into motion changes that led to a higher degree of decentralization at the level of provincial authority in the country. Washington's immediate response to this incident was an extremely embittered one and it reacted by imposing trade and investment sanctions.

However, by no means did Deng buckle under the pressure of US sanctions; he was a pragmatist whose bravado was rooted in practical reality. Liberalization in China did not come to a grinding halt, fortunately East Asia (Macau, Taiwan and Hong Kong) was an important source of investment in China and, in any case, by the early 1990s a sizable proportion of manufacturing activity had moved out of Hong Kong into the mainland as a result of higher labour costs. Although the repercussions of Tiananmen did not last very long its fall-out could have been much more damaging the if country had been heavily reliant on foreign investment from the United States.

*Insight*: In a sense China's economy had an advantage because the measures to make it more market-oriented had begun over a decade prior to the 1990s and this had resulted not just in higher levels of progress but also a degree of economic and perhaps even political resilience. Economic pragmatism for Deng Xiaoping did not include an accelerated process of democratization. China was not in a state of precipitous decline when Deng, by then an oligarch and a political stalwart, spearheaded liberalization in the country's economic dimension, which was conspicuously devoid of the usual prerequisite of having a democracy.

The end of the Cold War, coupled with the disintegration of communism in Eastern Europe, marked the beginning of a new era for international polity amid a fast-changing global equations. Deng's famous tour of South China was certainly well timed and, by the mid-1990s, China had managed to place itself as an important investor and production destination for practically every leading MNC or TNC in the world. China's market size and its significantly lower costs of production began to matter enough to relegate ideological considerations into the background.

## Conclusion

Over the last decade policies initiated in the Chinese economy have been overtly growth-oriented, but this has meant that developmental priorities have been not emphasized as much as they should have been. It is probable that China's subsequent phase of structural transformation will be propelled by policies, measures and changes that are oriented towards higher levels of development.

In essence, utilizing the benefits that emanate from high rates of growth to provide a fillip to an increased pace of development will be the next major transitional adjustment that the country will have make. An accurate visualization of the number of turnarounds that this will encompass is difficult but it will definitely be a process that will lend more insights into development economics.

## Appendix: fundamental lessons, in a nutshell

Economic imperatives transcend ideological demarcations, a message that rang and loud and clear when one views China's socialist market-based economy and its reverberating importance in contemporary geopolitics.

Despite the initial prioritization of poverty reduction in China there remains considerable scope for further cutbacks in the numbers of those who live below the poverty line. Yet there are numerous instances where poverty reduction is veritably an afterthought instead of being interwoven as an important element of strategy formulated and implemented. In such cases the battle against poverty is lost before it begins.

China effectively demonstrated that liberalization does not come with an autonomous ability to mitigate underdevelopment. It is the macroeconomic environment, policy framework and the structuring of liberalization that will determine whether or not it becomes an instrument of growth and development.

Structural transformation is a long haul: despite having achieved long strides towards economic progress, China is faced with the task of transforming economic growth into a process of sustainable development. Economic transition (to higher levels of growth and progress) encompasses much more than a handful of structural adjustments; it involves a prolonged period of continuous positive change.

# 15
# When Elephants Walk and Dragons Dance: A Comparison between the Indian and Chinese Economies

'In the same way that commentators refer to the 1900s as the American Century, the early 21st century may be seen as the time when some in the developing world, led by India and China, come into their own,' said a December 2004 study by the US National Intelligence Council.

East Asia gave the world what was, for a long time, described as the East Asian miracle during the 1970s and 1980s. Then it was South-East Asia's remarkable performance that began to unfold, in the mid-1980s and continuing up to to the mid-1990s. At the turn of the 21st century it became evident that India and China would be key players, if not the most important, on the global economy for a long time to come.

East Asia and South-East Asia didn't just surprise the world, the phenomenal progress of these regions evoked a rethink or reappraisal about some widely held interpretations and tenets of conventional economic belief. 'Following Japan's economic catching up episode between the 1950s and the 1980s the fast pace of economic growth, industrialization and growth of manufactured exports in the Republic of Korea as well as other Asian newly industrializing economies – Hong Kong, Singapore and Taiwan Province of China awarded these countries and by the extension of the region with the distinction of the forming the East Asian Miracle. China and India have entered this process most recently.' (UNCTAD, Trade and Development Report 2005).

Further according to the report China and India will have a much larger impact on the composition of world trade that Japan and South Korea. Miracle some would say, no miracle some would describe it, regardless it is undeniable that China-India are among the most important drivers of not only economic growth but also the next phase of globalization. If one were to describe the economic experience of both India and China with a literary undertone it would be: this is a story of chequered economic progress that gathered pace, of strategies that epitomized a blend or fusion of divergent ideological orientation, of adversity that was turned into opportunity, of untapped prospects and of developmental imperatives that need to be surmounted.

Unequivocally, India and China's economic advancement ushered in its wake a number of unanticipated occurrences, and it is probable that this will continue. Two decades ago not many would have anticipated that India and China would have the pivotal role that they do in the contemporary global economy. India and China are models of development in the making: taken together the empirics of development in both provide insights, lessons and aspects that are extremely relevant to the ills and deterrents that an entire gamut of developing countries continue to struggle against with varying degrees of effectiveness but without achieving escape from the trappings of underdevelopment.

On a theoretical plane the economic experience of these two nations gives to development thinking a distinctly new dimension or perspective on the subject.

Initial comparisons between India and China focused on the growth differentials between the two, this coupled with the assessment of economic liberalization on the basis of foreign investment inflows in both led to inferences that seem oversimplified in retrospect. As economic growth rates in India increased, and certain cutting-edge core-competences conferred on the country's manufacturing and services sectors a certain degree of international competitiveness studies explored the subject with more depth and incisiveness.

The India–China comparison extended beyond the purview of numbers, it viewed the sectoral strengths and weaknesses in both, the geo-political role that both have in the present and foreseeable global context and the other fundamentals of economic progress. The question about which of these two mega-economies has pursued a 'better' path becomes more difficult to answer (categorically at least) as comparative analysis becomes more detailed. Thus, the India and China story has to be evaluated not merely in terms of growth rate comparisons but in the larger context of formulating strategy that has much more applicability to the problems of developing nations. Crucial insights can be drawn from an analysis of integral aspects that pertain to the development experience of these nations.

When two countries with divergent political systems, stark differences in ideological underpinnings and growth strategies are currently heading towards outcomes that are not as dissimilar as many would have forecasted even just 20 years ago it tells us that there must be a common denominator. Although perceptions of what development means may have differed in India and China, the fact remains that building the fundamentals was the central objective of both nations.

When both set out on the path to development it was predictable at the outset itself that the journey would be a tumultuous one, one which would be interspersed with periods of uncertainty and even trauma. Both were saddled with a magnitude of poverty that can be described as extensive, both had to face the task of agrarian reform and the rather daunting mission of industrialization. From this point of broad convergence, insofar as the initial circumstances and challenges that prevailed in both nations about five decades ago are concerned, the route that India and China pursued towards the attainment of stated objectives differed and widely so. Having steered through economic upheavals, political turbulence and severe resource constraints, which could have driven economic progress to a grinding halt in both instances, India and China find themselves at centre-stage of the global economy and it is interesting to note both are grappling with the imperatives of reform and sustainable development.

Exuberance is a good thing, but it needs to be tempered, increasing growth rates in both countries cannot be disembodied from the larger goal of stepping up the pace of development, poverty reduction and an improvement in human development indicators; this means that an expansion of social infrastructure and reducing income and non-income disparities are problems that confront both. The severity of each of these ills may differ; however, there is a compelling need to translate the benefits of increasing growth to those who are barely able to eke out a means of sustenance. For both nations, although increasing growth rates is a crucial objective, achieving a faster rate of development happens is critical.

The comparison will begin with a brief overview of the historical circumstances, which will be followed by an examination of three distinct phases in the economic experience of both countries. These are:

1. The pre-economic liberalization phase in India and China. In China this spans a period of 1949–78 and in India it pertains to 1947–91.
2. Economic liberalization. This will view the period 1978 to the late 1990s in China. In India this spans from 1991 to the present period.
3. The current phase.

## An overview of recent history: India and China

Some centuries ago, when Christopher Colombus set out to find India and found America instead, he did this because the former was, at the time, a power to reckon with. Historically, there are few countries that have been as exposed to the 'winds of the globe' as India has been, as the nation was an important trading power a few thousand years ago. Trade was also the initial reason that a number of European nations, such as the British, Dutch, Portuguese and the French, expanded their interaction with the subcontinent. This was a land that bore the cruel onslaught of several invasions for many centuries and, for the last millennium at least, there has hardly been a period where a single political authority or a centrally run state ruled the entire nation. India was a melange of kingdoms and, at various points in time, this also included regional dominance by foreign powers. Interestingly, even during British rule, which was about as close as India got to having a singular political administration (rather than authority) at the helm of affairs it had over 550 kingdoms and monarchs.

In contrast, China has had a centrally run state presided over by a monarch throughout most of its recorded history. This is not to say that this dominant feature of its governance was not interrupted by the ravages of barbaric invasions and tyrannical intrusion by powers that came from outside; however, the frequency with which this happened was certainly limited (relative to India).

The passage of history and the cultural changes (however subtle these maybe) that emanates from this evokes ideological responses. A particular ideology is born out of a series of ideological processes, some of these are extremely short-lived, while others become the underpinnings of major transitions. Perhaps the most distinctive trait of India's legacy was its multi-lingual and multicultural character. This is a country that exemplifies among the most illustrative instances of pluralism and it was only democracy (no other imaginable alternative system) that could have accommodated and been compatible with this central characteristic of Indian ethos. Some would view democracy as an ideological response; be this as it may, the larger reality was one where a democratic process of governance was the most prudent political option and continues to be in the Indian context.

A dominant feature of China's history was long periods of rule by a single dynasty, although imperial authority changed hands and dynasties were overthrown. China has had its wars and spans of turmoil but it had at its centre of its governance an emperor who ruled it as a single national entity. At a political level, thus, communism spearheaded a transition from a situation where imperial authoritarianism was faltering to a hardliner, non-imperial, authoritarian state – one that would be able to effectively deliver the adjustments that modernization would compel. One such adjustment was the transformation of what can be described as the prevalence of feudalism in most parts of the mainland to a modern framework.

## Liberalization: the initial stage

India has been a country where transitions, some subtle and others profound, are made with regularity. However, if the extent of change is to be gauged by the number of transitions that occurred in India and China over the last few decades then one cannot state that either changed much more or (much less) than the other. Over the last 60 years, there were three distinct phases of fundamental change for both India and China. For the former the first phase began with the end of colonization in 1947 and continued for two decades thereafter (1947–67); the second began with the inception of partial liberalization during the mid-1980s, under the premiership of Rajiv Gandhi; and the third was ushered in by a much more discernible process of economic liberalization after 1991.

The Mao era that heralded the beginning of the communist regime in 1949 in China initiated the first phase of transformation. The second turning point began when Deng Xiaoping took on the mantle of governance in 1976 and the third was heralded in 1992 with Deng's historic tour of the South, during which he spearheaded the process of liberalization and reform.

The impact of a transitional period in China manifested itself much sooner and more overtly than the change in India. This is hardly surprising when one considers that the forces of transformation and the course that it took in China were wrought with upheaval, the disruptive effects of which were considerable. Consequently the outcomes of an economic transition on the social system in China were more profound than those for India.

By the early 1950s, or even earlier, the imperatives of industrialization were viewed with the utmost seriousness by the leaderships in both countries. This was understandable given the historical circumstances from which these countries were extricating themselves during the same time span. Colonization, in the instance of India, and China's humiliating defeat at the hands of the British during the 19th century and its subjugation by the Japanese gave to both an overwhelming apprehension about foreign dominance.

Thus, an avowed objective of the economic agendas in both countries was to eliminate any vestige of dependency and the attainment of self-reliance and self-sufficiency in the production of basic goods would entail setting up heavy industry. State-controlled industrialization, with an emphasis on the production of steel and cement, was the central characteristic of modernization programmes in both countries. In India it proceeded within a democratic context and in China it was propelled by totalitarian dictate.

Setting up heavy industry was a tall order, and the paucity of resources was a recurrent problem that had to be coped with it at the outset and in the course of industrializing. Relatively speaking, however, India seemed better equipped to take on the task of industrialization than China. Undeniably, imperialism had taken a heavy toll on the Indian economy because it had led to a drain on the treasury, a diversion of agriculture into commercial crops and a process of deskilling. Equally true is the fact that, at the time of independence, India did have a railway network, a world-class textile industry and a proficient and well-trained civil service. Unlike China, India had some rudiments of modernization and the challenge of creating the framework of national development appeared less insurmountable at the time than China's.

Throughout the two decades ensuing after independence India did manage to lay the foundation for a number of industries in the basic goods sector, such as steel, cement and engineering. The process of industrialization was linked to the accumulation of home-grown technical expertise, a feat that India was close to accomplishing by the end of the 1960s. The country had managed to create a reservoir of professional and technical talent within two decades of independence and it was this vital input that enabled it to acquire a competitive edge in a wide range of skill-intensive activities and industries. For instance, the phenomenal expansion of the information technology sector in India is attributable, among other things, to the presence of a highly skilled indigenous manpower base.

Despite its achievements, India did not embody a stellar instance of resource mobilization. Although there may have been criticism about the thrust that the country's economic policies placed on the expansion of heavy industry, the sound rationale underlying this has been validated and repeatedly so. This is a fact that becomes all the more evident when it is viewed in the context of the country's developmental goals over the longer term.

In the Indian context, a host of problems stemmed from the highly flawed manner in which policies were implemented and this was a pervasive ill that impeded the efficacy of potentially beneficial measures. It was absolutely necessary that resource mobilization and its deployment would be guided by economic priorities. Instead these were being superseded by political considerations that were simply about preservation of position and not much else. The fall-out of this was a plethora of inefficiencies, sagging levels of productivity, inordinate delays in decision-making about vital issues and superfluous bureaucratic interference, all of which were becoming a prominent feature of the many public-sector enterprises. Inevitably, there was a spillover of this to the private sector, which encountered the malaise of red tape-ism at every level of its operational and production process. This put the brakes on technical upgrading and, by the end of the 1970s, instead of being characterized by a reasonable pace of modernization Indian industry was riddled with technical obsolescence.

India's industrial policy had its weaknesses and, though some of these may have been difficult to avert, there were other shortcomings that were certainly avoidable. For instance, industrialization as it proceeded in India did not have to stifle the world-class textile industry that the country was endowed with at the time of independence. As mentioned, the emphasis was on large-scale heavy industry and the production of labour-intensive consumer goods was relegated to the small-scale industrial sector. Consonant with this, certain concessions and incentives (which included tax exemptions) were provided to this sector; the assumption underlying this measure was that setting up small-scale industries would provide an impetus to employment generation.

It is not as if assigning the production of consumer goods to a residual sector that would be deemed as small scale was without merit. If the performance of small-scale industry had been an encouraging one it would have conferred a distinct advantage to India; instead it did not serve most of the objectives for which it was originally created. Many of these units were adjuncts to large scale manufacturing enterprises and, more importantly, a fair proportion of small-scale industry was, in fact, capital intensive. There was gross misappropriation of the incentives granted to this sector, wherein small-scale production units were set up with the primary purpose of being able to avail of the tax concessions granted to this sector. Once again, mishandled policy formulation and the inability to remedy flawed implementation nullified the potential benefits that could have accrued from the consistent expansion of labour-intensive manufacturing.

It was not surprising that employment-intensive growth in India began to lose its pace by the early 1970s and this was not because the government lacked the intent to generate jobs. Policy formulation was not accompanied by expedient and smart implementation. Measures that were conceptually sound and could have brought forth significant gains to the country's economy were rendered almost ineffective as a result of a blatant deficiency in the execution of an entire range of policy initiatives. Predictably, resource mobilization in the initial stages of industrialization in India was constricted by the limited availability of financial capital; in subsequent years the score on expediency in the realm of project and policy implementation ran so low that it became as, if not more, constricting than the availability of capital.

China managed its resource mobilization much more effectively than India. However sound a strategy might be conceptually, insofar as implementation was concerned China had an edge, one which was evident in the realm of industry and agriculture. This is not to say that by the early 1970s it had an industrial economy that was more diversified and more advanced than that of India. As a matter of fact India had been able to propel the expansion of certain key sectors, particularly those related to the production of basic goods and heavy manufacturing. In doing so, the country had achieved, by the mid 1960s, a higher level of industrial advancement than China at the time. However, the moot point of the present comparison is not about asserting the superiority of a particular industrial strategy but about the relative ability of India and China to implement and adapt strategy in a manner that facilitates a productive and expeditious deployment of inputs harnessed.

Having proceeded on track to build its basic goods sector, China realized the importance of expanding its consumer goods sector a few years after it embarked on its endeavour to set up heavy industries. Had China's approach to its consumer goods sector been similar to that of India's it is very probable that its economic performance in the previous decade would not have been impressive. Also, China could have had much more success with the industrial policy that it formulated, despite all the flaws that it may have had or the input shortages that it was confronted with, if the resources garnered were utilized efficiently.

*Table 15.1*   Enrolment ratio (%) in China and India (2002–3)

|        | Primary  | Secondary | Tertiary  |
|--------|----------|-----------|-----------|
| China  | 100      | 70        | About 18  |
| India  | About 90 | 50        | 10        |

*Source*: UNESCO data.

China and India began their climb towards economic progress with similar per capita incomes (India's was slightly higher); by 1973 it was evident that human development indicators (such as life expectancy, infant mortality rates and levels of educational attainment at the primary level) had exhibited an improvement in both countries. (Table 15.1 compares educational attainment.)

In 1950, India's human development index (HDI) was 0.160 and China's was 0.163. By 1973 China's HDI was 0.407 and India was lagging behind with an index of 0.289. It must be noted that the per capita incomes of both were fairly similar, even at this time. With regard to human capital accumulation, be it in the realm of educational attainment, infant mortality rates or life expectancy, China has performed much better than India. In a comparison between the two economic giants it is this aspect of China's trajectory of development, and not so much the spectacular success of its trade and investment liberalization, that needs to be noted.

India did begin with a head start over China and, during its first decade, it seemed to be heading in the right direction. However at some point after the mid-1960s or the early 1970s, development seemed to grind to a halt in India; India found itself almost bereft of any significant economic progress throughout the early 1970s. Arguably, the upside during this period was that India did not have to cope with traumatic disruptions in its trajectory of economic progress. As such, the nation proceeded with a Hindu rate of growth that hardly mirrored its potential.

A good proportion of the gains that accrued to China during the initial phase of modernization were eroded by the rather colossal and tragic waste of human capital and other resources as a result of the Cultural Revolution and the Great Leap Forward. The imminent reversal of economic progress that ensued positioned China's economy on a downward spiral. The situation could have become an irreversible catastrophe but it did not. When Deng Xiaoping assumed the reins of government in 1976 it heralded a new beginning. The political stalwart understood that ideology and political considerations could not hold at bay economic imperatives and geopolitical realities. In any case, at the time China found itself reeling as a result of some terrible mistakes and errors of judgment.

## Liberalization: India and China's variant

Ideologies evolve and adapt, so do economic prescriptions. In essence neo-liberalism upheld free markets and linked practically every parameter of economic progress to unshackling market forces. Transition is not an easy task. Although the possibility of eliminating the pain and costs that emanate from transitional adjustments is remote, it is essential to mitigate the difficulty and, in certain instances, trauma that arises from this. Empirical evidence has demonstrated that disrupting a precedent framework without having in place another that works better is extremely damaging.

The nature, timing and pace of liberalization were charted out differently in the instances of India and China. During its initial stage liberalism enabled the Chinese economy to embark on trade-led expansion of its manufacturing sector. The country has met with remarkable success in using selective liberalization as an instrument that will catapult it to achieve unprecedented levels of economic progress. Comparatively, in the instance of India's liberalization foreign investment has had a role that is in quantitative terms more subtle and less exceptional.

This apart, liberalism did pave the way for a transition in the Indian economy that made competitiveness and higher levels of efficiency paramount if business houses were to remain in the fray. Thus, economic liberalization in India had a qualititative impact on its macroeconomic environment, besides which it also provided an impetus to a spectrum of spheres in the ambit of the service sector, such as financial services, information technology and, in a smaller way, bio-medicine.

India's rather gradualist stance in the initial stages of liberalization may have elicited criticism from some quarters; however, it is likely that undue haste to implement every constituent of neo-liberalism would have been detrimental. Thus, both India and China demonstrate that successful liberalization is possible and it is even more likely if a country does not proceed at a breakneck speed, particularly during the initial phase.

Economic liberalization in China was selective in scope, confined as it was to the special economic zones, and it was one of a number of initiatives, such as decentralization and a higher degree of autonomy, that were directed towards making its state-owned enterprises and agriculture more market-oriented.

Action speaks louder than words; this was an adage that certainly held true of Deng Xiaoping, who did not fritter away any time in launching agricultural and industrial reforms, which would facilitate the creation of competitive market structures. China demonstrated a unique possibility for the first time: it managed to combine communism with a fair degree of economic liberalization; this was a blend that a number of Eastern European countries, including Russia, could not achieve. Notably, this came before the collapse of the Berlin Wall, which symbolized the disintegration of communist denominated systems.

Stating that communism survives in China, despite the operation of capitalist forces, is misleading because the survival of the communist system can be attributed partly to its becoming market-oriented. Undoubtedly, market orientation is an integral characteristic of capitalist functioning and it was traditionally regarded as the exclusive feature of capitalism until China began its selective inception of liberalization.

Communist or socialist systems were considered, with good reason, to be highly centralized and fervently totalitarian. By the early 1980s it was apparent that the well-defined demarcations between the two could get blurred in reality, where the combination of a capitalist orientation and communism was a possibility, not quite as far-fetched as it may have seemed. Rigid and unflinching centralization that preempts any initiative directed towards adaptation would disintegrate sooner or later, as was frequently the case with countries in Eastern Europe. The empirics of China's experience depict that it might be difficult but it is possible for centralized systems of governance and policy-making to be resilient and embody a certain degree of flexibility. For instance, communism as it prevailed during the Maoist era was different from what came into being during Deng's tenure. In the case of both variants, centralization is a dominant characteristic; however, Deng Xiaoping's use of central authority was deft because he was able to mesh authoritarianism with liberalism.

Differentiated though its role may be in both nations, the context and circumstances within which economic liberalism worked in India and China has led to the evolution of a variant of liberalization that is compatible with a wide range of economic systems. This fact is a positive aspect for strategy formulation in developing countries because it means that a particular country does not have to dismantle its economic system in total in order to ensure that liberalization is effective.

Liberalization was seen, until very recently, as compatible with the prevalence of democratic systems. The impact that liberalization had in China brought into question the generality of the widely held belief that liberalization would be incompatible with a non-democratic political framework. It would be erroneous to state that China's experience implies a refutation of this notion: it does not. However, it compels us to take note of the fact that democracy is not always the precursor to economic liberalization. Having said this, it is also true that, once liberalization is initiated, democracy makes the adjustments entailed much easier. In the Indian context, however, the existence of a democratic system of governance did not translate into a quicker pace of economic liberalization.

China's economic experience demonstrates that it is possible to have a process of economic liberalism that does not translate into a commensurate political change. This has been the status quo in China so far; however, given the expansion of private-enterprise economy and the need for institutional reform in the Chinese context, it is likely that certain elements of political change will exert an influence on communism, or what some would describe as the socialism-liberalism combination.

Comparisons between India and China usually lend themselves to a discussion about which country embodies the 'superior growth strategy'. Not too long ago, the export-led manufacturing boom in China was extolled by prominent members of the global business community and some sections of the academic diaspora. Undoubtedly, China's economic performance has been impressive, particularly in terms of the growth rates and rise in per capita income that it has managed to achieve, the phenomenal expansion of its manufacturing sector and concomitantly its export competitiveness and the discernible improvement in human development indicators, such as education enrolment ratios, life expectancy and poverty indices. The advantages of India's economic course have become manifest over the last few years: its vibrant private sector, which is home to some world-class companies, such as Bharat Forge, Wipro and the Aditya Birla group, to name but a few; its institutional framework and financial-sector fundamentals give it an edge that China is yet to acquire.

Cutting across the quantum of economic achievement in China and India there exists a remarkable similarity between the two. The presence of world-class companies, such as Lenovo in China and Infosys in India, across a range of industrial spheres, which include automobiles, information technology, pharmaceuticals, telecommunications and household appliances. In both instances, policy orientation had a distinct role to play in encouraging the expansion of certain industry leaders; however, it is an observably different context and ownership structure that led to the corporate success stories in India and China.

According to the study by the Boston Consulting Group, (2006) two-thirds of Chinese firms are state-owned or-controlled, some have a mixed-ownership structure and only four are privately owned. However, the ownership of most leading Indian companies is divided between private owners, a strategic investor (such as a foreign investor) and shareholders from the market. In the study only one Indian company is state-controlled. China's experience tells us that commercial success is possible even if a company is government-owned or -controlled; this apart, the interesting point about Indian and Chinese companies is that both need to move beyond cost-based differentiation. This means that value creation will be the sine qua non of competitor advantage in both. This is a feature that exists in some sectors in both India and China; however, it needs to become more pervasive and this defines a need to step up the pace and extent of innovation and skill development.

Another commonality between the two is that resource mobilization is not a hurdle for both India and China; this fact is more obvious in the case of the latter. This is an interesting fact, some would even say uncanny, because compared to India, it is in China where liberalization has had a far more significant role as far as resource mobilization is concerned. Furthermore,

India's significant increase in growth rates has been achieved with a rate of capital accumulation that is much less than that of China's, not to mention that its levels of foreign investments are a fraction of China's.

Thus, although, at this point in time, the numbers in may be more impressive in the instance of China, from a macroeconomic perspective both have converged to a scenario where mobilizing huge amounts of financial capital is not a problem. The reason: if China is an economic powerhouse and India is an emerging one, both India and China have a sound balance of payments situation and are unequivocally the most attractive foreign investment destinations. Perhaps the edge that China has over India as far as garnering huge amounts of investment goes is less pertinent than the exigent task that both have, which is the mobilization of other kinds of resources – harnessing a wide range of capabilities –organizational, technical and innovative, the cornerstone of sustainable development. Ensuring that prosperity continues relies on the management and organization of these intangible resources.

Over 4 per cent of China's GDP growth was accounted for by capital accumulation and this was possible because of China's high saving rates. India, on other hand, had a much lower capital accumulation of about 1.5 per cent during the 1990s. However, India's growth is explained largely by its total factor productivity of capital, which is marginally lower than that of China. Despite being constrained by infrastructural bottlenecks, a significant aspect of India's productivity-driven growth is that it managed to achieve the present levels of economic progress with a much a lower savings rate and quantum of foreign investment than China. (Table 15.2 indicates total factor productivity increases in both countries.)

*Table 15.2* Contribution of consumption, investment and trade to GDP growth in China and India (%)

| Country/Decade | Consumption | | GDFK* | Trade | | GDP Gr.[†] |
|---|---|---|---|---|---|---|
| | Private | Public expenditure | | Exports | Imports | |
| 1st Decade | | | | | | |
| China (1979 onwards) | 4.88 | 1.39 | 3.05 | 0.61 | −1.06 | 10.10 |
| India (1980 onwards) | 3.25 | 0.75 | 1.33 | 0.32 | −0.57 | 5.89 |
| 2nd Decade | | | | | | |
| China (1979) | 3.88 | 1.10 | 3.62 | 2.03 | −1.96 | 9.41 |
| India (1980) | 3.11 | 0.70 | 1.51 | 1.16 | −1.38 | 5.70 |

* Gross domestic fixed capital formation. [†] Annual average GDP growth.
*Source*: UNCTAD, *Trade and Development Report* (2005).

Thus, the fact that India was unable to attain higher levels of capital accumulation reflects a weakness in its growth strategy; however, the ability of its industrial sector to manage the resources that it had with a higher degree of probity or efficiency is a strength. At this point, India has to step up its rate of capital accumulation, which has been constrained by its high revenue deficits and consequently negative public savings. This has to be accompanied by massive investments in physical and social infrastructure provision, a lack of which has constricted its progress so far. China needs to manage the huge quantum of resources that it has mobilized from its domestic economy and external investors, for which it has to spearhead measures that will reduce the sizable pile-up of non-performing loans and the proportion of non-viable investments in its state-owned sector.

For both India and China, a fundamental challenge stems from the need to optimize capital accumulation. The manifestations of a suboptimal allocation of capital may differ in both countries but the problem concerns the same parameter.

Thus, in response to the question raised earlier about which nation embodies a growth strategy that is more effective than that of the other (the question is a straightforward one, the answer, however, is not as easy), if there is an answer to this then it would at best be on the basis of the efficacy and expediency with which both India and China tackle reform.

## Present reform imperatives in India and China: a comparison

Theoretically, the task of reform agendas in both India and China may be clear-cut; however, the initiatives that these require are held back by the political economy of underdevelopment that exists in India and the politics of control in China. In the Indian context, the tacit formulation of policies that will catalyze the expansion of infrastructure and will do so while protecting the interests of those who may be displaced and need rehabilitation is an imperative that cannot be glossed over on any pretext. Furthermore, in so far as fiscal policy is concerned, striking a balance between trimming fiscal deficits and an increase in public investments towards expanding physical and social capital is yet to happen. In China, understandably, the compulsions of reform in the state-owned sector have to be addressed without a dilution of developmental interests; this does not make it any easier. As a matter of fact, having a faster pace of reform in China does become slightly complicated because the attempt would be to do so in a context that is largely authoritarian. In both nations, political considerations impede the expediency with which reform occurs, and working out a way around this limitation is an issue that confronts both.

Comparative studies about China and India use the phrase 'competing models of development' to describe the paths that these nations have pursued towards increasing their growth rates. Be this as it may, the approach and scenario pertaining to economic reform in both countries can be illustratively termed as 'complementary models of reform'. It is evident that China has before it a long road to institutional reform, which includes putting in place a well functioning legal system and a well-controlled and healthy banking system coupled with a broad-based capital market. India, on other hand, has before it the crucial task of expanding its physical infrastructure. China's expenditure on infrastructure (electricity, transportation, telecommunications, real estate and construction) is about eight times as much as India.

Labour productivity in China is higher than in India and a significant part of this differential can be explained in terms of the inadequacy of infrastructure provision that continues to hamper operational efficiency and lengthen delivery time in India. Labour productivity is inextricably linked to the persistence of certain constraints and, inevitably, this translates into higher costs.

At this point it would be useful to make a comparison about some aspects of the Indian and Chinese banking sector. The fundamentals of India's banking sector and its capital market are certainly sounder than that of China. However, a parallel maybe drawn between the prevalent situation in China's banking sector and the main characteristics of this sphere in India about a decade ago. Even as China finds itself in the initial stages of creating a sound institutional framework in its banking and financial sector, it is reminiscent of the reform initiatives that were set into motion in India's banking sector over a decade ago.

The sounder fundamentals of the banking sector are indicated by the higher capital adequacy ratios in Indian banks compared to those in the Chinese banking sector. According to a report by Morgan Stanley Research Division of Morgan Stanley & Co. (2004) the Indian banking sector (which includes the state-owned and non state-owned banks) has a capital adequacy ratio of 12.6 per cent. The state-owned banking sector in China has a capital adequacy ratio of 4.6 per cent and non state-owned banks have a capital adequacy of 6.8 per cent.

Until the early 1990s, nationalized or state-controlled banks dominated the banking sector in India and concomitantly there was minimal private-sector participation. Inevitably, a lack of competition ushers in a host of inefficiencies. Similarly, China is saddled with a stack of non-performing assets, as was the case with India about a decade ago. The advent of liberalization in India facilitated the entry of private-sector banks (domestic and foreign) and this compelled the nationalized banks to tighten their belts. Understandably, this was an uncomfortable situation in which banks found themselves and the result was that these had to recapitalize by an amount of US$5 billion during the mid 1990s. During the last few years, the combination of increasing levels of competition and declining interests has enabled state-owned banks to improve and strengthen their capital base.

In China too the government has recapitalized the banks twice: once during the late 1990s with an amount of RMB270 billion and, in the second instance, in 2004 by US$45 billion. Evidently, as the Indian instance corroborates, although it is extremely likely that performance improvements in state-owned banks would require an impetus from the government this is an interim measure. Sagging levels of efficiency cannot be remedied by bail-out packages; the solution begins by easing those controls that make it difficult for state-owned banks to reduce their non-performing loans. A frequently cited reason for the proliferation of non-performing assets is that profitability cannot be the only basis for lending in a developing country. Even though this is a valid fact, it does not explain (not in entirety, at least) the allocative inefficiencies that pervaded the state-owned banks because priority-sector lending or development-oriented lending can be managed better and disbursed more prudently. Plausibly, this may not have eliminated the accumulation of non-performing assets but it certainly would have reduced them. Thus, reform in China's banking sector is not merely about relinquishing controls but using the policies to direct an increased proportion of loans to sectors that are more productive and employment-intensive.

Despite having liberalized their financial markets, in India and China liberalization has a controlled pace and a limited extent. This is a similarity that the two nations share despite the differences in their approach to liberalization. Concomitantly, the stance towards full fledged capital account convertibility by the monetary authorities in both is cautious. Perhaps one of the most interesting outcomes in the empirical evidence about both is that their foreign exchange reserves have increased at an unprecedented pace.

This tells us that the path of controlled financial liberalization can work rather well given the presence of certain other fundamentals such as a relatively sound fiscal and monetary management practices. The lesson here is that financial development does not require an accelerated pace of financial liberalization, this was a fact that was evidenced by the Asian crisis and more recently by the processes underlying international financial integration in India and China.

Reform initiatives in China's banking sector have begun and some of the outcomes have been positive; however, the process needs to be spearheaded, a measure that is invariably deterred by excessive control. In this context, the reform of India's banking exemplifies a useful lesson: that it is possible to have a process of successful banking sector reform even in a context where government controls have reduced but continue to exist. Notably, the predominance of state-owned banks in the Indian banking sector continues because these enjoy the largest market share of loans. Alternatively expressed, government control and a competitive environment in the banking sector are two aspects that need not be mutually exclusive; however it is important that the degree and mechanism of control does not stifle measures directed towards increasing levels of efficiency.

It is not as if the Indian banking sector is without its weaknesses; there continues to be scope for further reform in this sphere. However, the banking and finance sector is among the fastest-growing sectors in India currently. China's first stock exchange began in Shanghai in December 1990 and India's first stock exchange began over 129 years ago. Over the last decade the Indian capital markets have witnessed a rapid expansion and the highlight of this has been stock markets that are among the most buoyant globally. In the absence of a regulatory authority that is vigilant and ensures a certain degree of transparency, it is unrealistic to expect capital markets to function efficiently.

Stock market scams and other financial malpractices did happen, even as capital markets expanded; however, stricter monitoring procedures and better enforcement of standards set by the Stock Exchange Board of India (SEBI) reduced the scope and the extent with which irregularities could occur. As a matter of fact, there has been an enhancement in SEBI's ability to sniff out scams in the making and take counter-measures that prevent them from happening.

## Conclusion

At this point it would almost be juvenile to pick out the winner, as it were, in terms of which country adopted the 'better strategy'. China's economic prescription cannot be adjudged as superior on the basis of its higher growth rates or sizable inflows of FDI into the country, nor can India's strategy be considered the smarter course of action because it has facilitated the emergence of a rather vibrant home-grown corporate sector.

Lauding China's FDI – export-led orientation as the generalized prescription for other developing countries would be a half-baked inference, as would upholding India's pattern of growth as the way to go for other less developed countries. Describing China's experience as one that was based on the tenets of neo-liberalism is a brutal simplification of the country's growth strategy. (As depicted in the previous chapter, liberalization was one constituent, albeit an important one, in a much larger context of growth-directed instrumentalities.)

Similarly, ascribing to India's economic progress the presence of world-class manufacturing companies in its organized sector would be an incomplete fact because the emergence of these companies was partly an outcome of certain policies that were focused at the outset from creating an edifice for a home-grown industrial sector. These policies were ensconced within the licence Raj and it must reiterated that, at one point in time, a number of companies in India struggled against the odds, having to function in a system that was being choked by the excesses of bureaucratic intervention and all the shackles that come with it. A few years after liberalization some of these companies emerged even stronger and more resilient.

If one were to extract the most important elements of developing strategy from both it is this: both countries are evolving their distinct paradigms of growth. A comparison between these two mega-economies is a useful one not because it endorses generalizations about advocating this or that strategy of growth but because it corroborates that each country needs to determine its sphere(s) of comparative advantage and it is on the basis of this that a nation evolves its core competences. Thus, it is the process of identifying its strengths and building upon them that defines what the drivers of growth should be. The variables that spurred growth in India were different from those that propelled growth in China.

Both these nations have to face developmental challenges and the task of spearheading their reform processes to the next stage. Traversing the economic experience of both underscores that increasing growth rates is a necessary condition but not a sufficient condition for development and, thus, both have before them the compelling need to build transmission mechanisms that will enable the benefits of growth to percolate to the lower rungs of the socio-economic hierarchy. The key advantages and disadvantages that characterize the economic systems and structures of both of these powerhouse nations have been discussed. In the larger context of globalization it is the levels of growth and development in India and China that will have a considerable role in shaping economic trends in the ensuing decades.

From a sectoral standpoint the challenges that confront the two nations differ; however, from a broader perspective both have similar problems to surmount. Poverty reduction and quickening the pace of development are two objectives that both need to attain. Furthermore, if India has the politics of underdevelopment to contend with, China has the politics of control to grapple with. Both India and China have loss-making state-owned or public-sector enterprises and in both countries the interplay of political considerations with economic imperatives does, in many instances, lead to a misdirection of a certain proportion of resources. Measuring the size and scale of the political economy of underdevelopment in India or that of control in China would be a contentious exercise and one that is rather unnecessary in the present context. The more vital point is that this is a deterrent that holds back expediency insofar as implementation of infrastructure-building initiatives in India and constraints and delays institutional reform in China are concerned. The manifestation of both outcomes is a slower pace of development.

The Chinese economy, characterized by over-investment, coupled with its high savings rate and in veritable contrast the need for India to step up its rate of capital accumulation if it wants to have a growth rate of above 7 per cent, does indicate the difference in the problems confronting the two countries.

Interestingly both represent supply side concerns, in the instance of China an increase in the availability and accessibility of social goods that will increase consumer spending and greater efficiency in the allocation and utilization of investment is required if economic progress is to be sustained at present levels. In the case of India higher economic growth entails higher levels of investment. For both the Chinese and Indian economies addressing supply-side issues require a more expeditious and more effective process of reform.

Having demonstrated two rather disparate paths towards economic progress, it is the pace and effectiveness with which India and China weed out the vestiges of underdevelopment that will determine the efficacy of their strategies. Furthermore, in charting out measures that will step up the attainment of developmental targets it is likely that there would be a greater degree of similarity in the initiatives undertaken in both.

On a conceptual plane, a comparative analysis also helps one to visualize that an ideal growth paradigm would embody the strengths of both India and China. However, even if a country managed to achieve this rather pheno-menal feat it would have to face the unfinished task of development. It would have to face the challenge of poverty reduction, disparities of income, social security issues and institutional reform. However, the magnitude of these problems would be much less.

# Part II

# Globalization: A Process of Incomplete Economic Integration

# Introduction to Part II

This section will examine the present role that globalism has in economic development and, in doing so, ascertain the importance of transforming it into an effective strategy of development. It will elucidate that, for globalism to exist, much more than economic liberalism is required.

As will be demonstrated in the following three chapters (Chapters 16–18), rhetoric about the importance of economic integration stands in stark variance to the structure and policies that deter it. Instead of having strategies that would ensure a consistent and continuous process of economic integration we seem to be moving further away from this by adopting patterns of growth that are almost disembodied from development. Against a backdrop where poverty and glaring inequalities, not just of income but also of opportunity and resource accessibility, have acquired grave proportions, the prospects of economic integration are becoming less tenable. It is even more alarming to note that this happens amid and despite cognizance about the fact that the world cannot really afford to endure the risks and costs of polarized growth and the marginalization of millions any more.

# 16
## Globalization: Vision and Reality

We have an uneven, lopsided process of liberalization that exists against a background of asymmetries, economic distortions and restrictions that is not globalization. Then what is?

If we consider one blatant fact, which relates to the overarching global influence that a few control groups, such as the World Trade Organisation (WTO) have exerted on policy-making across the developing world to alter fundamental parameters, it becomes evident that globalization is not about unleashing opportunities worldwide but about consolidating access to global markets by a few privileged players. The consequence of this for the developing world has been a trend of clustered or negligible overall opportunity creation and enclaved benefits.

**It would not, therefore, be too early to ask ourselves the question: What are we globalizing? Is it availability, accessibility or opportunity?**

**Perhaps this point may be better illustrated as follows: globalization of financial systems (financial liberalization), globalization of the availability of a wide range of products and services and global utilization of information and communications technology have not added to globalized opportunity creation and a generalized increase in per capita incomes across the global economy.**

The third wave of globalization, as the current phase is described, may also be defined as a period during which the scope of corporate activities have increased at an accelerated tempo. The pressures brought on by cost-cutting and the need to for expanding markets have shaped the emergence of an internationalized mode of production. This was catalyzed by the advent of communications and information technology, which enabled the breaking down and relocation of processes involved at various stages of production to different countries. Although the benefits of this have been substantial, the beneficiaries have been few.

Another aspect of this process is that a diverse range of production processes and services were globalized in a manner whereby the disadvantages or costs ensuing from it has an impact which is borne worldwide;

however, the accruals or benefits emanating from it are reaped by a few. More often than not, those who acquire the maximum profits bear the minimum cost (in this context the cost includes both the pecuniary and the non-monetized aspects of commercial activity). This represents a negative externality the quantum and proportion of which is unbelievably massive; the far-reaching ramifications of this threaten the sustainability of the present patterns of globalization.

## Economic history: lessons in restrospect

It would be extremely convenient to place the blame for failure on a single variable or instrument. Two decades ago it was import substitution and the underpinnings of centralized planning that were cited as the fundamental reasons for the inefficient, resource misallocations and slackened pace of growth that pervaded most of the developing countries. Currently, we are witnessing an intensifying rhetoric against globalization and it is interesting to note that it has taken considerable time to articulate concerns and problems that were obvious even at the time the neo-liberal strategies were fervently propagated.

Whether the strategies consisted of import substitution or neo-liberal policies the non-fulfilment of vital developmental objectives was rooted not so much in their intrinsic principles as in the manner in which these were designed and implemented. Evidently, the adoption of policies structured to suit the ideology, interests and the investment strategies of a handful of institutions and corporations has culminated in the present stand-off between growth and development.

This fundamental fact can be demonstrated by considering the past. In this context, if we view recent economic history spanning a 50-year period, beginning in 1950, by which time most countries had obtained independence, we can extract from it some fundamental lessons that can guide analysis and decision-making. These are as follows.

(i) In the context of economic strategy, this has been a phase of experimentation. From having systems that were based on the closed-economy, highly protectionist and centrally planned models many countries moved towards the adoption of economic liberalism. Yet from a global perspective we still have to surmount the same ills. Interestingly, both these contrasting strategies have had their share of success and failure. It should be noted that, besides the Soviet Union and countries of Eastern Europe that had opted for the socialist-communist model of governance in its entirety, a number of developing countries such as India and Sri Lanka did not go in for the long haul and adopted some (but not all) of the fundamental tenets of socialist governance.

View the instance of Russia and China. At a deeper level, for instance, the collapse of the socialist-communist model in Russia was not so much the result of an ideological failure as it was of the inadequate fulfilment of vital objectives. More than the principles of socialism, this was rooted in the process of implementation wherein politics took precedence over economics. Over a decade after the transition to the market economy the political-institutional nexus has not weakened and a consistent increase in growth rates continues to elude the nation. So was it a failure, or communism, or was it liberalism gone wrong, or was it some other aspect that was not accounted for?

At the other end of the spectrum we have increasing evidence that China's dynamism does not stem merely from the fact that its market reforms took off; in all probability this would not have been as successful if, in the prior period, China had not made remarkable strides in poverty reduction and the consequent improvements in socio-economic indicators (life-expectancy, literacy etc.). The crucial point that emanates from this is that ideology itself is no longer sacrosanct. This has been perhaps one of the hardest-hitting lessons of the previous century – that it is ultimately the delivery of objectives that clinches the fate of strategies, policies and, of course, ideologies. Thus, to flaw the strategy and not the implementation is itself seriously flawed. How successful or unsuccessful central planning and import substitution may have been or how positive or negative the impact of liberalization may have been if these were structured differently or implemented in a manner that was not partisan is anybody's guess at this point in time.

(ii) If we revert to the instance of Russia's tumultuous economic experience we find that it reveals some vital points:

(a)  Unfortunately, in Russia the shift from communism to market economy has coincided with its deceleration from a developed country prior to 1989 to a developing one. This was country that had natural resources, infrastructure and technical expertise. Despite this, standards of living have plummeted quite sharply; consequently a nation that had minimal levels of acute poverty prior to 1989 had about 20 per cent of its population living below US$4 a day during the economic transition. An environment of uncertainty, financial instability and institutional decadence is the backdrop of present-day Russia.

(b)  It would be easy to chronicle Russia's experience as an instance where privatization or liberalization failed; however, this would at best be a half-truth. In the absence of institutional reform, privatization provided the scope for asset-stripping and accentuated rent-seeking activity. Had privatization been preceded by institutional measures that curbed or deterred local and state governments from abusing their wider discretionary authority, the consequences of liberalization would have been different. Moreover, the response to the crises that have occurred Russia has not included adequate institutional reform.

(c)  I would say that the main theme of Russia's experience has been that economic transition is a multidimensional process that should have brought in its wake commensurate institutional and political change. Unfortunately, this did not happen and Russia is yet to witness institutional glasnost. Regardless of ideology or a change in it, in the absence of systemic reform and stability power blocs and oligarchs will thrive and the scope of controlling interest to manipulate will be determined by the magnitude of resource misallocations and distortions within a system.

(iii) Theory may have pitted protectionism and liberalism as the two opposing ends of trade policy. However, the fact that both these features can coexist is one of the fundamental causes of the discrepancy between the anticipated gains from liberalization and its actual consequences. East Asia and South-East Asia are perhaps the most successful exemplifiers of export-led growth and this serves as a stolid reminder that the composition of a nation's trade flows and how lucrative this is depends largely on the effectiveness and nature of government intervention.

We have to understand, therefore, that the meaning of liberalization does not just concern the untempered and unconditional working of market forces, it concerns the relative freedom of the market to determine decision-making. As a matter of fact, there would not have been any talk of any East Asian economic miracle if the Washington Consensus had been blindly adhered to by East Asia.

(iv) The pace of liberalization has been a subject of contentious discussion; however, empirical evidence drawn from the experiences of Latin America, Russia, East Asia and, more recently, China and India provides enough endorsement of the fact that it is the speed of reform (or the lack of it) that should determine the expeditiousness of liberalization. In other words, musings about the gradualist approach vis-à-vis the dramatically expedient 'shock therapy' variant of liberalization should not be isolated from the broader context of reform. In the absence of reform, liberalist policies accentuate distortions within the system. The East Asian crisis is etched in recent economic history as a stark reminder of this fact; regardless of weakness in fundamentals that these countries may have had, a crisis of the nature and extent that occurred would certainly not have taken place if the IMF prescription of speedy liberalism had not been pursued.

(v) There are a number reasons to which the Asian crisis is attributable and these have been cited by the extensive analysis and research that it elicited. However, it would be useful to consider some of the vital aspects pertinent to it:

(a) When the Asian Crisis began the weaknesses that existed in the banking and financial sectors of most South-East Asian nations (such as the laxity of the regulatory regime) came to the fore. In this context, one frailty that has frequently been cited is crony capitalism. Admittedly, institutional weaknesses have a role in causing or aggravating a crisis and, as such, the banker and politician nexus that prevailed in

South-East Asia also had a negative fall-out in some countries, such as Indonesia. However, we cannot detract from the fact that this was a feature that existed much before capital-account liberalization had been aggressively advocated. The removal of restrictions on capital flows was done despite cognizance that this feature existed.

This evokes an imminent question: in the absence of the faulty-sequenced, ill-timed capital-account liberalization, would the weaknesses of the banking and financial sectors, however entrenched these may have been in some countries of the region, such as Thailand and Indonesia, been sufficient to unleash the volatility and instability that ensued? It is improbable.

(b) One of the resonant lessons of the Asian crisis was that a flawed sequencing of financial liberalization, when accompanied by capital-account liberalization, increases the likelihood of domestic banking and exchange rate crises. This conclusion shouldn't have taken decades to arrive at, given the incidence of recurrent financial and exchange-rate instability that had occurred in Latin America, Russia and Mexico during the 1980s and 1990s. Regardless of the differences in the innate causes and circumstances, a reason common to all the crises was a misjudgment about the timing, sequence and extent of financial liberalization.

(c) For instance, quite unlike Latin America, Russia and Mexico, where financial and economic fundamentals were rather shaky during the 1980s and 1990s East and South-East Asia was a region that had performed impressively for over a decade and had done so while building its infrastructure and improving its socio-economic indicators. Thus, it hardly seemed that a crisis was looming on the region's horizon. Yet, despite some rather contrasting features in both regions, comparisons of crises in the two reveal a basic similarity. Be it the pattern of financial deregulation in Latin American countries or the rather ill-timed full convertibility of the Thai currency, Baht, the propellant in both instances stemmed from the imperatives of the finance and money markets of the United States and some European countries.

(d) Increasing economic growth rates in Latin America during the 1950s and 1960s made it an attractive financial proposition for international lenders. The surpluses of oil importers and the expanding eurodollar market led to a surge in liquidity and this fuelled the demand for additional avenues and outlets into which it could be ploughed. The inflows of liquidity were far in excess of the absorptive capacity of many Latin American countries and the consequence was inflationary pressures that snowballed out of control after the mid-1970s.

Matters became worse after the rapid change in US monetary policy to control its own levels of inflation led to the beginning of a massive outflow of liquidity and, during the ensuing debt crisis, the net resource transfers from the region were unprecedented. East Asia, which had been among the most buoyant economies for about two decades, did not have either a liquidity or a resource constraint. Once again, it was the need for higher returns that led to the build-up of excessive liquidity in East and South-East Asia and not the external financing requirements of the nations concerned.

(vi) Joseph Stiglitz remarks in his book, *Globalization and its Discontents*, 'Intellectual consistency has never been the hallmark of the IMF' (2002, p. 107). Thus, it follows that policies advocated by the IMF, and even the World Bank, were not rooted firmly in the underpinnings of economic logic. There are several instances of these intellectual inconsistencies and vacillations. For instance, the assumption that the benefits of liberalization will trickle down is itself absurd because to presume the existence of an autonomous transmission mechanism that would ensure the percolation of 'these advantages' is unrealistic. Furthermore, to assume that the trickle will suffice and make a significant difference to society can at best be described as a ridiculous mistake.

An illustrative instance of the IMF's blatant misjudgment was its 'remedial' prescription of excessively contractionary, fiscal and monetary policies to counter the financial instability that occurred during the Asian crisis. These measures served to aggravate the downturn even further. The basis for the imposition of these policies was its stilted presumption that the curative for the crisis should be similar to the one implemented to counter the crisis that occurred in Latin America during the 1980s. Profligate governments, overspent finances and excessive debt characterized most Latin American countries during the 1980s and undeniably this stands in striking contrast to the relatively sound fiscal and monetary management of the South-East Asia region. Notably, Malaysia stood apart and did not pursue these policies and, contrary to the anticipation of the IMF and its 'advocacy', the results of doing this were a speedier recovery and a shallower downturn.

The fervent recomendations of the IMF's liberalization prescription shows itself even more overtly as a set of measures that was rooted in the institution's inconsistent interpretation about the need to adopt measures that would expedite the pace of liberalization. Despite the fact that some of these policies were obviously inappropriate, particularly in the South-East Asian context, its pursuit by some of the nations in the region reflected an institutional weakness that I would say took the heaviest toll.

(vii) Unbundling a system that doesn't work effectively and transplanting it with a perceptibly contrasting strategy will not provide it with a corrective. Thus, abandoning globalization will not resolve the present problems because, firstly, its potentialities to mitigate underdevelopment were hindered and obstructed; and, second, claims about doing away with something that has never existed in totality (except as a half-baked and diluted variant of what it was supposed to be) seems inappropriate.

In no uncertain terms, among the most important insights that empirical evidence gives us is that it is not reversal of strategy alone but a removal of all those impediments that perpetuate its structural deficiencies and deter its effective implementation that will pave the way to a positive and significant impact. In the context of globalization this would involve strengthening its link with economic integration and development.

## Globalization and economic integration: the dichotomy

Globalization is an instrumentality of economic integration. However, a distinct differentiation needs to be made between facilitating processes and the resultant outcomes; and although the multiplicity of linkages and interconnectedness among countries set the ball rolling towards a higher degree of global integration it remains one facet of a multifaceted objective. Economic integration continues to remain an unfinished task. Plausibly, this fact is highlighted when one consider that economic integration consists, basically, of five instruments. These are: i) international trade and monetary regimes; ii) international capital flows; iii) international ecological considerations; iv) asset distribution and human development; and v) gender justice.

The last three instruments have been the subject of many a discussion, but have not been prioritized by policy practice. It is this lacuna that is a manifestation of a pattern of globalization that hardly focused on developmental concerns and assigned an overwhelming emphasis to the first two constituents.

In the enumeration that follows the some of the fundamental reasons underlying the stark dichotomy between globalization and economic integration will be elucidated. It is evident that global policy and practice prioritized trade and financial liberalization and the other three have either been or are at best residual goals.

## Financial and trade liberalization: an overview of its impact

A few months before the Asian crisis in 1997 India was under considerable pressure from certain developed countries to opt for a course of expeditious capital-account liberalization. At the time, not undertaking this measure symbolized to its proponents a lack of dynamism. Perceptions changed dramatically with the onset of the Asian economic crisis in mid-1997. Undoubtedly this tempered the relentless advocacy of capital-account liberalization

The possibility of having combinations of limited capital mobility and a degree of financial liberalization has been explored only in the recent past. Thus, recent trends, coupled with the oversights of the past, underscore that financial integration entails much more than easing the curbs or restrictions on capital flows and empirical literature questions the theoretical under-pinnings on the basis of which unhindered capital flows were advocated and sheds light on certain aspects that were overlooked earlier. These are as follows.

(i) The dangers wrought in accelerating the pace of capital-account liber-alization in the absence of mature and broad-based financial markets, as is the case with most developing countries. Even prior to the Asian economic crisis empirical evidence did not uphold or even point to a general causality between financial liberalization and economic growth. There were instances where financial liberalization has been aided and been a stimulus to the growth process and there are those where it hasn't. As a matter of fact, we are still without conclusive evidence to infer a significant and positive relationship between the two variables.

(ii) Financial capital is not a homogeneous entity and it includes in its purview various kinds of capital flows, such as foreign direct investment, portfolio equity flows, portfolio bond flows, long-term bank credit, short-term bank credit and official flows. As such, each type of inflow will have an impact on growth that may differ from the other. There have been studies that have analyzed the effects that different types of capital flows have on domestic investment. Bosworth and Collins undertook one such study in 1999 and data used was for the period 1979–95. The central finding was that bank lending and FDI are positively associated with increases in domestic investment. Although the association between portfolio capital inflows and domestic investment is positive it is not statistically significant. In 2001 the World Bank report on global development finance endorsed this inference after one of its studies found that the association between FDI or other long-term inflows or bank lending is stronger than short-term debt and domestic investment.

(iii) Financially-integrated economies with higher growth rates have been repeatedly misinterpreted as examples of financial liberalization that have promoted or aided the process of economic growth. A strong and robust correlation does not exist between financial integration and growth. Either research findings pertinent to this subject do not find a distinct correlation between financial integration and economic growth or, even in instances where empirical findings indicate a link, it is difficult to arrive at a definite inference. The reason for this is the positive effect that financial liberalization has had on growth in certain instances and the rather negative outcomes it has had in certain others.

(iv) The positive effects of financial integration require the support of other features. According to some studies on financial liberalization and integration there are certain threshold effects, such as a certain minimum level of human capital formation, that influence the outcome that a higher degree of financial integration has on growth. For instance, it is unlikely that the imposition of financial liberalization will yield discernible benefits if the country or region has a rudimentary industrial sector, which lacks specialization and is characterized by the predominance of low skill-intensive activity, such as the production of primary goods. Gains aside, the situation could be one that exacerbates economic vulnerability and volatility if the country concerned is in the initial stages of development. Furthermore, if the composition of external debt is such that it constitutes a high proportion of short-term liabilities it could render a country even more susceptible to financial crisis. As we have seen in the case of Latin American countries and Mexico, the recurrent crises and the ensuing economic contraction that happens as a result interrupt the process of financial integration. Over the last ten years, recurrent financial crises in Latin America, Russia and Mexico have resulted in a flip-flop of the views and contentions expressed about the timing and sequencing and degree of capital account liberalization that should be adopted.

(v) Generalizations about causality between financial integration and economic growth do not always hold up. It is likely that financial integration itself could be the result of higher economic growth rates; thus, even if findings indicate a robust correlation between the two it does not always mean that financial integration provides the impetus to growth, the reverse may also hold true.

(vi) China and India have achieved higher growth rates despite having a limited degree of financial liberalization. Easing the curbs on capital mobility has resulted in increasing levels of efficiency and specialization in the ambit of the banking and financial services sector in India. This is an interesting feature because it exemplifies much more than just the positive impact of opening up capital markets. It also demonstrates that successful financial liberalization is possible without accelerating the pace at which all restrictions on capital flows are removed. It is not merely the extent/quantum but the timing and form of financial liberalization that determine its success or failure.

Mauritius and Botswana are other instances of countries that had rising economic growth rates over the last decade or so but are not characterized by a high degree of financial liberalization.

Stanley Fischer says:

My own view is that in the course of their economic development all countries will want to liberalize the capital account and fully integrate with global capital markets. This is based on the fact that all the advanced economies have very open capital accounts. And it is based on what I believe to be the correct reading of the existing economic evidence: which is that the economic benefits of a well sequenced orderly opening of the capital account on balance outweigh the costs. However countries should approach capital account liberalization with great care. We have been reminded in recent years that overly rapid liberalization of the capital account – especially at the short end – holds risks for any country and enormous risks when macroeconomic stability, the domestic financial system and domestic financial regulation are not yet strong enough. In addition countries need good data to be able to monitor inflows and outflows. All of which is to say that countries need to calibrate their access to international capital to the capacity of their domestic economies systems safely to absorb it ('Further Liberalization of Globalization of Financial Services', Institute for International Economics, Washington, DC, 5 June 2005).

China and India demonstrated the rather effective impact of what may be termed as a middle-ground stance insofar as capital account liberalization is concerned. Both countries initiated a certain degree of liberalization in the domestic financial sector, to a greater extent in India. At the same time, India has retained its controls on capital flows. Over the last decade or so capital controls have been eased in India and, to a lesser extent, in China but both continue to have restrictions on capital flows.

If the rather fervent advocacy of financial liberalization had included in its agenda a concerted effort to increase the access of the poor to the benefits of freer money and capital markets it is very likely that there would have been a higher degree of financial integration. However, there seems to have been a pronounced propensity to propagate a particular variant of financial and trade liberalization. Typically, until not too long ago this ignored the fact that the generic presumption about the causality or correlation that financial liberalization has with growth was seriously flawed.

Access to the financial system by those in the unorganized and unprivileged sector is an integral constituent of the process of financial integration. A vital function of the facilities provided by the finance and banking sphere is to enable or aid those in the lower income groups to upgrade their skills and earn their livelihoods. The provision of instruments that would bridge the credit requirements of all those who cannot afford to borrow from conventional sources of funding is an imperative. For instance, micro-credit specifically serves this purpose; however, although the gains from micro-finance schemes have been impressive, much more needs to be done in the context of utilizing it for those who have little or no recourse to any source of finance.

The considerable range of possibilities for marking out a course for financial integration that is more appropriate for developing and underdeveloped countries has hardly been explored. Initiatives in this direction have been too little and too slow, despite the irrefutable evidence that micro-credit is an extremely vital input that can empower millions of micro-entrepreneurs to carve out for themselves a livelihood option. However positive or remarkable the impact of financial liberalization may be, if the percolation of its gains does not extend beyond the enclave of the relatively privileged it leaves the objective of having an integrated financial system an unattained one.

## Trade liberalization: is it about free or fettered trade?

It has taken about two decades and extensive empirical evidence to dispel the myth of the 'magic wand' approach underlying trade liberalization. An unfettered movement of goods and services between nations may have contributed towards higher degree of economic integration and with it poverty reduction; however, the basis underlying contemporary trade liberalization stands in stark contrast to the archetypal descriptions of free trade. As the reality unravels itself we find that this measure has left in its trail a host of benefits for a few countries, an insignificant impact on many and adverse consequences for some others.

The impact of trade on growth could have been a profound one; empirical evidence has revealed that in most instances this has not been the case. Has the role of trade been overestimated or misjudged? Answering in the in the affirmative is convenient; however, it still does not take us to heart of the matter. It is the lopsided manner in which globalization has been made to work and the overriding pursuit of the agendas of special interest groups that have taken the wind out of the sails of what could have been a rather powerful instrument of growth and development.

Empirical evidence about the impact of trade liberalization on growth and poverty reduction is vast. However in conjunction with a diverse range of other research findings, this does not give us a basis to generalize that trade liberalization will always lead to higher economic growth. The link between trade and growth and the role that this has in the improvement of socio-economic indicators has been the subject of numerous studies. Although the inferences that have emanated are varied, a commonality is the concurrence by research about the discernible influence that other macroeconomic policy variables exert, not just on growth but also on the course and consequences of trade liberalization.

According to a working paper (Berg and Kreuger, 2003) by the IMF on trade and poverty growth:

> Openness is not a magic bullet, trade policy is only one of the determinants of growth. Thus, it should not come as a surprise that even though trade is an important determinant of growth and there has been substantial trade liberalization in the last twenty years, growth in the 1980s and 1990s has been disappointing, resulting in a correspondingly modest (if unprecedented) decline in poverty.

Dani Rodrik, who has undertaken some important research in the ambit of trade reform, elucidates that the efforts assigned to the implementation of trade reform may be better spent on other sorts of reform, primarily institutional. However 'open' a country's trading regime, the impact of it on growth and development rests on the preconditions that exist, the expediency and effectiveness of other reform measures and the presence or absence of other complementary features. Perhaps this explains a recurrent problem encountered in measuring the precise impact of trade on growth because it becomes difficult and, in some instances, almost impossible to disassociate the effect of trade from that exerted by the other determinants of growth.

As in the case of financial integration so also it is not uncommon to find that interpretations of trade liberalization are whittled down to mean reductions in tariffs. This misdirects final conclusions about what needs to be done to have an open trading regime. For instance, dismantling the distortive effects of import substituting, inward-oriented regimes that existed through the 1970s and 1980s requires much more than the reduction in tariff barriers. It should be noted that even in countries where trade has provided an impetus to growth rates it does not make it an instrument of economic integration unless it complements or aids efforts directed towards poverty reduction. If the benefits of trade liberalization are enclaved or the inequalities of incomes worsen as a result of the measures it entails the process of integration may even be hindered.

In the instance of most developing countries trade has not been a facilitator of either poverty reduction or economic integration. These observations are underscored even further in studies that view the impact of trade on those in the lowest income groups. Furthermore, there are hardly any instances where income distribution improves as a result of trade liberalization; in most cases either it worsens or it remains unchanged.

In this context Sachs-Warner's findings reveal that openness is negatively correlated with growth among the poorest 40 per cent but strongly and positively correlated with growth among the relatively higher income groups. This observation has been corroborated in a number of countries where trade liberalization has skewed inequalities of income and assets.

Inevitably, the predominant inference that comes forth from the evidence about the link between trade and poverty is that there is no significant link between 'openness' and the income of the poor. Dani Rodrik, in a working paper on trade and development (2001), stated:

> In this alternative view a development friendly international trading system is one that does much more than enchance poor countries access to markets in the advanced industrial countries ... It is one that enables poor countries to experiment with institutional arrangements and leaves room for them to devise their own possible divergent solutions to development bottlenecks. ('The Governance of Trade as if Development Really Mattered')

According to a report on poverty by UNDP (2003), studies, particularly about South Asia and China, indicate that the growth in per capita GDP over 2000–1 and trade as a percentage of GDP had a rather low correlation coefficient. Furthermore, this weakened correlation between per capita GDP increase and trade as a percentage of GDP was also evident throughout the

1990s. As a matter of fact, studies indicate that changes in trade openness over the 1990s and the growth in per capita GDP have a high negative correlation coefficient, implying that trade openness has been associated with a lower increase in per capita incomes.

Against a backdrop where trade is controlled largely by the WTO, international financial institutions and the G7 (the former two subserve the interests of the latter), it was obvious that the policies that would underpin trade policy would not be balanced and advantageous to less developed countries. Constrained by debt and dependency on the export of primary products, many LDCs can barely afford to have production patterns that are determined by their comparative advantage. The terms of trade are weighted against the major exports of the developing countries. Although poorer countries are supposed to adhere perforce to the principles of 'open markets', their market access is unduly restricted by the tariff and non-tariff barriers imposed on their exports to developed countries. Perhaps few instances demonstrate the double standards that are encountered by the poorer countries as lucidly as the trade barriers that the US imposes on imports of goods that are made in developing countries and the standpoint of the WTO on the subsidies granted to the producers of agricultural commodities. As a result of the increase in commodity prices and a decline the US dollar, exports from low-income countries have increased, imports by these countries have also risen over the last few years. Be this as it may, more important than the expansion of trade in the developing world is the preponderance of primary commodities in the export baskets of the less developing world. Although the terms of trade are not exactly favourable as far as agricultural products are concerned, it is certainly made more adverse by a pattern of trade liberalization that lacks reciprocity and is pronouncedly one-sided.

According to the Global Economic Prospects Report (2005), the estimated average overall trade restrictive index (OTRI) for high-income OECD countries is 12 per cent for all trade; however, it stands at a much higher 44 per cent for agricultural trade. Thus, on average, the world has an OTRI of about 35 per cent in agriculture, three times that of 12 per cent in manufacturing. As such, amid the existent market barriers on a wide range of product exports from the less developed countries the impact of trade liberalization was a foreseeable one.

The report also cites that recent US cotton subsidies have ranged from U.S\$1.5 billion to almost U.S\$4 billion annually. Even if there were to be an elimination of only US cotton programmes it would reduce US production by 25–30 per cent and its exports by 40 per cent. The average annual losses for cotton producers from the less developed countries resulting from US and EU support policies are in the range of US\$150–200 million. This is just one indicator that the present dynamics of trade liberalization are weighted against the less developing world with regard to a wide range of its exports.

*The Rich World, Poor World Guide to Global Development* (Centre for Global Development) cites an interesting finding that the United States collects more tariffs on goods from poor countries than from rich countries even though it imported a much higher value of goods from richer countries.

Further the report states that if the richer countries were to scrap their tariffs and other non-tariff barriers currently imposed on the imports from developing countries it would result in a discernible increase in the value of income for developing nations. Interestingly the rise in income would be almost double that of the development assistance received by these nations.

The protests and outcry at the WTO meetings in Seattle and Cancún and, more recently, the impasse that WTO negotiations encountered in Doha during 2004 are not random outbursts of activism, instead these are reactions by those individuals who realize the way in which the WTO blatantly disregards the considerations of most developing nations. One such issue, vital to the interests of developing nations, concerns the subsidies granted to the agricultural sector. At the outset one cannot overlook that, besides the EU, the US allocates large subsidies to its agricultural sector. The US farm bill of 2002 gave US$12 billion in subsidies and 80 per cent of the recipients of this were large producers who had more than 500 acres of land. If developed countries find it necessary to provide subsidy support to their farmers it is obvious that the need of the agriculture sector for subsidies in developing countries is certainly more exigent.

Understandably, the proposition to phase out these subsidies elicited opposition from the developing countries. In many developing countries the richer farmers take up a sizable proportion of subsidy support allocated to agriculture. So far this is a feature that local administrations have not been able to curb. Given this situation, it is very likely that it is the small and subsistence farmer who will eventually bear the brunt of a reduction of subsidy support, however minimal this might appear at the outset.

## Conclusion

Clustered opportunity creation was an inevitability given the incomplete process of economic integration. As we have seen, there could have been a greater degree of integration if a fairer system of trade and financial liberalization had evolved and poverty reduction, instead of being an afterthought, was a consideration at the outset. Interestingly, this could have been achieved without dampening the special-interest agenda.

Be it financial or trade liberalization, the resultant outcomes have not spearheaded the process of economic integration enough to resolve the growth–development trade-off. One of the most unfortunate consequences of this has been that the liberalization of markets and trade has left consumption requirements practically untouched of almost 2 billion people who find themselves enmeshed in abject poverty globally. This has been a grievous mistake, to say the least; however, perpetrating the vicious circle of low consumption and incomes is a disastrous folly that the global community cannot afford to make, not any more. The discussion about economic integration continues in the following chapter. The attempt therein will be to demonstrate the manner in which vested interests led commerce and politics to scuttle (generally speaking) the developmental dimension of progress; it is the perpetuation of these interests that entails integrating the task of money-making with socio-economic considerations.

East Asia is one of the most successful instances of trade liberalization, particularly because the policies that these countries initiated at the outset of liberalization enabled not just a phenomenal expansion of trade but also had a rather positive impact on developmental outcomes: trade liberalization in East Asia was a comprehensive course of action that involved much more than reducing tariff barriers and opening the floodgates to imports. The next chapter will view some of the important aspects of the economic success of East Asia.

## Appendix

Subsequent to protracted negotiations, the developed countries who also allocate significant subsidy support to their farmers agreed that, in view of the pivotal importance of the agricultural sector in a number of the poorer nations, these should be given certain concessions. The methodology specified for calculating the reduction in subsidies is complicated and, even if developing countries are provided with concessions and a longer time frame for the cutbacks, it does not offset the losses that would be incurred by those farmers who depend on this subsidy support.

According to the Agriculture Agreement finalized at the meeting of WTO in Doha (2004), the Doha Ministerial Declaration calls for 'substantial reductions in trade-distorting domestic support'. One of the most blatant oversights of the agricultural agreement is that subsidies are just one of many trade-distorting measures. What about the slew of polices that distort patterns of trade in a manner that is detrimental to the interests of the less developed nations? It would be interesting to note that dismantling these has not been a consideration of any import on the WTO agenda.

Another rather tricky issue pertains to the tariffication of agricultural products. (This is in accordance to the commitments made during the Uruguay Round of the WTO meetings, wherein the imposition of tariffs was to replace quantitative restrictions in farm trade.) The Doha Ministerial Declaration states, 'substantial improvements in market access' are needed. Members also agreed that special and differential treatment for developing members would be an integral part of all elements in the negotiations. Despite a series of informal meetings in the months of April and May, the tiered formula was not finalized. The reason quite observably was a lack of consensus among the small forum of powerful nations. Developing nations would not have been represented if Brazil and India were not included in the meetings, which constituted EU countries, the US and Australia.

There are some other issues pertinent to the Agriculture Agreement that will be discussed in Box 16A.1.

## Box 16A.1   Excerpts from the WTO Ministerial Declaration (2004)

1. The starting point for the current phase of the agriculture negotiations has been the mandate set out in Paragraph 13 of the Doha Ministerial Declaration. This in turn built on the long-term objective of the Agreement on Agriculture to establish a fair and market-oriented trading system through a programme of fundamental reform. The elements below offer the additional precision required at this stage of the negotiations and thus the basis for the negotiations of full modalities in the next phase. The level of ambition set by the Doha mandate will continue to be the basis for the negotiations on agriculture.

2. The final balance will be found only at the conclusion of these subsequent negotiations and within the Single Undertaking. To achieve this balance, the modalities to be developed will need to incorporate operationally effective and meaningful provisions for special and differential treatment for developing country Members. Agriculture is of critical importance to the economic development of developing country Members and they must be able to pursue agricultural policies that are supportive of their development goals, poverty reduction strategies, food security and livelihood concerns. Non-trade concerns, as referred to in Paragraph 13 of the Doha Declaration, will be taken into account.

3. The reforms in all three pillars form an interconnected whole and must be approached in a balanced and equitable manner.

The Doha Ministerial Declaration calls for 'substantial reductions in trade-distorting domestic support'. With a view to achieving these substantial reductions, the negotiations in this pillar will ensure the following:

- Special and differential treatment remains an integral component of domestic support. Modalities to be developed will include longer implementation periods and lower reduction coefficients for all types of trade-distorting domestic support and continued access to the provisions under Article 6.2.

There will be a strong element of harmonization in the reductions made by developed Members. Specifically, higher levels of permitted trade-distorting domestic support will be subject to deeper cuts.

7. The overall base level of all trade-distorting domestic support, as measured by the Final Bound Total AMS plus permitted de minimis

level and the level agreed in paragraph 8 below for Blue Box payments, will be reduced according to a tiered formula. Under this formula, Members having higher levels of trade-distorting domestic support will make greater overall reductions in order to achieve a harmonizing result. As the first instalment of the overall cut, in the first year and throughout the implementation period, the sum of all trade-distorting support will not exceed 80 per cent of the sum of Final Bound Total AMS plus permitted de minimis plus the Blue Box at the level determined in paragraph 15.

8. The following parameters will guide the further negotiation of this tiered formula:

- This commitment will apply as a minimum overall commitment. It will not be applied as a ceiling on reductions of overall trade-distorting domestic support, should the separate and complementary formulae to be developed for Total AMS, de minimis and Blue Box payments imply, when taken together, a deeper cut in overall trade-distorting domestic support for an individual Member.
- The base for measuring the Blue Box component will be the higher of existing Blue Box payments during a recent representative period to be agreed and the cap established in paragraph 15 below.

## Final Bound Total AMS: a tiered formula

9. To achieve reductions with a harmonizing effect:

- Final Bound Total AMS will be reduced substantially, using a tiered approach.
- Members having higher Total AMS will make greater reductions.
- To prevent circumvention of the objective of the Agreement through transfers of unchanged domestic support between different support categories, product-specific AMSs will be capped at their respective average levels according to a methodology to be agreed.
- Substantial reductions in Final Bound Total AMS will result in reductions of some product-specific support.

10. Members may make greater than formula reductions in order to achieve the required level of cut in overall trade-distorting domestic support.

Developing country Members will benefit from longer implementation periods for the phasing out of all forms of export subsidies.

---

## Box 16A.1   (Continued)

### De minimis

11. Reductions in de minimis will be negotiated taking into account the principle of special and differential treatment. Developing countries that allocate almost all de minimis support for subsistence and resource-poor farmers will be exempt . . .

Developing countries will continue to benefit from special and differential treatment under the provisions of Article 9.4 of the Agreement on Agriculture for a reasonable period, to be negotiated, after the phasing out of all forms of export subsidies and implementation of all disciplines identified above are completed.

### The single approach: a tiered formula

To ensure that a single approach for developed and developing country Members meets all the objectives of the Doha mandate, tariff reductions will be made through a tiered formula that takes into account their different tariff structures.

To ensure that such a formula will lead to substantial trade expansion, the following principles will guide its further negotiation:

Tariff reductions will be made from bound rates. Substantial overall tariff reductions will be achieved as a final result from negotiations.

Each Member (other than LDCs) will make a contribution.

Operationally effective special and differential provisions for developing country Members will be an integral part of all elements.

---

### Some comments about the Agiculture agreement

The basis on which concessions will be given to developing countries lacks clarity and is rather complicated. One of the main loopholes wrought in this is that it would involve a procedure of cautious monitoring about whether the recipients or end users of the subsidies can actually be categorized as poor or subsistence farmers. It is difficult to visualize a situation wherein developed countries will reduce subsidies to their farmers without compensating them with what maybe conveniently termed as non-subsidy support. Would this be viewed as a trade-distorting measure by the rule-makers of the WTO?

# 17
## Revisiting the East Asian Miracle

Goh Keng Swee was one of Singapore's leading economists, who served in the Ministries of Finance and Defence between 1959 and 1971. Addressing the opening of the International Labour Seminar, held in Singapore in 1965, he said:

> I will be the last, being by training an economist myself, to deny the importance of economic factors but the process of development and modernization does not begin and end with economic factors alone. It is necessary that we pay regard to them, but it is not sufficient merely to do so.

Four decades ago not many would have anticipated that the countries of Japan, South Korea, Taiwan, Hong Kong and Singapore would achieve a phenomenal trajectory of economic progress, which some would describe as a miracle. These countries were characterized by a trend of sustained rapid economic growth, industrialization and structural transformation and within a relatively short span of time the region was catapulted into the league of the fastest-growing nations. The dramatic ascendancy of East Asia and South-East Asia has been a subject that has been widely discussed, debated, lauded by many and criticized by some; regardless it is a milestone in the annals of socio-economic development.

Through the 1970s and 1980s, East Asia was the most buoyant region globally. Japan, Korea, Hong Kong, Taiwan and Singapore had an impressive growth performance and with it these nations scored rapid gains on the frontier of development. Perhaps even more remarkable than the performance per se was that it occurred at a time when the world was confronted with the problems of economic slowdown, unemployment and inflation. The 1980s in particular have been described by many as the era of stagflation. These countries, referred to as HPAE (High Performing Asian Economies) by the World Bank (in a study in 1993), were characterized by high rates of physical and human capital formation, infrastructure provision and poverty reduction.

Broadly speaking, there are three basic reasons that are commonly used to undermine the contention that the East Asian experience has significant relevance to contemporary developing countries. First, it is argued that present circumstances differ from those that existed during the period that the countries transformed themselves into HPAEs; for instance, the increased capital mobility in current times would limit the efficacy of government policy as businesses have the option of relocation and outsourcing. Second, there are trade practices that these nations could engage in that contemporary developing nations would find difficult or even impossible undertake, given the role that the WTO has. Thirdly, the Asian crisis is invariably used as a pointer to regate the positive features of the path pursued by East Asia.

Notably time and circumstances have changed but prerequisites of development have not. The structure of underdevelopment and the constraints that come with it are not very dissimilar from those that existed three decades ago. The task of increasing economic growth rates while retaining macroeconomic stability is an imminent challenge confronting most developing nations.

On the subject of the Asian crisis, it must be noted that unhindered financial liberalism was not a policy constituent of East Asia in the initial stages. As a matter of fact, through the 1970s and the 1980s, the HPAEs pursued a policy of selective or managed liberalization, wherein creating a conducive environment for domestic private investment and foreign investors did not necessarily mean a relinquishment of capital controls or a dilution of government regulation and control. The Asian crisis was partly the outcome of an accelerated pace of financial liberalization, particularly in South-East Asia, and citing it as an example depicts the downside of adhering to a particular prescription of neo-classical market economics. Recurrent crises in Latin American countries (such as Argentina), Mexico and Russia demonstrate the inextricable link between macroeconomic stability and economic progress and it is this vital aspect that was one of the cornerstones of the East Asian model of development.

This sets the stage for exploring those elements of the East Asian model of development that apply to contemporary developing nations.

The classic lessons that can be drawn from the East Asian miracle have been enumerated exhaustively by substantive research on the subject. (One point of clarification that needs to be made is the distinction between replication and application. As mentioned earlier, these countries had discernible differences in the specifics of their policies and this precludes, at the outset, the feasibility of replicating the economic experience of one country in another. However, as this chapter will elucidate, there are aspects of East Asia's economic experience that continue to be relevant or applicable in the context of the contemporary developing world.) According to a study by the World Bank about East Asia's progress (2001), the four 'keys' of the East Asian miracle are:

1. Adherence to a sound macroeconomic policy.
2. The importance of having an efficient bureaucracy, which can formulate and execute policies that are needed for development over the longer term.
3. Pursuing activist government policies to industrialize and export an increasing proportion of industrial output.
4. The adoption of a flexible pragmatic policy approach, which incorporates therein an error correction mechanism.

East Asia demonstrated that the achievement of these goals is critical for sustaining growth and development; however, the merit of analyzing the empirics of the region's economic experience lies in the path it pursued and the systems that it evolved to ensure that critical preconditions for economic growth were attained. At a time when ideological orientation clinched the policies and strategies that countries pursued, the East Asian miracle stood out as an instance that did not allow economic progress to be shackled either by the demarcations of ideology or the scarcity of natural resources. Instead, it added a new dimension of thinking to the meaning of resource generation by illustrating that countries need not be constricted by the endowments that they lacked because it is the initiatives to harness resources that ultimately steer the course of economic progress.

## Analysis

The East Asian model of development does not embody a single homogeneous strategy pursued by countries in the region, rather it is a collective term that encapsulates models of growth and development, each of which were characterized by certain unique features and attributes. Having said this there were fundamental similarities in the economic and political underpinnings of the strategies and policies that these countries pursued. A common strand running through the experience of the HPAEs was that all these managed to evolve a dynamic combination of government intervention, entrepreneurship and development.

The economic experience of the HPAEs lucidly demonstrated that it was possible for interventionist policies and a vibrant market economy to coexist as complements to each other and in a manner that can be highly productive. It cannot be overlooked that this possibility of having a judicious blend between the market and the state was cited against a backdrop of ideological polarization wherein countries were divided on either side of the 'ism'. Interestingly, India's attempts at achieving this blend of sorts by having a mixed economy is another instance of such a combination. However, the gains from having this approach in terms of economic growth became more evident during the post-liberalization phase.

The World Bank study about the East Asian miracle (EAM) (1993) used the term 'embedded autonomy' to describe the nexus between business and government. Vested interests and concomitantly special-interest agendas are ubiquitous; however, the East Asian and, to a lesser extent, the South-East Asian experience is illustrative of the manner in which this feature was utilized to increase growth rates.

There is hardly anything surprising about the vast sums of money and powerful positions that are accumulated and acquired by certain individuals and industries in the course of economic growth; what is undoubtedly worth looking at is that the combination of effective governance and institutional management was able to direct powerful and deeply embedded vested interest groups to become instrumental, in harnessing increasing levels of economic progress for a long period of time. In discussions about the EAM, reams have been written about the important role that cultural attributes have had in enabling this; however, it is plausible that a section of the embedded interest groups in East Asia would have indulged in rent-seeking and capital repatriation and not much else had the business environment been a different one. Thus, an exploration of this aspect could provide useful insights into the manner in which policies play a pivotal role in tapping strongly entrenched special interests groups to serve larger national economic objectives.

Export-led growth is an integral aspect of the East Asian model; more often than not it is singled out as a major cause underlying high growth rates in the region. Notably, increasing exports was a constituent of a larger trade policy package; perhaps even more pertinent than this are the underlying mechanisms that made trade the conduit of growth in the region. This is a vital issue for developing countries, given the emphasis on trade liberalization coupled with the rather disappointing impact that it has had in a number of countries. Tables 17.1 indicate the expansion of trade.

*Table 17.1*   Exports to the world from East Asia (US$ billions)

| Year | First-tier NIEs | ASEAN 4 | Total |
| --- | --- | --- | --- |
| 1985 | 82.7 | 10.2 | 102.2 |
| 1994 | 483.8 | 102.5 | 483.8 |

Please note first-tier NIEs or newly industrialized countries are South Korea, Singapore, Taiwan and Hong Kong. The ASEAN 4 or Association of South East Asian nations are Malaysia, Indonesia, Thailand and The Philippines.
*Source:* UNCTAD Trade and Development Report, 1996.

Trade policies pursued by the HPAEs have elicited criticism on the premise that government intervention, whether it manifested in the form of subsidies or any other measures, was protectionist or distortionary. However, this argument is not convincing enough to distract us from the reality that trade liberalization is not merely the outcome of fair competition or market forces; it also requires appropriate policies. As a matter of fact, the HPAEs were among the first developing nations at the time to exemplify that outward orientation involved a wide gamut of measures, of which easing trade barriers may be a single one. As such, import-substituting industrialization and export promotion were the two pillars on which their trade strategy was based and both these aspects were interlinked.

Marking out an industrial policy, which would define the priorities and specify the measures therein, such as subsidies and incentives that would be utilized to achieve stated objectives, was an integral constituent of economic strategy in these countries. The sectors identified as important may have differed but in all East Asian nations a distinct similarity was a combination of protection and policy-determined competition that each of these evolved. This was a blend that was not without its problems; however, it spearheaded the region's rapid scaling up on the technological learning curve and this notably was one of the core objectives of East Asia's outward orientation strategy. Import-substituting industrialization in East Asia was encouraged by a certain degree of protectionism and, although this is a feature that has been the butt of criticism, it did not result in a breeding ground of inefficiency and sloth in the industrial sectors of the HPAEs.

There have been criticisms about the pursuance of interventionist measures and the role that industrial policy has had in East Asia and subsequently South-East Asia. In essence, studies have cited the distortions that arose did so as a result of implementation of these measures. Perfect policies exist conceptually; however, in reality it is the effectiveness with which policy constituents are implemented that determine the net impact of policy. If one were to place economic history in perspective it comes to light that the government intervention has had a role even in the avowedly liberal market economy of the United States. For instance, the US telecommunications industry was promoted by the government by establishing the first telegraph line between Baltimore and Washington in 1842. In recent times, both the role of public policy in propelling the widespread diffusion of internet usage in the US and its influence and interventions in the country's capital market endorse the fact that the impact public policy has on market forces is a fact that cannot be overlooked or dispensed with.

Generally speaking, to quantify the precise contribution of policy inputs is an extremely difficult task; however, it is undeniable that the contribution of these, whether perceived as impressive or not in the quantitative sense, has proved to be an extremely valuable instrument of East and South-East Asia's progress.

A critical question pertained to whether it as simply an increasing trend of productivity or huge amounts of investment that spearheaded the economic expansion of East Asia and subsequently South-East Asia? In essence, there are two schools of thought on the issue. Simply expressed, one contends that it was the sheer quantity of investment that drove growth rates in the region; the other line of thinking elucidates that it was the productivity of capital and other inputs that underpinned the high levels of investment and the increasing growth rates that these countries had for almost two decades. This has been a matter of considerable debate, the micro-foundations of which may offer some interesting insights but overall it is evident that both productivity and factor accumulation were important contributors to the rapid and consistent economic progress of the region. (Table 17.2 indicates the buoyant economic growth of the region.)

Regardless of whether factor accumulation had a more or less crucial role to play than total factor productivity in East Asia'sprogress, empirical evidence tells us that high levels of investment cannot be sustained in the absence of pay-offs, supportive policies and a stable macroeconomic environment. Furthermore, it is extremely doubtful that these nations would have managed to achieve levels of investment that constituted over 20 per cent of GDP without an increase in total factor productivity. Estimates about total factor productivity in East Asian countries differ; however, the stimulus that it gave to economic progress is indisputable. Furthermore, it demonstrated that it is the increments in productivity, however small these may be, that comprise a rather significant determinant of how sustainable economic growth would be. On the subject of the significance that productivity had in East Asia's economic progress, the United Nation Conference on Trade and

*Table 17.2*  Economic growth rates in East and South-East Asia (per cent)

| Country | 1980 | 1985 | 1990 | 1992 | 1994 |
|---|---|---|---|---|---|
| Indonesia | 7.90 | 2.60 | 7.20 | 6.90 | 7.30 |
| Malayisa | 7.50 | −1.10 | 9.80 | 8.70 | 8.70 |
| Philippines | 5.30 | −4.50 | 2.70 | 0.30 | 4.50 |
| Singapore | 9.70 | −1.80 | 8.40 | 6.00 | 10.10 |
| Thailand | 4.70 | 3.50 | 11.60 | 7.60 | 8.40 |
| Vietnam | | | 5.40 | 8.70 | 8.80 |
| | **1971–80** | **1981–90** | **1991–96** | | |
| Korea* | 7.67 | 9.08 | 7.35 | | |
| Taiwan* | 9.70 | 7.96 | 6.48 | | |
| Hong Kong* | 9.38 | 6.63 | 5.21 | | |

* These estimates are from the Asian Development Bank Institute, MG Quibria's East Asian Growth Miracle report, February 2002
*Source*: East Asia Analytical Unit, Department of Foreign Affairs and Trade, Commonwealth of Australia.

*Table 17.3*  Ratio of foreign direct inflows to gross fixed capital (%)

| Country | 1971–80 | 1981–1990 | 1991–93 |
| --- | --- | --- | --- |
| Japan | 0.1 | 0.1 | 0.1 |
| Hong Kong | 5.1 | 9.9 | 5.7 |
| South Korea | 12.0 | 0.9 | 0.5 |
| Singapore | 15.8 | 26.2 | 37.4 |
| Taiwan | 1.3 | 2.6 | 2.6 |
| Indonesia | 3.5 | 1.5 | 4.5 |
| Malaysia | 3.6 | 11.3 | 24.6 |
| Philippines | 1.0 | 3.8 | 4.6 |
| Thailand | 2.3 | 4.8 | 5.0 |

*Source:* UNCTAD, Trade and Development Report 1996.

Development (UNCTAD) report (2003) states: 'The close correlation observed in East Asia between high rates of investment, rising shares of manufacturing in GDP and strong export performance is underpinned by a rapid growth in productivity.'

A critical input that underpinned productivity increase in East Asia was a rapid diffusion of technical progress and the assimilation and adaptation of technology acquired to suit the innate requirements of the industrial sector (including those of its potential export markets). This was facilitated by significant investments in social infrastructure provision. The resultant increase in educational attainment was, thus, closely intertwined with its industrial policy.

Scaling up the value chain through an extensive and accelerated pace of human capital formation entailed the rapid creation of new comparative advantages and, once these were transformed into core competences, another set of advantages were identified and built upon. Throughout each phase of its economic progress and at each stage of its industrial advancement East Asian economies created core-competences in various industries. Thus from being an exporter of low-skill labour-intensive manufactures these countries became exporters of high technology products. Over the period 1963–93 high technology products to the OECD region increased by 180 per cent.

Furthermore, the rapid industrial transformation and transition that Japan and subsequently Korea and Taiwan made from light industries to heavy and chemical industries to electronics and presently to high-technology industries would not have been possible without the extremely active and dynamic role of public policy, a feature that has characterized all these nations. This is also the case with Singapore, where the evolution of core competences in trade, finance, electronics and some other spheres of industry is inextricably linked with the policy framework.

Policies in Korea, Taiwan and Japan may have been wrought with certain deficiencies and distortions and, in the course of industrialization, there were instances of enterprises and projects that failed. However, if viewed over a longer term this still does not alter the crucial role that domestic industry has had in the economic progress of this region. In the countries of East Asia, the approach underlying industrialization may be described as a sector-by-sector, bottom upwards strategy, from downstream to upstream. Downstream industries comprised the export-oriented units that engaged in the specialization of those products that would have an international market. In the initial stages of export promotion the focus was on the production of light consumer goods such as textiles, and at this time domestic industry was oriented towards the production of intermediate goods. As economies of scale evolved in the intermediate goods sector this segment was oriented towards the external market and domestic industry made its foray in the sectors that had a high degree of technological intensity.

Despite the protectionist policies that the import-substituting industries availed of these were, by and large, efficient and competitive because the counterbalance came from policy stipulations that required these industries to export a certain proportion of the output and do so within a specified time frame. Consequently, companies had to reduce costs and this provided the impetus to higher and faster rates of technological advancement and skill upgrading. Although the association between rent-seeking and rampant inefficiency is a rather infamous one, and with good reason, the East Asian growth strategies demonstrated that this connection need not always hold. It is not that these nations were without rent-seekers (it would be utterly naive to expect to find a society without these), the impact that this feature had differed from the usual profane, unproductive rent-seeking activity that is invariably a deterrent to development.

Incentives, privileges and subsidies were not granted to businesses in East Asia randomly or without any criteria. Through the use of these specific concessions, such as subsidized financing, tax advantages and even access to external financing, governments in South Korea and Taiwan steered and fostered the expansion of industries that were envisioned to play an important role in the future. Concessions were provided in consonance with the priorities of industrial policy and were used to promote and encourage the setting up of certain industries. Notably, incentives were not granted unconditionally given that these were linked to certain performance criteria. Interestingly, these privileges were not handed over directly to firms 'on a platter'; prospective recipients in the private sector had to compete for subsidies and the duration of these was temporary.

## Box 17.1  Industrial policy: choice of sectors

The choice of sectors that industrial policy set out to promote differed in each country. During the late 1960s, in South Korea for instance, it comprised ship-building, petrochemicals, steel, non-ferrous metals, electronics and machinery. Through the specific incentives and short-term export targets provided it was expected that these sectors would become competitive internationally within a decade. By the eighties the emphasis of South Korea's industrial policy had shifted to high technological activities, small and medium enterprises. Further the industrial development law in 1986 specified industries across a spectrum of spheres that included, shipping, foreign construction, ferroalloys, fertilizers and dyes that required rationalization.

There were undoubtedly demerits in granting the maximum incentives to a small group of business houses (chaebols), this became pronouncedly manifest after the Asian crisis in 1997. However the government-business nexus worked rather well for three decades, and this is a feature that held true for East Asia.

The result of this was the evolution of certain knowledge- and skill-intensive core competences, such as the production of semi-conductors. It must be noted that each country in the HPAE category formulated an industrial policy that defined the spheres of importance in accordance to their innate features, strengths and targets. However, the common characteristic in the strategy of industrialization that these nations pursued was the emergence of a sequential pattern of industrial evolution wherein the inception and expansion of the various segments in the manufacturing sector were closely interlinked.

In the context of developing countries the issue is not whether East Asia's pattern of sequencing is applicable or not. The more pertinent aspect that emanates from the region's industrial pattern is that, although the sequence of industrial expansion may vary from country to country in accordance to their indigenous attributes and endowments, sequencing has a discernible role in determining whether the process of industrialization is a productive and efficient one. An effective strategy of industrialization requires that policies accord importance to the composition, timing and the productivity of industrial expansion stated to occur during a particular period. Whether or not initiatives to do so are referred to as sequencing is hardly an issue.

If in the initial stages of its modernization East Asia had adopted a pattern of industrialization that emphasized investment merely in the expansion of heavy manufacturing without assigning any importance to the production of light consumer goods or to increasing agricultural productivity it is doubtful that we would have witnessed what was called, for many years, a 'miracle'.

Circumstances and timing may have spelt a different set of considerations; however, a vital lesson demonstrated by the underpinnings of economic progress in the HPAEs is the role that domestic industrial capabilities have in the development process of a region.

The relevance of this fact becomes most vivid when we view the South-East Asian countries. The mid-1980s witnessed the resonance of Indonesia, Malaysia and Thailand. Similar to their counterparts in East Asia, the next tier of newly industrialized economics (NIEs), which includes Malaysia, Thailand and Indonesia, also exhibited a pattern of industrial change that was formulated and driven by an extremely active, or rather interventionist, policy. However, in the instance of South-East Asia the downside of this has been the fall-out of crony capitalism, which has ushered in its wake a process of decision-making that upholds the interests of powerful lobbies at the cost of developmental considerations. This point of differentiation between the growth experiences of the two regions is simply a manifestation of fundamental differences in the creation of industrial and technological capabilities between East Asia and South-East Asia. An elucidation of this point follows.

(i) Foreign direct investment has had an important role to play in South-East Asia's progress, much more so than the part it played in Japan, South Korea and Taiwan. This was partly the result of the role that FDI has played in the industrialization of the region. Whether FDI crowds out domestic investment is not the only issue; even more important than this are the implications and conditions that stem from having a composition of investment that has a much higher proportion of FDI relative to domestic investment. Evidently, these may not be entirely conducive to indigenous requirements, whether industrial or otherwise, in a country. There have been instances wherein profitability of the foreign investor or TNC entails measures that could deter or retard the pace of policies that are in the larger interest of the nation.

(ii) The mode of technology transfer and the political economy of protectionism and incentive allocations in Malaysia, Indonesia and, to some extent, in Thailand define the main distinctions between the economic course pursued by these nations and in Japan, South Korea, Taiwan and Singapore. Technological upgradation in the latter entailed an extended process of learning and adapting. For instance, Singapore's evolution of core competences in the electronics sector was preceded in the initial stages by advances in pre-electronic activities, such as mechanical, electromechanical and precision engineering. However, policy prescriptions, particularly in Indonesia and Thailand, have attempted to accelerate the process of technology transfer.

Having a consistent trajectory of technical progress involves creating an environment that enables assimilation, absorption and, at some stage, adaptation of technologies acquired. This entails much more than utilization of state-of-the-art technologies. Predictably, in the absence of sufficient increases in the levels of educational attainment and vocational training in South-East Asia (with the exception of Singapore), technological transfer has not led to the generalized process of technological sophistication that North-East Asian nations were able to acquire.

The reasons for the East Asian miracle were high rates of saving and investment and rapid increase in exports, this explains the surge in growth rates that occurred in the region by the early seventies. However, the impetus to the critical inputs underlying the economic performance was the link between its institutions, business and policy. According to the trade and development report (1996), 'At the core of East Asian success lies a set of institutions which keep policy-makers connected to business while still enabling governments to propose and implement appropriate measures directed at tackling a series of interrelated institutional and structural obstacles that can seriously hold back the process of investment, technical progress and exporting in a late industrializing country.'

When one views the disappointing and rather negative impact of trade liberalization in a number of developing countries the commonality is the lack of a productive and dynamic link between the institutional framework and business. It is not infrequent that one finds instances where the enclave of powerful vested interests exert an influence on policies and institutions that reduces their scope and nullifies the benefits that these can have.

Crony capitalism is a phrase that was used frequently in the context of explaining the causes that led to the Asian crisis in 1997; this was a negative aspect of the business policy nexus that existed in East and South-East Asia. As such, institutions were weakened by crony capitalism that runs rife in the economic system as in the case of some other developing countries.

According to John Weiss (February 2005) 'Individual promotion policies may have been misplaced and led to resource misuse in high cost products (for example not all of the investment in the heavy chemical industry in the Republic of Korea can be adjudged successful) but in these countries there was a strong stimulus to private manufacturing investment since regardless of the precise impact of such policies they would have raised profitability of manufacturing in other sectors.'

(iii) As we have seen, the efficacy of government intervention relies crucially on the ability to ensure measures that will curb or minimize forces that will generate unproductive rents. More often than not, the good intent of policy-makers is undermined by the stranglehold of powerful lobbies and the political economy that eschews as a result is inimical to a merit-based society. In Malaysia, for instance, the privatization programme that the government embarked on in the late 1990s was structured in a manner that would facilitate the transfer of valuable assets to a coterie of influential businessmen who were connected to the United Malays National Organization.

Thus, subsidy allocations in South-East Asia were hardly linked to performance criteria; instead these were overtly influenced by political patronage. This has resulted in the emergence of a system where the dictates of economic development are superseded by cronyism. The explanation of industrial policy and its outcomes in South-East Asia extend beyond the purview of an undue reliance on foreign investment to the quality of governance and institutional structures that existed. This, coupled with the business–political nexus, was not one that would encourage the implementation of policies that would serve developmental imperatives.

## Comparisons: East Asia and Africa

When countries that are disparate in more ways than one pursue apparently similar strategies and have extremely divergent results the issues that come to light on close inspection give us useful insights. One such instance is the comparison between East Asia and Africa. Given the situation in most parts of Sub-Saharan Africa (SSA) and other countries outside of SSA, there are those who would view such a comparison an oddity; be this as it may, it highlights some of the crucial principles and prerequisites that decide the course of subsequent development (or underdevelopment).

Before proceeding with the comparison we have to view recent growth trends in the region. Africa witnessed moderate growth for over a decade from the mid-1960s to the end of the 1970s and this was a period during which investment exceeded 25 per cent in some countries. (Table 17.4) indicates the average growth rates in Africa and Sub-Saharan Africa over 1965–99.) The precipitous decline of growth and investment in the continent occurred in the era of structural adjustment during the 1980s and the restoration of investment rates to their pre-1980 levels continues to elude a number of countries. Most of these countries witnessed a growth upturn during the mid 1990s and this seemed a watershed because the average income growth exceeded population growth rates in the region for four years. An exception

*Table 17.4*   Average annual GDP growth in Africa, 1965–99

|  | 1965–9 | 1970–9 | 1980–9 | 1990–4 | 1995–9 |
|---|---|---|---|---|---|
| Africa | 4.5 | 4.2 | 2.5 | 0.9 | 3.5 |
| Sub-Saharan Africa | 2.4 | 4.0 | 2.1 | 0.8 | 3.9 |

*Source:* UNCTAD Report on Economic Development in Africa, 2001.

to this was Nigeria and Republic of South Africa (RSA), where growth rates were about 2.2 per cent per annum over the period 1995–9. However, the spurt in economic progress could not prevent a slowdown towards the end of the decade in the region and growth rates in Sub Saharan Africa (SSA) reduced to 2.7 per cent. Furthermore, SSA's per capita income at the end of the century was about 10 per cent below the level attained in 1980 and significantly less than what was attained about three decades earlier (estimates cited are from the UNCTAD report on Economic Development in Africa, 2001).

A frequent misconception that arises is that Africa's growth shortfall has been the result of inadequate investment. An exploration of this claim takes us to the several reasons that have culminated in a situation wherein some countries have an increase in economic growth rates that is too low and short-lived, while others finds themselves in the throes of economic stagnancy.

Notably, during the 1950s, most of East Asia was not significantly more prosperous than the African continent; however, the overwhelming impetus to its policies stemmed mainly from the compulsions of achieving rapid economic progress. This conferred on it a position of strength because it did not deter it from implementing measures that would enable it break through the trappings of underdevelopment.

Most African countries epitomize instances of unsustainable growth, and it is this characteristic that starkly contrasts its economic experience from that of East Asia. Low returns on capital and the persistent paucity of domestic savings will ensure that an increase in capital accumulation or growth rates will peter out sooner rather than later. Undoubtedly, Africa has a vicious circle of investment and growth. Simply stated, this means that low incomes constrain savings and investment and this in turn impedes any increase in the low growth rates. The rudiments of this rather chronic feature (which exists in a number of underdeveloped countries in and out of Africa) stems from the use of external financing as a substitute for domestic resources instead of as an interim measure.

Investments that are financed predominantly by external financing, irrespective of whether this is foreign aid, external debt or even foreign investment, may bridge the resource gap over the shorter term. However, if unaccompanied by concerted initiatives to step up the pace and quantum of domestic resource mobilization an increase in capital accumulation and growth cannot be sustained over the longer term.

The debt crisis of the 1980s and the continued reliance of a number of countries on foreign aid and investment have created what I term as a dependency spiral/syndrome (see Figure 17.1).

The transition from the dependency spiral, which most African countries find themselves enmeshed in, to having a virtuous circle of investment and growth stands as the most crucial prerequisite of development.

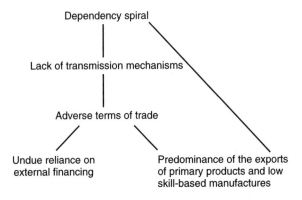

*Figure 17.1*   External financing includes in its ambit overseas development assistance, various forms of aid and foreign investment

In this context there are aspects of East and more recently South-East Asia's economic experience that could be drawn upon.

First, a continued increase in the levels of capital accumulation cannot be achieved in the absence of rising levels of productivity. In the initial stages of development it will not be possible to spur a consistent increase in the productivity of labour and capital without investments in infrastructure, education and skill upgrading. It is almost impossible to sustain an upswing of capital accumulation without the creation of transmission mechanisms. Furthermore, in situations of extreme disparity countries generally have clusters of extreme affluence, together with a large pool of untapped savings. Policies must be formulated so that domestic savings are tapped. One effective way of doing this is to increase the quantum of investment opportunities. In the absence of this there is capital flight and this, added to the debt-servicing obligations, continues to aggravate the reduction in domestic resources.

Yet even the more competent governments in Africa have limited capacity to manage simultaneously multiple new investments and social delivery programmes as well as better auditing, introducing the rule of law, undertaking judicial reform and so on. Their biggest challenge may well be to set priorities in the deployment of their scarce administrative resources which large infusions of aid cannot easily buy. Fortunately the experience of successful countries – Korea, India, Chile is that doing a few things right in particular to encourage local private sector investment can trigger a sustained growth process and that avoiding privileging insiders (i.e. getting the policies reasonably right) goes a long way to ensuring that the poor capture some the resulting growth gains. (Testimony for the Senate Committee on Foreign Relations, Nancy Birdsall, Centre for Global Development, 17 May 2005)

Thus regardless of the quantity of external financing that a developing country might be able to obtain, it is extremely unlikely that it would be able to unshackle itself from the dependency spiral unless it manages to increase the efficiency of resources acquired. For instance, it has been estimated that for each dollar of capital inflow into Sub-Saharan Africa 25 per cent was used to make interest payments and profit remittances overseas, over 30 per cent leaked into capital outflows and reserve build-up and 51 per cent constituted terms of trade losses. If the resource inflows that this region received, either as aid, grants or loans, had been available for domestic investment it would certainly have led to an increase in growth. It must be noted that the share of SSA in total capital inflows to developing countries declined to 10 per cent in the 1990s from 20 per cent in the 1980s.

Furthermore, there has been a decline in the proportion of aid flows from 37 per cent in the early 1990s to 27 per cent at the end of the decade. According to a report on Africa, in 2001 Sub Saharan Africa had not received any net transfer of real resources over the previous two decades.

The consequence has, of course, been a process of growth that is either discontinuous or one that decelerated. Thus, be it aid or any form of external financing the objective should be to use these as instruments to raise the levels of domestic saving and investment.

Thus, at the heart of Africa's stubbornly persistent underdevelopment is a resource crunch that will need much more than infusions of external financing (however massive these maybe) to be overcome. Obtaining finance represents one critical aspect of the solution; however, the larger and more fundamental issue is to ensure the presence of complementary inputs and dynamically supportive policies, which will ensure the utilization of funds procured to build a framework that will enable the build-up of structures (i.e. productive capacities and transmission mechanisms) that will enable development. So far this has not happened in a number of Africa's countries and attributing this merely to a dearth of external funds provides us with an extremely incomplete explanation.

There have been several studies that have attempted to calculate the quantity of external financing required to accelerate the rates of growth and the pace of poverty reduction. Having ascribed quantitative estimates of the resources required, most such studies emphasize the macroeconomic environment and the policy framework required to enable the growth rates to increase. For instance, according to a UNCTAD report (2001), increasing the rate of growth to about 6 per cent per annum in Sub-Saharan Africa requires doubling of official capital inflows into the region, along with policies directed at increasing the efficiency of investment, the propensity to save and the proportion of capital inflows that are retained.

East Asia's judicious use of policy and institutions to attain rising levels of capital accumulation and productivity and with it create a virtuous circle of investment, savings and growth demonstrates the importance of governance and an institutional framework in harnessing local resources. Both East Asia and Africa did implement policies of export promotion and import substitution; inevitably the outcomes of apparently similar policies were startly different in both regions.

If import substitution failed in many African countries during the 1960s and 1970s, the underlying cause was its inability to build transmission mechanisms that would enable the percolation of the gains that stemmed from industrialization to the larger mainstream. Infrastructure provision, rising levels of educational attainment, efficient institutions with a highly trained and effective civil service and bureaucracy continue to be conspicuous by their absence in many African countries even to date. The consequence of this was small domestic demand, low levels of productivity and investment and constricted or negligible poverty reduction.

In a comparison of Africa with other developing nations it must be noted that the endeavour to build an industrial base was successful in those nations where transmission mechanisms existed. In East Asia infrastructure was provided more expansively and institutions functioned with greater efficiency than those in India and, for that matter, even in China. However, the commonality was that all these regions did manage to create the mediums through which gains from industrialization could percolate to the mainstream. Undoubtedly, the inefficiencies that arose in the industrial sector in India, particularly during the pre-liberalization era, may have reduced the gains forthcoming from the country's process of industrialization; however, unlike the African case, the transmission mechanisms were created.

Attributing the failure of import substitution in Africa to protectionism or lack of capital is a rather shallow interpretation, a fact that is corroborated by comparisons with other nations that have managed to use protectionist policies to evolve an industrial base, which in turn has spearheaded the process of development. Be it the pursuit of measures directed towards industrialization or those intended to achieve agricultural liberalization, policies adopted were almost disconnected from the macroeconomic environment. Thus, the implementation of piecemeal strategies that would create enclaves of modernization whether in the ambit of agriculture or industry without complementary support structures have inevitably failed to deliver a consistent trajectory of growth. The consequence of this has been a decline in the share of industry in Africa's GDP from 39 per cent to 32 per cent between 1980 and 1997 (United Nations Economic Commission on Africa estimates). Furthermore, 17 of Africa's 20 most important non-fuel goods consist of primary commodities and resource-based manufactures. Once again this stood in sharp contrast to the increasing proportion of industrial goods in the total exports of East Asia.

Modernization is inextricably linked to technical progress; however, initiating and sustaining a process of technical upgrading requires much more than the utilization of modern technology in certain sectors.

In most parts of Africa the medium of technical progress consisted of turnkey technological transfers and in East Asia technology transfers were undertaken through technical imports and licensing. However, even more important than the medium of obtaining the technology was the fact that, for the first tier of newly-industrialized economies, procuring a particular technology marked the beginning of a multi-tiered process, which included learning, adopting and adapting. Thus, mastering technologies acquired with a view to achieving the fundamental goal of evolving local core competences was the central feature of technical upgrading in East Asia.

As a matter of fact, there is a debate about whether the process of imitation, improvization and adaptation of foreign technology can be described as innovation. I use the term 'derived innovation' because the framework and incentives, which were created to facilitate a dissemination of technical progress in East Asia, did not rely primarily on the superimposition of 'apparently modern' technology.

In this context, Japan, Taiwan and South Korea in East Asia were pronouncedly cognizant about the fact that modernization extended beyond the purview of technology imports. It must be noted that this was hardly the case with developing countries during the 1950s and 1960s.

Africa's inability to attain competitiveness was certainly not the result of insufficient liberalization or trade openness. It was the larger backdrop in which trade policies were implemented and the failure to link these measures with the imperatives of national development that underlies the rather discouraging impact of 'openness' in a number of African countries. For instance, agricultural liberalization can benefit the small and subsistence farmer; however, often agricultural trade policies are structured in a rather skewed manner, which benefits a minority and does so by overlooking important considerations. An illustrative instance of this is the liberalization of the cashew sector in Mozambique during the early 1990s. In the initial stages the curbs on exporting cashews were replaced by export quotas and an export tax.

However, in 1998 these were removed; the immediate consequence of this was a rise in the export of raw cashews and the impact of this had adverse repercussions for many. Mozambique had begun a cashew-processing industry in 1980 and it had 14 cashew processing plants. As resources were ploughed into the export of cashews it inevitably meant an end to processing and this resulted in unemployment of about 11,000 workers, most of whom were unemployed until 2001. Thus, the gains in terms of higher levels of efficiency were offset by the losses that arose as a result of the policy change.

Such situations are not uncommon and developing countries are confronted with a trade-off between the developmental considerations and short-term efficiency gains. In many instances, as was the case with Mozambique, policies emphasize the latter. Having said this, economic growth does not have to suffer a setback if a proportion of the benefits that may ensue from higher levels of efficiency are invested in the creation of physical or social infrastructure. Striking a balance between competitiveness and development is not an easy task. However, if policies directed at enhancing competitiveness in an industry or a particular sector have adverse ramifications on other sectors and there is a loss of welfare and a decline in incomes, particularly of the lower income groups, the net gain from the attempt to become competitive is minimal. Furthermore, the extent of competitiveness that a particular country attains over the longer term is inextricably linked to rising levels of economic progress. For instance, East Asia and subsequently South-East Asia could not have attained the present levels of competitiveness in certain sectors without investments in infrastructure development.

Agricultural liberalization in Africa is replete with instances where the outcome has been a reduction of wages, increased levels of unemployment and contraction of domestic production. Despite not being able to 'afford' a variant of competitiveness that has the negative impact just described, present policies in a number of countries fail to link market reforms to poverty reduction. The antecedents of this persistent feature stems from the circumstances that compelled Africa to opt for policies of trade liberalization that were inimical to development. It must be noted that those developing countries that are mired in debt and heavily reliant on foreign aid are more likely to opt for choices that will compromise development. When policy choice is constrained by short-term considerations these have the most adverse implications for a country. If a nation's capacity to tackle the problems emanating from underdevelopment head on is impeded, it denotes among the most serious deterrents to sustained economic growth.

Observably, the growth dynamics of East Asia were the result of smart policies, but this was not all. Policy implementation was even smarter. Furthermore, it was not the benevolence of the system created but the pragmatism that it embodied that underpinned its remarkable progress. Many African countries have neither benevolent leadership nor pragmatic policies. One of the most likely consequences of these lacunae are episodes of growth deceleration, which require much more than infusions of external financing to be overcome.

When political compulsions override economic logic the result is dramatic reversals in progress and the inevitable consequence of this is a withdrawal of aid, external financing and a contraction of investment. This rather grim scenario is not uncommon to countries of Africa; Zimbabwe's present economic collapse is among the most recent reminders of the disastrous outcomes that can arise from a malevolent political economy. Once a vibrant and diversified economy and an exporter of food, the country has witnessed an unprecedented contraction of its incomes over the last five years. The culmination of this has been a catastrophic impact on socio-economic indicators, such as a rise in infant mortality rates, exports that have been halved and a severe decline in the production of maize, one of Zimbabwe's most important commodities. The regressive course that the country has taken from being a food exporter not so long ago to one that has a compelling need of food aid is largely the result of blatant neglect of economic imperatives for the sake of political mileage. The present leadership in the country has used coercive and drastic measures to repress a rising opposition movement, using land seizures and chaotic disruption of farms to achieve this end. Those in government have attempted to place blame on the drought that the country has had to experience and, for a time, even some visiting IMF missions corroborated this. However, Zimbabwe has had droughts in the past that were even more severe and not left the country teetering on the edge of a breakdown as it is at this time.

Zimbabwe has been in arrears with the IMF since February 2001 because it failed to pay interest on its $4.5 billion loan and the institution has considered the expulsion of the country from its membership. However, in September 2005 it decided to defer a final decision about the matter for six months and this provided a temporary reprieve that the present leadership of the country welcomed. However, the crux of the problem is not whether the country will or will not be expelled from the IMF but whether it will be able to reverse the extensive damage that has been inflicted by misgovernance and disastrous macroeconomic management. (Zimbabwe narrowly escaped expulsion from the IMF in January 2006.)

## Conclusion

Viewing the East Asian miracle from a developmental perspective brings forth some interesting insights. The East Asian model of development embodied a model of poverty reduction, which may not depict an ideal instance of pro-poor growth but, over a period spanning three decades, it is among the few instances of growth that had an impact on poverty reduction. Building transmission mechanisms that would translate the increases in growth to the mainstream continues to be a crucial input in the process of development and the challenge confronting developing countries and less developed nations is to be able to achieve this.

Herein, its combination of extremely high rates of investment, which included increasing rates of human capital accumulation, pragmatic institutions and the selective application of government intervention, is a feature that developing countries can draw upon. East Asia vividly demonstrates that it is not just what causes growth but what is done (or not done) when growth rates increase that will decide whether economic progress will be a sporadic phenomenon or a consistent process. The impact of growth on poverty reduction in the region can be explained by the creation of meso-variables, which were conduits through which the effects of macroeconomic policies were transmitted to the household. One important meso-variable was educational attainment. Thus, although in conventional terms income inequalities in the region may not have reduced as much as poverty, we cannot overlook that there would have been a significant reduction of disparity in the non-income sphere, for instance, the rising levels of educational attainment did reduce the skills gap.

To ascribe a sustained and rapid increase in growth rates merely to high levels of investment or export promotion is an extremely partisan interpretation of economic progress. First, a trend of increasing levels of investment and technical progress cannot be maintained in the absence of proactively supportive policies and complementary measures.

It is not as though East Asia began with all the trappings of a sound investment climate. However, all these countries grasped in the initial stages of their development the inextricable link between governance and investment climate. During the 1940s and 1950s there was widespread concurrence that the preeminent task of charting the development strategy and the processes to achieve these cannot be relegated to the market mechanism. As such, during the post-colonization era the norm that prevailed in most parts of the developing world was systems that were highly centralized, as such the formulation of economic strategy used models of planned economic growth. Resource allocation was undertaken through the use of import quotas, export subsidies, fixed exchange rates and price controls. Undeniably, these measures were flawed because there were more than a few instances where these provided a breeding ground for inefficiencies and rampant corruption. There are also examples, however, that exhibited the positive outcomes and the overall gain (in terms of growth) of having a system based on a model of planned economic development.

As the downside of excessive centralization became overtly evident it lent credence to the advocates of minimizing government intervention. The consequence of this for economic thinking and strategy formulation may be termed as ideological polarization wherein government intervention and market forces were pitted opposite each other as two extremes. It is in this context that East Asia demonstrated that the most important issue was certainly not one of minimizing intervention but the challenge was to get a package of interventionist policies that would encourage and step up the pace of development. Joseph Stiglitz was among the first economists to highlight the role that institution building played in the effective implementation of policies in the East Asian and subsequently the South-East Asian context. Herein, the link between interventionist policies, the proactive functioning of institutions and governance were the parameters within which economic strategies were drawn out and executed.

Thus, the region's political economy of development was a vibrant one that provided an instance of pragmatic intervention, which contrasted starkly with those countries where an overdose of centralization impeded

progress. In doing so, East Asia underscored that it was not excessive government intervention per se but the excesses of ineffective and inept government functioning that explained the adverse impact that interventionist
policies had in certain countries. Moreover, when the global resonance of
neo-liberal strategies (over the last two decades) failed to eliminate or significantly mitigate unproductive rent-seeking activity, as was the case in Russia,
it dealt a blow to the presumption that equated the minimization of rent-
seeking behaviour with the minimization of government intervention.

It must be noted that initial neo-liberalist interpretations about East Asia's
miracle highlighted the classic role that the market mechanism of these
countries played in facilitating economic development. However, even elab-
orate citations of this tell us only one part the miracle story because the
existence of buoyant market forces in these countries were not a stand-
alone feature that appeared out of nowhere. Perhaps it is even more vital
to understand the reasons markets worked in the way that these did in
East Asia and conversely did not work as buoyantly elsewhere. Interestingly, and some might say even paradoxically, it was the interventionist
policies that steered markets to deliver the outcomes that they did. Economic
strategies that encompassed a package of protecting infant industries, subsid-
izing exports, building export-oriented institutions, maintaining low level of
interests could not have been implemented in the absence of interventionist
policies.

There are hardly any countries globally that can boast of having an investment climate that can be described as absolutely unflawed. However, there
are certain fundamentals that need to be in place if a country is to have an
investment climate that is relatively sound without which it is not possible
to step up and sustain the pace of capital accumulation.

According to the World Development Report (2005), a good investment
climate is one that benefits everyone in two dimensions. First, it serves
society rather than just firms through its impact on job creation, lower prices
and broadening the tax base. Second, it embraces all firms not just the large
or influential ones. The report cites the various indicators of a country's
institutional and policy variables, which include an entire gamut of variables
such as secure property rights, rule of law, corruption, openness to trade,
legal origins, financial sector and good governance and it states that it is
difficult to distinguish the effects of specific policy action from the broader
background institutions that influence the impact of these actions.

Interestingly, it is the limitations in governance and a glaring lack of transparency that have propelled the enforcement of measures that are not rooted
in a sound evaluation procedure of what would be good for the country. At
this point it must be noted that good or effective governance would have
ruled out at the outset the implementation of many measures consistent
with what was once a widely advocated prescription of neo-liberal market
economics. For instance, tempering the pace of financial liberalization or

the prescription of ceilings on foreign-ownership requirements in certain sectors did elicit criticism on the grounds that these were not consistent with the principles of having open markets. It is highly probable that economic liberalization will have a structure different from the IMF-styled prescription in an investment climate that is comparatively sound.

Empirical evidence and research about the impact of interventionist policies and economic liberalization on development provide us with a diverse range of findings on the basis of which we can broadly classify interventionist policies in two categories:

1. Government interventions that induce higher growth rates over the medium and longer terms.
2. Interventions that reduce growth rates over the longer term.

Undeniably, a government that would have a discernible role in inducing a virtuous sequence of investment and growth will be an extremely productive and vital input in a contemporary developing country.

As empirical evidence has demonstrated to us repeatedly, the solutions to development do not come forth by making watertight demarcations between the government and the market. Problems are not resolved by seeking a refuge in contrasts because a scenario that appears to be the opposite of what prevails could very well be the breeding ground of the same ills that a country set out to mitigate. Contrary to expectations, liberalization was not the antidote to the wide gamut of inefficiencies and distortions that arose from excessive centralization. The irony that has emerged in recent times is that there are contexts in which economic liberalism could result in market failure. This may not be a spectacular revelation at this point in time but over three decades ago the East Asian model stood out as one of the few instances that recognized that markets and government are not mutually exclusive domains.

What was particularly striking about the East Asian model was that it achieved a level of progress through measures that were neither advocated, recommended nor viewed very kindly by the influential and advanced nations of the time.

The Economic Report on Africa (2007) also underscores the importance of having what may be termed as a heterodox stance on economic liberalization. It is rather significant that the report cites the relevance of the East Asian economic experience. In doing so it states: 'The Asian experience is an example of how a strategic trade policy cannot be limited to a choice between liberalization and protection. Rather, a strategic trade policy is one that can be used in a dynamic and adaptable way to support specific development choices. Therefore in order to realize the benefits of diversification, countries in Africa should use trade policies as dynamic instruments towards chosen diversification ends.'

# 18
# The Stilettoization of Economic Progress

The elephant embodies tremendous potential and capacity. It is the colossus of the animal kingdom and it can perform an entire gamut of difficult tasks almost effortlessly. For a moment, let us imagine something ridiculous, that we attempted to compel an elephant to wear stilettos. Inevitably, the result would be one of two possibilities: either the elephant violently resists our attempt, in which case we will have to flee, or it concedes, in which case, however hard we tried, we would not be able to prevent it from taking a first step without stumbling.

This seemingly peculiar analogy tells us what happened to the fate of development over the last two decades. In the realm of economics, the elephant symbolizes the untapped potential and promise of developing countries and the stilettos signify the quick-fix growth package that a host of countries in the developing world pursued over the last decade or two (more under duress and less by choice).

Stilettoization of economic progress has been one of the predominant trends of geopolitics over the last decade. As elucidated in the previous chapter, economic growth is not a straightjacket and yet a number of underdeveloped countries were cudgelled into 'fitting' economic progress into a standard policy package that essentially comprised liberalization of trade and financial markets. The rather negative consequences that this would bring in its trail were no less predictable than the inevitable fall that the elephant would have if he wore stilettos. (Incidentally, the phrase denotes the attempt to define and measure economic progress in terms of standard policy prescriptions that are deemed appropriate for the developing world.)

When not much is done for long enough we cannot attribute it to merely to an oversight, an insufficiency of resources or mistakes in policy stance and priorities. Surmounting the imminent challenge confronting developing countries involves exploring various issues of underdevelopment. In consonance with this, we proceed with our elucidation about the causes and circumstances that perpetuate the incomplete process of economic integration and in doing so have even stymied trends of development. A crucial aspect of the present discussion would be the pivotal role that the political economy of underdevelopment has had in perpetrating and exacerbating the disconnect between issues of integration and those of development.

## The political economy of underdevelopment: a macroview

The emergence of a vibrant political economy that thrives on every vestige of poverty and deprivation is one of the most binding shackles that obstructs resource mobilization, impedes its efficient allocation and lowers productivity of investments. This is a rather perverse fact but it is one that has prevailed for a considerable period of time and the reason for this is rooted in extremely powerful special-interest agendas and lobbies that either propel policies that perpetuate poverty or that have a set of priorities, which do not do much in the ambit of serving developmental imperatives.

For purposes of better understanding, I will describe the political economy of underdevelopment in terms of its two constituents. These are: (i) the political economy of poverty and inequity; and (ii) Geopolitics of the global economy. A concise enumeration of each follows.

It almost seems that the phrase 'long term' is the bête noire of die-hard commercial considerations; this is one of the main reasons that the dictates of short-term commerce have been allowed to relegate the rationale rooted in development and the aspects related to it to the periphery of policy practice.

The inextricable link between development, sustainability and profitability as viewed by the hard-nosed doyens of commerce may have been understood initially but the importance of having strategies and decision-making that reflects this fundamental linkage appears to have been grasped only in the recent past.

### The politics of perpetuating poverty and inequity

It is rather interesting to observe the imaginative and often convincing manner in which policies that are not rooted in any concern for development are couched as strategies that offer the promise of alleviating or mitigating development. This was largely facilitated by the existence of a vast number of people who live on the margins of existence and the consequences of this have been manifold. In essence, the glaring lack or non-accessibility to opportunities of livelihood enfeebles the evolution of productive capacities and the bargaining position of huge sections of society. Taken together, these factors compress wages, particularly for unskilled workers, and enable certain control groups to take advantage of the deficiencies in income and human capital formation because ultimately these culminate in the lack of scope, awareness and influence in politics and policy-making. One of the most startling contradictions of many developing country democracies is the apparent power that the poor have in electing the leaders but their complete lack of any influence in steering policy. In nations that are non-democracies the problems arising from the distribution of power is even worse because leadership is not determined by public choice.

There has been quite a squabble in economic theory about estimates of poverty and the extent of reduction. The only useful purpose that this can serve is enabling the formulation of a methodology that would help to obtain estimates that are more accurate. One of the most important initial steps (and this is largely overdue) would be to revise the $1 a day basis for defining the poverty line to a $2 day basis. It seems rather difficult to comprehend that, although inflation is accounted for in practically every commercial activity, a number of studies continue to use the $1 a day definition of the poverty line. As indicated in Table 18.1, poverty estimates vary, in some cases quite significantly, according to the basis used for defining the poverty line. However, by any standard measure, the maximum progress in the direction of poverty reduction has been made by China, India, Bangladesh and, to a lesser extent, Pakistan. On the other hand, there were significant increases in extreme poverty in Nigeria, Sub Saharan Africa, South Africa and Tanzania.

It is widely acknowledged that a number of poor countries find themselves stuck in a poverty trap. The term 'poverty trap' is not a new one in economics. Basically, it means that low incomes result in low savings and this in turn constrains investment, consumption and productivity. The net outcome of this is the perpetuity of low incomes. It must be noted that, in the hierarchy of developing countries, there are a number that may not find themselves enmeshed in a poverty trap but have all the same the constraints and ills of underdevelopment.

*Table 18.1* The story of income divergence annual average compound growth rates of per capita GDP%

| | -fold increase | | | | | |
|---|---|---|---|---|---|---|
| | 1820–2001 | 1820–1913 | 1913–1950 | 1950–73 | 1973–80 | 1980–2001 |
| Developed world | 19.0 | 1.3 | 1.2 | 3.3 | 1.9 | 1.9 |
| Eastern Europe | 8.8 | 1.0 | 0.6 | 3.8 | 2.1 | 0.2 |
| Former USSR | 6.7 | 0.8 | 1.8 | 3.3 | 0.8 | −1.6 |
| Latin America | 8.4 | 0.8 | 1.4 | 2.6 | 2.7 | 0.3 |
| Asia | 6.9 | 0.4 | 0.1 | 3.6 | 2.8 | 2.3 |
| China | 6.0 | −0.1 | −0.6 | 2.9 | 3.5 | 5.9 |
| India | 3.7 | 0.3 | −0.2 | 1.4 | 1.4 | 3.6 |
| Japan | 30.9 | 0.8 | 0.9 | 8.1 | 2.3 | 2.1 |
| Africa | 3.5 | 0.4 | 0.9 | 2.0 | 1.2 | −0.1 |

*Source*: United Nations, *World Economic and Social Survey 2006*.

The IMF has described the 'persistent failure to break the cycle of stagnation and poverty in the poorest countries as perhaps the most striking exception to the otherwise remarkable economic achievements of the twentieth century'. By any yardstick of evaluation, be it policy measures, strategy or politics, in the national and international context it is evident that endeavour to mitigate poverty in the developing world has been overtly inadequate. The Millennium Development Goals could very well be the next instance that bears testimony to this fact. In recent times, the best known instance of an agenda that has set out to formulate a global compact to end underdevelopment are the Millennium Development Goals. Perhaps the most recent revelation that, despite all the brouhaha and honourable intent, far too little is happening on this frontier; this is evidenced by the fact that by 2015, which is the deadline set for meeting the MDG, many developing countries will not have met the goals that were enumerated at the beginning of this century.

These goals set targets that are essential for surmounting poverty, not merely in terms of income but also taking into account the other denials and consequences of low incomes, such as high infant mortality rates, gender discrimination in education and health care. As regards the progress made towards the attainment of the MDG by different regions, some facts are presented below:

- Sub-Saharan Africa is off track in terms of its performance on the criterion of income poverty and other non-income targets. However, one of the encouraging signs from this region is the discernible progress made towards the objective of gender parity, wherein the gap between the enrolment of girls and boys into primary and secondary schools is narrowing. Furthermore, in the Middle East, South and West Asia gender disparities in the ambit of school enrolments has eased. Latin America has made rapid strides towards achieving the primary education target.
- In some countries of Europe, Central Asia and in the former Soviet Union rising malnutrition dims the prospects that these nations will achieve the required reduction in the number of people who suffer from hunger.
- In the context of making considerable progress towards the attainment of the maximum number of MDG, East and South-East Asia have been stellar performers.

Achieving the MDGs would mean overcoming the toughest hurdle to unleashing the forces of economic progress. Even fulfilment of all the targets would not be enough to eliminate poverty. However, it would mean drastically reducing the massive extent of extreme poverty that we are witness to today.

At its core, the political economy of poverty is perpetrated by inequalities in income and opportunity. Traditionally, economics did not have an amoral approach to inequality and discussions about values and ethics have inevitably conditioned studies and research about issues pertinent to equity and development. The multidimensional approach to economic development was narrowed down rather indiscriminately merely to a growth-centric approach. From thereon, the maximization of growth has been viewed as an end in itself and all considerations that would ultimately impact development, such as equity and poverty reduction, were relegated to the background by the early 1980s. There are two main reasons for this: these were the geopolitics of the time (the 1970s and 1980s) and the politicization of equity. The advent of structural adjustment programmes, which dealt a severe setback to a number of developing countries, evokes an imminent question: what were the considerations that propelled the implementation of policies that certainly did not bring in their wake a consistent revival of growth, rather putting the brakes on development for over a decade?

The answer is that regardless of the 'requirement' of such measures, the more important aspect was evidently the special-interest agendas of a minority (of certain institutions, individuals and corporations) that paved the way for the structural adjustment policies. In a sense, this was the precedent to the pursuit of neo-liberalism during the 1990s.

Inevitably, broader perspectives about growth, which delved into what caused it and what happened, receded into the background and in its place we had a quick-fix package of growth. Economic theory could have ensconced itself comfortably with the idea that nothing but growth matters; however, many countries that attempted the attainment of fast-paced growth found that they were saddled with a huge problem of inequality. These measures were not the only reason for income disparities but there are many countries in which inequalities have worsened partly as a result of quick-fix policies.

Equity has been misconstrued and even botched so that it can be used as a medium to extract political mileage. It is wonderfully tempting to talk about equality and all that goes with it and even easier not to do much about it. The quest for this has culminated in many an uprising and revolution. The unfortunate fact is that redistributive justice has been used as a pretext for the enforcement of policies that stifle entrepreneurship and choke competition and a recurrent outcome of this has been the prevalence of excessive bureaucratization and red tape-ism in a number of developing countries. Furthermore, the promise of creating an egalitarian society has been used, in more than a few countries, as a pretext for the ascent of totalitarian and oppressive regimes.

As one gleans through contemporary economic experience, it almost seems that, instead of being viewed as an imperative, the concept of equity and all its connotations have been used as a political ploy. There has been a contentious debate on whether the inequalities of income have reduced over the last two decades. Estimates vary in accordance to the methodology of calculation. In essence, a substantive amount of research indicates that inequalities of income have increased within several developing countries and the disparities between countries have also risen. There are studies that dispute this inference and state that within-country inequalities of income have reduced in a number of less developed and developing nations. These also state that disparities between the developing and developed countries have not increased, not significantly at least.

An assessment of inequality begins with an attempt to measure disparities in income; however, it has to proceed by analyzing how a skewed distribution of income impacts the access to education, health care, other forms of infrastructural provision and, ultimately, the availability of employment and opportunity creation. (Tables 18.1 and 18.2 indicate the trend in global inequality. As indicated, it is the disparity between the developed regions and the rest of the world that has contributed most to global inequality.)

Inequality is a collective term for a host of denials and it is very likely that a high degree of inequality brings with it a certain 'distribution' of power and structure of politics that abets its perpetuity. There is ample evidence

*Table 18.2*  Decomposition of international inequality by region (2000)

|  | All economies | | | All economies without China | | |
|---|---|---|---|---|---|---|
|  | Contribution to overall inequality (%) | | | Contribution to overall inequality | | |
|  | Between regions | Within regions | Total | Between regions | Within regions | Total |
| Developed countries | 0.69 | 0.01 | 0.70 | 0.72 | 0.01 | 0.73 |
| Eastern Europe | 0.00 | 0.00 | 0.00 | 0.00 | 0.00 | 0.00 |
| Latin America | 0.00 | 0.01 | 0.00 | −0.01 | 0.01 | −0.01 |
| East Asia* | −0.17 | 0.05 | −0.13 | −0.14 | 0.05 | −0.09 |
| Rest of East Asia | −0.01 | 0.00 | −0.01 | −0.01 | 0.00 | −0.01 |
| Western Asia | 0.00 | 0.00 | 0.00 | −0.01 | 0.01 | 0.00 |
| Africa | −0.05 | 0.01 | −0.04 | −0.06 | 0.01 | −0.05 |
| CIS | −0.01 | 0.00 | −0.01 | −0.02 | 0.00 | −0.02 |
| Total inequality | 0.45 | 0.08 | 0.53 | 0.48 | 0.09 | 0.56 |

*Note*: * This includes the countries of China, India, Indonesia, Philippines, Republic of Korea, Taiwan province of China, Singapore, Thailand, Bangladesh, Hong Kong Special administrative Region, Malaysia, Myanmar, Nepal, Pakistan and Sri Lanka.
*Source*: United Nations World Economic and Social Survey (2006).

of the fact that a skewed distribution of income stokes political populism. The promise of freebies (such as free rations or electricity) to those with extremely low incomes, or even no incomes at all, has become, for many political parties in South Asia, a winning formula for clinching power in the elections. It is this aspect that forms the cornerstone of the political economy of inequity and there would probably have been an upside to it if the sops promised to the poor were delivered to them. Instead, more often than not this is not the case and the amenities are availed by those who certainly are not in the category of low incomes.

The corollary of this is that inequality has multivariate dimensions and a given reduction in income inequality has to translate, at the very minimum, into an increased accessibility of the individual or community to an entire range of basic goods and services that it previously lacked.

Tables 18.1 and 18.2 indicate the income inequalities and divergence between the developing and the developed world. The World Economic and Social Survey also cites that if we exclude China between 1960 and 1980 the share of world population living in countries with GDP per capita of half the mean had stayed constant at about 47 per cent. By 2001, however, the share had increased to 52 per cent.

## Box 18.1  Trends in inequality

According to the UNCTAD report (2002) *Escaping the Poverty Trap* over the period 1995–9 81 per cent of the population in the less developed countries lived on less than $2 a day as; 50 per cent of the population in the less developed countries lived on less than $1 a day; the average per capita consumption of those 50 per cent that live below the $1 a day poverty line is 64 cents a day (1985 purchasing power parity); the average per capita private consumption of 81 per cent of the LDC population that lives below the $2 a day poverty line is $1.03 day (in 1985 PPP dollars)

Economic stagnation and low levels of growth perpetuated poverty but this was not all. In a number of less developed nation the prolonged deficiency of resources required to finance investment and infrastructure has resulted in the existence of what is termed as a 'poverty trap'. The report cites that over the period 1995–99 there were on an average only 15 cents per person per day available for the expenditure on private capital formation, public investment in infrastructure and the continuity of public services such as health and education. Consequently the dependence by the poorest nations on

---

## Box 18.1   (Continued)

external financing to bridge the resource gap has not shown much sign of reducing (external finance includes overseas development assistance, loans, grants and foreign direct investment)

According to the UNCTAD Least Developed Countries Report (2006) the average ratio of aggregate net external resource flows to GDP in the least developed nations has increased from 7.8 per cent in 2000 to 12.7 per cent in 2004. Region-wise the ratio has increased discernibly for the African LDCs, where it has risen from 10.8 per cent in 2000 to 18.9 per cent in 2003. However, the dependence of least developed nations has reduced from 3.5 per cent in 2000 to 2.9 per cent in 2003. Similarly the ratio has also declined for the other developing nations from 3.5 per cent in 2000 to 2.5 per cent in 2003.

Not surprisingly, despite the increase in real GDP growth, a number of less developed nations have had the ratio of domestic savings to GDP remaining too low in these countries compared with other low and middle income developing nations. Evidently the better growth performance of the least developed nations was facilitated by an increased reliance on external finance.

*Source*: UNCTAD, *Least Developed Countries Reports* (2002, 2006).

---

The main point that emerges when we take into account rates of poverty reduction and the disparities of income is that, although there has been a tremendous increase in global income over the last four decades it has not acted as an instrument of development. By any yardstick of evaluation, be it policy measures, strategy or politics, in the national and international context it is evident that endeavour to mitigate poverty in the developing world has been overtly inadequate.

### Geopolitics of the global economy

The clout and influence that some advanced nations have enabled them to steer and, in certain instances, veritably determine the course of economic action in a number of underdeveloped nations. A facile question that could be asked about contemporary economics is: has geopolitics been weighted against the underdeveloped nations? The answer is yes. The overt manner in which WTO is used to serve the interests of a coterie of a few wealthy nations or the fervent propagation of quick-fix growth prescriptions by the IMF and World Bank are some of many instances affirming this fact. The power wielded by a few nations and the impact that this has in tilting policy to suit the vested interests of select lobbies is obvious, even in international organizations. The World Development Report (2006) states:

> Even when each country has equal representation in an international body such as the United Nations system or the World Trade Organization (WTO) powerful forces can chisel away at developing country interests (through separate bilateral agreements for example). And the capacity to make informed decisions can be limited.

However, the deeper issue underlying the rather skewed nature of the global political economy pertains to the extremely limited capacity of a host of less developed nations to formulate strategies that would engender national development. The globalization of corporations and international financial institutions has in a number of instances preempted the implementation of an entire gamut of initiatives that are required for national development. A perspective that criticizes the organizations that perpetrate and benefit from this may lend a dramatic undertone to the discussion but it really doesn't do much to retrieve the situation in which the developing world finds itself.

Perhaps it would be more useful to view the factors that constrain the choice of strategies available to underdeveloped nations. It is easy to understand that countries that are reliant on aid and debt will have their course of economic action 'shaped' by considerations and conditions (linked to debt and aid), which invariably conflict with the imperatives of local or indigenous development.

Dependency compromises the prospects of national development. In the unipolar global economy the geopolitical distribution of power became even more skewed after the end of the Cold War and this would predictably influence and discermbly so not just on the structure but also the outcome of neo-liberalism. A clear instance of this was that the pursuit of trade and financial liberalization by a number of less developed and developing countries was more the outcome of compelling circumstances than independent or strategic choice aimed at auguring well for the interests of the country. The rules of neo-liberalism were determined largely in accordance to the requirements of developed countries and its rather indiscriminate advocacy to the developing world did not accelerate growth rates. Instead, it left in its trail rather adverse and in some cases disastrous results.

Having spoken about the unequivocal role that geopolitics has in determining policies pursued, it is important that we account for the crucial role that weak and inept governance in certain countries has had in destabilizing and reinforcing the dependency syndrome that a host of underdeveloped nations are confronted with in current times. Among the most damaging manifestations of fragile governments and institutions is the emphatic endeavour of the leadership (however frequently this might change) to do all it can to preserve its constituency of power, regardless of what it does to enfeeble a country. There are numerous instances of countries with brittle foundations of governance being thrown out of gear. Recurrent failures in the government machinery of a nation herald the beginning of an overarching dominance of geopolitics in the vital affairs of the country concerned. This is a situation that pre-existed contemporary times; historically one of the basic causes of colonization and conquests has been fragile or crumbling leaderships.

The neo-liberal tradition emphasized an increase in economic growth (and not must else). Growth maximization was its hallowed centrepiece, to be obtained even if it involved sidelining all other priorities; now, this approach looks even less attractive than that which existed in the era preceding it. A few exceptions aside, the credibility of the policies that neo-liberalism pursued falls apart when one views the growth rates that occurred in most countries of the world during the 1980s and 1990s. On average, economic growth rates achieved by most countries in the world during the 1980s and 1990s were below those achieved in the 1960s and 1970s. The exception to this was the encouraging growth performance in many parts of Asia. The former Soviet Union, Central and Eastern Europe, Africa and Latin America had very low growth rates or no growth at all.

Market forces would determine resource allocation, this was the sine qua non of economic liberalism. Expectedly, liberalization should have enabled markets to function with higher levels of efficiency, expediency and a higher degree of 'completeness'. This was not the case. Neo-liberalism did not result in the creation of free markets or fix market failure.

Be it geopolitics of the global economy or the national political economy, in any country it is evident that the stranglehold of vested interests shackles market forces. Classical economics recognized the problem of market failure and it was obvious that neo-liberalism was not going to provide practical solutions to this. Even more importantly, markets fail if they exist; what about situations where markets don't exist? It is the inability of liberalization to provide solutions that will overcome the latter that has proved to be its most serious flaw. There exists a vast terrain of opportunity across spheres such as infrastructure, public health and agriculture for which markets either don't exist or, where they do, are highly inadequate. It was obvious that there is an inextricable link between an increase of incomes across socio-economic groups and an expansion of markets; despite this neo liberal measures failed to create markets for the 'underserved'.

Among the most interesting revelations of economic experience over the last 50 years is that countries that have made maximum progress, such as those in East and South-East Asia and, more recently, China and India, have evolved their distinctive blend of market economics.

As has been substantiated so far, economic integration within countries and between nations remains a fragmented and pronouncedly incomplete process. The present magnitude of global income inequality is one fact among others, that evidences this point.

Increasing levels of trade by developing and underdeveloped nations has resulted in a small increment in their external economic integration but this has not changed the acute disparities that characterize a large part of the developing world. Narrowing this substantive income and non-income differential that exists between the poorer income groups and more affluent stratas, which are generally endowed with more skill and accessibility to social infrastructure and employment opportunities, lies at the core of any measure directed towards stepping up the pace of economic integration.

This chapter will conclude with an elucidation of a modified version of the Arthur Lewis model. The purpose of this will be to explain one method by which the extent and pace of economic integration can be stepped up.

## Economic integration: altering its partial approach

Before the discussion proceeds it would useful to describe the main proposition of Arthur Lewis's model (1954). The multisectoral structure of contemporary developing nations is not a disadvantage, as a matter of fact it provides these countries with a means of expanding opportunity creation and employment. This was a critical insight that emanated from the economic experience of India and China. Traversing the strategies and measures implemented by both nations does elucidate an important facet about economic dualism and the relevance of the Lewis model to the present scenario of underdevelopment, which pervades a large part of our world.

Arthur Lewis's model has been extensively used as a basis for understanding the dynamics of development. It assumed that most developing nations have two sectors – one a small modern sector where production entails the use of capital and labour, the other a large traditional sector, which used mainly labour that had, at best, some rudimentary tools of production. Entrepreneurs in the modern sector saved a part of their profits and invested them; in contrast, the producers in the traditional sector do not save or invest. The central proposition of Arthur Lewis's work is that the traditional sector is a reservoir of surplus labour for the modern sector. The expansion of industry results in an increasing demand for the labour from the agricultural sector. The increase of employment in the modern sector continues until there is no surplus labour in the traditional sector; thereafter, output growth in the modern sector would imply a decline in the traditional sector, where a reduction of labour would result in a fall in output. If real wages began to rise in the modern sector before the point of full employment is reached it could apply a brake to the increase in profits and consequently investment in the modern sector.

This model has its flaws, as all models do, but one of its strengths is embodied in its rather incisive and simple understanding of the primary cause of underdevelopment. Its rather rudimentary two-sector framework and the differential that exists between the traditional or agricultural sector and the modern or industrial sphere also presents a fairly accurate depiction of dualism, which characterizes practically every developing country and, to a lesser extent, the developed nations.

Its weakness stems from the invalidation of what seems, in present times, Lewis's wishful assumption that there would be a continuous transfer of labour from the agricultural to the modern sector, which would eliminate the situation of surplus labour in the country concerned. This did not happen. The reasons are obvious, the most important one being the sheer size of the underemployed and unemployed labour force in the rural regions of many developing countries. Thus, even a rapid expansion of the industrial sector cannot be a source of employment provision to all those that can be described as surplus labour. If, however, the central assumption of Arthur Lewis's model had been validated, the world would have found itself with monumentally less underdevelopment than exists currently.

Realistically, though, the proposition or assumption that that economic dualism will be eliminated seems unfounded. The existence of dualistic economic structures does not have to add up to dramatic disparity. In this context, the framework and the main principle adopted by Arthur Lewis's model can be constructively used to elucidate that economic dualism can be made into a facilitator of employment provision in the contemporary developing world.

For this purpose, one adaptation of the Lewis model is the application of its main tenet to each sector within a country. Thus, each sector, agriculture, manufacturing and the services, can be divided into traditional and modern segments in terms of the per capita income, access to human capital formation, occupational profile, utilization of technology and other criteria that each segment has. This would be more in consonance with ground-level realities because each sector, be it primary, secondary or tertiary, is characterized by the existence of dualistic economic structures, concomitantly divergent political equations across socio-economic stratas and pluralistic socio-cultural patterns.

Thus, a sector-based or sector-specific application of Lewis's model could prove useful in the context of understanding the connection intersectoral linkages have with a higher degree of economic integration.

There exists a modern and traditional sphere within the rural economy that comprises the non-farming and farming sectors. The agrarian sector itself consists of large-scale commercialized farming and subsistence-oriented cultivation. We could assume that the non-farming sector has a higher proportion of relatively more skilled or less unskilled labour, which works at wages that exceed the average income earned by the subsistence farmer. If the non-farming sector expands as a result of increasing demand and an easing of infrastructure bottlenecks the result will be rising levels of employment which would inevitably draw upon labour from the traditional farming sector. It must be noted that a transfer of workers from the farming to the non-farming sector would not necessarily be from the category of surplus or underemployed labour. The workers concerned could also be from the group of those that do manage to eke out a livelihood through farming; however, better remuneration in non-farming activities could result in a relocation of a fraction of the workers from the sphere of subsistence farming. Plausibly, the provision of employment to workers in the agricultural sector would occur for as long as the expansion of non-farming sector continues. As the supply of surplus labour dwindles in the farming sector its wages will begin to increase and the transfer of workers to the non-farming sector will slow down and taper off.

The industrial sector in most developing countries has provided employment to some of those who migrated from the rural regions in search of possible jobs. However, those left behind in the race for employment with industry often work in the informal economy or the unorganized sector. Workers in this segment toil amid Dickensian conditions: lower levels of wages, hazardous working conditions in a number of spheres and the absence of any security or legal protection. Employment in this segment is provided by small-scale enterprises that are ancillary production units of large and mid-sized manufacturing companies. It is not uncommon to find larger firms subcontract a part of their production to small-sized firms. Insofar as the industrial sector is concerned, it is unrealistic to expect that it would be able to provide employment to the entire strata of labour in the unorganized sector.

In a scenario where there exists a sizable informal economy, an expansion of labour-intensive manufacturing will provide an impetus to employment opportunities to some workers in the unorganized sector. Despite this, the industrial sector will be unable to absorb the pool of surplus labour in its entirety. Similarly, there also exists an unorganized segment in the services sector. At the higher end of the tertiary sector are highly skilled professionals and doyens of technical expertise, where as at its lower end is an entire gamut of service providers, many of whom are self-employed; these include hawkers, salespersons, delivery persons, caterers, cleaner, domestic workers and so on. It is heartening to note that not all of those working in the unorganized segment of the services sector have low incomes; however, there are those involved in tedious and backbreaking jobs, such as construction workers and stone breakers, that require greater access to at least the basics of social infrastructure i.e. health care services, education for their children, social security and insurance.

The rapid expansion of the services sector over the last 20 years in India, for instance, provides an eye-opener to the entrepreneurial potential that it embodies and the unequivocal exigency of extending human capital formation to those in the lower income groups. Despite the limitations that the manufacturing sector has in providing employment to the greater proportion of workers in the informal economy, it is likely that as it expands its demand for individuals with varying degrees of skill intensity will increase. Plausibly, this would also provide employment those in the unorganized segment of the services sector. Furthermore, skill upgrading in the informal economy would increase the prospects of those who have managed to become semi-skilled to find employment in the manufacturing sector and in instances where this does not seem likely it would enable them to carve out more remunerative avenues of livelihood for themselves.

Thus, a modified version of Arthur Lewis's model can be used to shed light on the importance of building upon intersectoral linkages in order to achieve a faster pace of economic integration. Lewis observed that it was the transfer of labour from the traditional sector into the modern one that would enable absorption of surplus labour. The principle underlying this is not erroneous but theoretical possibilities are not always practical options that can be realized. Given the scenario that exists in most developing nations, the feasibility of eliminating dualism is remote; this apart it is questionable whether doing away with dualistic structures would be advantageous in certain contexts. For instance, had India and China pursued a pattern of growth that impinged on a single sector the outcomes could have been catastrophic. Thus, it is the extreme disparity that arises as a consequence of economic dualism that needs to be mitigated.

Understandably, given the simpler structures that constituted economic systems when Arthur Lewis propounded his model, he assumed that it was only a transfer of surplus labour into the modern or industrial sector that would facilitate a reduction and eventually an equalization of wages between the two sectors. The present mechanics of growth preclude the achievement of a highly equal distribution of income, as would have been the case if the findings of the Lewis model were completely corroborated. Demonstrably, the modification enumerated would render the findings and framework of the Lewis model more realistic and less idealistic. The central proposition of the modified Lewis model is: it is not economic dualism but the striking disparity that it ushers in its wake that need to be eliminated.

Transfer of surplus labour to the relatively more advanced and faster-growing sectors needs to be supplemented by other measures that will increase the accessibility of those involved in subsistence farming and in the unorganized segment of the industrial and services sector to social infrastructure. This means it is important to increase the accessibility of workers in the unorganized segment to health care and education, added to which they should be provided with some form of social security and medical insurance.

## Conclusion

The crux of dealing with underdevelopment rests essentially on bridging the gap between the intent to improve matters and implementation of the measures that this entails.

As we have seen, although some progress has been made in this direction many countries find themselves straddled between cognizance about meeting certain economic imperatives and the inability to do so. For much more to happen in the ambit of mitigating underdevelopment and at a much faster pace, I suggest:

1. Adopting a multidimensional approach to growth maximization.
2. The evolution of a development paradigm standard or benchmark on the basis of which growth and development strategies can be formulated and assessed.

This is discussed further in Part III.

## Poverty and human deprivation: some startling facts

More than 1 billion people in the world live on less than $1 a day. In total, 2.7 billion struggle to survive on less than $2 per day. Poverty in the developing world, however, goes far beyond income poverty. It means having to walk more than one mile every day simply to collect water and firewood; it means suffering diseases that were eradicated from rich countries decades ago. Every year 11 million children die, most under the age of five, and more than 6 million from completely preventable causes like malaria, diarrhoea and pneumonia.

In some deeply impoverished nations less than half of the children are in primary school and under 20 per cent go to secondary school. Around the world, a total of 114 million children do not get even a basic education and 584 million women are illiterate.

- Every year 6 million children die from malnutrition before their fifth birthday.
- More than 50 per cent of Africans suffer from water-related diseases such as cholera and infant diarrhoea.
- Every day HIV/AIDS kills 6000 people and another 8200 people are infected with this deadly virus.
- Every 30 seconds an African child dies of malaria, a total of more than 1 million child deaths a year.
- Each year, approximately 300–500 million people are infected with malaria. Approximately 3 million people die as a result.
- TB is the leading AIDS-related killer and in some parts of Africa 75 per cent of people with HIV also have TB.
- More than 800 million people go to bed hungry every day ... 300 million are children.
- Of these 300 million children, only 8 per cent are victims of famine or other emergency situations. More than 90 per cent are suffering long-term malnourishment and micronutrient deficiency.

- Every 3.6 seconds another person dies of starvation and the large majority are children under the age of five.
- More than 2.6 billion people – over 40 per cent of the world's population – do not have basic sanitation, and more than 1 billion people still use unsafe sources of drinking water.
- Four out of every ten people in the world don't have access even to a simple latrine.
- 5 million people, mostly children, die each year from water-borne diseases.
- In 1960, Africa was a net exporter of food; today the continent imports one-third of its grain.
- More than 40 per cent of Africans do not even have the ability to obtain sufficient food on a day-to-day basis.
- Declining soil fertility, land degradation and the AIDS pandemic have led to a 23 per cent decrease in food production per capita in the last 25 years, even though population has increased dramatically.
- For the African farmer, conventional fertilizers cost two to six times more than the world market price.

*Source*: Millennium Project (2005).

Developmental targets have seldom been achieved within the specified time frame and in many instances these have never been attained. Simply expressed, the approach has been to identify certain goals and make projections about the funds that would be needed to achieve the specified objectives, identifying a wide gamut of aspects that constitute the composite of what is termed as development and calculating investments needed to mitigate the ills of underdevelopment. Instead of being viewed as one of the most rewarding investments, poverty reduction has been viewed, until very recently, as an investment-intensive endeavour. In retrospect, this was inevitable when we consider that the approach until very recently has been to view poverty reduction as a residual expenditure. Poverty is a bind, abject poverty is a tighter one. Cutting through this requires much more than increments in public expenditure. It needs a system that supports and sustains it and this is most certainly a globalized imperative.

# Part III

# Bridging the Gap between Growth and Development: Evolving a Paradigm

# Introduction to Part III

The empirics of growth and development over the last three decades provide useful insights to contemporary development strategy. Be it the economic experience of India and China or the impact that economic liberalism and globalization has had on the developing world, the dimension that it lends to economic thought and strategy formulation needs to elucidated.

Push the frontiers of thought and we could arrive at a school of thought or proposition that could be a watershed for development strategy. It is an exploration of this possibility that is the focus of the concluding section, Chapters 19–20.

# 19
## The Production Function of Development

### The nature of economic growth

*Many of us would probably have lived prosperously for a long time to come if development was a quick fix. But the simple truth is that it isn't.*

It is not surprising that economic convergence did not occur. The contemporary era unravels before us the manifestations and outcomes of adhering to and pursuing a myopic approach to growth. Inevitably the assumption that as countries develop their incomes will converge to those prevalent in the developed world was invalidated.

There is, however, another form of economic convergence occurring in the global economy: regardless of their divergent levels of economic achievement, be this underdeveloped, developing or developed nations, countries in the global economy are converging to an imminent challenge – that of sustainable development.

Sustainability, in principle is an evocation of long-term considerations.

Proficient analysis by many about what makes growth rates escalate has not enabled us to ensure that an increase in growth rates will invariably lead to a rise in levels of development. This is the critical issue of our times and the hotbed of most ills, including the recent one of terrorism, which seems to be spreading its tentacles in a rather globalized manner. The nub of the problem is translating this cognizance into reality on the ground by creating the mechanisms that will facilitate the diffusion of development once economic growth begin to increase.

Suffice it to say at this point that by definition the feature of globalization should have upheld the principle of reciprocity. Beyond a glimmer of rhetoric and the occasional signing of development co-operation pacts, even a cursory glance at the dynamics of trade liberalization, environmental protection or the mutuality of economic welfare among nations tells us that much more needs to happen on this frontier before countries take each other's developmental interests into consideration.

As explained in the previous chapter the pronouncedly flawed presumption that growth is the primary and singular input that is required for development lies at the base of the rather disembodied approach to economic progress. Although this assumption has been invalidated by the overwhelming reality of persistent underdevelopment, a more holistic approach to economic progress continues to elude us. A rather myopic approach to growth continues to override the implementation of measures that are rooted in fundamental considerations. The culmination of this is that economic growth that should always be the precursor to development can sometimes be inimical to it. (The manifestation of this is a trade-off between growth and development, which is almost endemic in certain regions and exists in smaller and subtler measure elsewhere.) Perhaps the most straightforward indicators of this problem are the magnitude of poverty reduction and income and non-income disparities, as indicated in the preceding chapters.

This rather adverse disconnect between growth and economic development makes it necessary to classify economic growth into two categories: economic growth that is pro-development and that which does not encourage development. It should be noted that the latter includes economic growth that does not do much for underdevelopment and could on occasion even deter it. We have to begin to distinguish growth in terms of its developmental impact or the absence of it. In this context there are three types of growth that can occur:

1. Growth rates that do not have any impact on development or the fructification of any of its objectives.
2. Growth rates that facilitate an increase in developmental objectives.
3. Growth rates that, in the course of increasing, have a regressive or negative impact on development. Thus, in real term such increases in the growth rates should be assigned a much lower value than their respective numerical magnitude.

In discussions about growth, when we cite that country A has had double-digit growth rates whereas country B has had, say, a 5 per cent growth rates, do we differentiate between growth that helps or even facilitates the achievement of developmental goals and that which doesn't? In sheer nominal terms, growth rate in country A is higher than in B. However, if the higher growth rate does not result in any changes that will help development, the question that arises is whether we can infer that A's growth performance is better than B's. Observably, we cannot. If the pursuit of certain strategies or the implementation of some measures does not help in tapping the reservoir of skills, talent, knowledge competences and inputs that a country is endowed with it represents, effectively, a loss of potential opportunity creation and consequently growth.

Thus, among the most frequent misjudgments in assessing overall economic performance arises from viewing a higher economic growth rate as equivalent to a commensurate increase in levels of development and vice versa. For all the rhetoric about development, growth-accounting estimates do not provide us with an indication of qualitative constituents of growth. This is a flaw that needs to be remedied for more accuracy in evaluations and inferences about economic performance.

The concept of growth in real terms should be expanded to include other socio-economic variables besides inflation. One of the counter-arguments to this may be that it is difficult to quantify qualitative changes; while it is true that to account for certain 'intangible' variables and qualitative improvements in a mathematically precise method is difficult, these can certainly be incorporated for growth assessments.

In order to ascertain and examine the nature of growth that is occurring in any country there are certain mathematical and econometric applications and tools. Besides this, the human development index is a fairly comprehensive indicator of the trends in development in any nation. Having said this, it is also true that there is scope for another instrument that would enable a more exhaustive understanding of the underpinnings of economic growth in a particular region. I suggest the construct of the production function of development so that it would be possible to make fairly accurate assessments about the impact that economic growth in a country will have on development indicators. One of its foremost applications would obviously be to facilitate a priori the differentiation between growth measures or initiatives that would make a negligible contribution to development from those that make a significant contribution to developmental parameters.

One of the distinct advantages of the production function would be its ability to provide a fair indication of the durability or sustainability of economic progress. Knowing some of the adverse consequences of inappropriate and unfavourable measures well before or shortly after implementation could spare poor countries the agony of having to wait until certain adverse repercussions begin to unravel. Conversely, the production function for development would also indicate the potentially favourable initiatives that a region needs to put into place if it is to expedite the process of development.

More often than not growth-accounting estimates do not include a very wide range of parameters, which affect the quality of growth and play a crucial role in the process of development. Conventional growth-accounting studies exclude some aspects that are important determinants of economic progress. For instance, the costs of opportunities foregone by the pursuit of strategies that do not do much for employment provision and poverty reduction lie outside the purview of growth accounting. Acceleration of growth-achieved at the expense of other sectors or by deceleration of progress in other socio-economic categories are crucial variables that are either excluded from growth-accounting estimates or not accounted for adequately. This is hardly surprising because there exist many non-monetized gains and benefits that arise from the pursuit of certain non-pecuniary activities, most of which are linked to social welfare provision and the advantages conferred by natural endowments such as forests and fertile soil, which enable individuals to eke out means of subsistence for themselves.

Even abounding economic progress is not a pretext to overlook those sections of society that have been stripped of their livelihoods as a result of measures that have destroyed their means of sustenance. A reduction in the source of non-monetized benefits results in an increase in non-monetized losses and the net outcome of this is a setback to the process of development. Excluding a terrain of important variables from growth-accounting estimates does not change either the significance that these have in the process of economic development or reduce the damaging and unrecoverable costs of reducing the quantum of these 'non-monetary' benefits; these need to be represented in growth-accounting estimates. For instance, soil erosion and indiscriminate deforestation have resulted in environmental degradation and estimates that did not account for these consequences (or, if they did, inadequately) did not alter the grave challenges that these have brought in their wake.

According to the World Resources report (2005), 'It is often difficult to assign a monetary value in the economic system to goods and services on which the poor rely. Some have a market value when sold abroad but many are consumed locally and do not enter into the formal economy. In effect the poor exists in an informal and often unrecognized economy. This has led to the systematic undervaluation of the assets of the poor and the under-estimation of the potential benefits of the sound eco-system management

The defining principle of the production function of development would be the juxtaposition of growth rate of GDP or any other denominator of national income considered appropriate as an input in the multidimensional process of development. Undoubtedly, the construction of such a tool would be a complicated exercise that would entail accounting for as inputs an entire gamut of variables, including those that are perceived as more intangible, such as the efficiency and effectiveness of with which institutions in a country function, the quality of governance and practices of gender-based social discrimination. Besides the inherent limitations of quantifying certain inputs, the methodology that would be used in calculations and the framework that will be adopted for an exercise in development accounting would need incisive thinking and considerable discussion.

The analytical framework of the production function would thus include a wide range of variables, some of which would be excluded by conventional growth-accounting studies. For purposes of illustration, a simple and some would even say rudimentary development production function can be written as:

$$D = \mathrm{f}(G) + (I) + (I^*) + Go + PR \qquad \text{(i)}$$

where $D$ denotes economic development; $G$ denotes growth rate of GDP or GNP (per capita); $Go$ denotes governance; $I$ denotes physical and social infrastructure provision; $I^*$ denotes innovation; and $PR$ denotes poverty reduction.

Undeniably, the measurement of a parameter such as governance would not be easy but, on the basis of the expediency and effectiveness of performance of government agencies, it would be possible to construct an index. This may not be as precise an indicator of the variable concerned but it would be a close approximation of the status quo.

In the context of development, an ideal scenario would be one where every increment in growth translates into an equivalent increase in developmental gain. Such a situation is veritably non-existent in contemporary times. Conceptually, this production function will be a useful principle because it provides a benchmark or yardstick in terms of which the current nature and impact of growth strategy can be evaluated. In terms of the production function of development, the prevalence of such a feature may be expressed as:

$$D = f(G) \qquad \qquad \text{(ii)}$$

The avowed prioritization of growth-maximization policies without an emphasis on ensuring that the other prerequisites of development are in place would provide a panacea for underdevelopment if there exists an autonomous transmission mechanism from growth to development. However a self-propelling transmission mechanism from growth to development does not exist, thus the priority assigned to increasing economic growth rates alone has not mitigated the problems confronting the underdeveloped world.

The production function for development would enable ascertaining the relative importance of each parameter or factor of production in the process of economic development. Thus, by enabling an assessment of the parameters involved in the process of development this production function would shed light on the existent and foreseeable deterrents that would reduce or whittle away at the impact that growth can have on development. Indicating the other variables that are more, or at least as, important as the rate of growth, would be a pointer to the other spheres that should be worked upon if the rate of development is to be increased. For example, in a scenario where poverty-reduction initiatives and institutional reform needs to be stepped up the production function of development would indicate that the impact of growth-inducing measures on development would be limited in the absence of concerted initiatives towards poverty reduction and institutional reform.

Visualize another instance: an increase in GDP growth that arises as a result of an expansion of investment that is financed by aid inflows or external borrowings. As corroborated by empirical evidence, it is likely that the gains that ensue in such a scenario would be transient unless some benefits of enhanced incomes are transmitted to a larger proportion of the population instead of being confined to a minuscule proportion. Furthermore, the structural adjustments that external borrowings invariably compel usually decree negative implications for economic development.

Evidently, once such a production function is complete, however tenuous a task it may have been, its usefulness to economics will be profound. It would enable us to estimate the development quotient of growth that has occurred or will occur in a country or region over a certain period of time. Extrapolating the development quotient of growth would, thus, provide us with an important basis for classifying the nature of growth. The production function of development would be an important tool that would enable the differentiation, with greater precision, of the probable impact that growth enhancing measures will have. Conservatively speaking, it would then be possible to arrive at a fairly accurate approximation of what may be termed as growth elasticity of development, or the responsiveness of development to increments in growth. For instance, if the highest growth elasticity of development is 1 it is most likely that most elasticity estimates will be greater than 0 and less than 1.

As such, if estimated growth elasticity is between 0 and 0.5 it means that the increments in growth will result in an improvement in development indicators but the extent of this progress will be less than proportionate to the increase in economic growth rates. On the basis of empirical evidence about the subject so far, a fair number of countries in Asia would fall into this category.

If the estimated growth elasticity of development is between 0.5 and 0.8 this clearly denotes an instance where the link between growth and development is a strong one; this would indicate that the country or region concerned has achieved a certain level of economic progress or reduction in underdevelopment. The presence of transmission mechanisms, such as poverty reduction, human capital formation and effective institutions, strengthens the link between growth and development because it facilitates easier percolation of growth benefits to lower income groups.

If the growth elasticity of development is equal to 1, it means that every increment in growth will result in a commensurate increase in the extent of development. Sadly, this is a feature that is conspicuous by its absence. Growth matters; perhaps even more important, however, are the mechanisms or measures underlying it. This is an issue where the saying that 'the end justifies the means' is appropriate. In the context of economic progress the underpinnings of growth will determine the extent or magnitude of ensuing gain.

Thus, the development quotient of growth will make it easier to make a cogent and quick assessment of the relative importance of other variables towards economic development. If a country has a low growth elasticity of development it means that it has a low development quotient. This implies that there are other variables that are more significant than, or at least as crucial as growth and not assigning importance to these inputs would deter growth from having a greater impact on economic development. This sheds light on the other spheres that need to be worked upon if development is to be stepped up. The thrust of policy measures to induce growth in a region or country that has a low development quotient will not do much to step up the pace of development.

Having thus enumerated the principle and the framework of the production function of development, we proceed to the next chapter which will elucidate the evolution of the development paradigm.

# 20
# The Development Paradigm: Its Evolution and Importance

Victor Hugo once spoke about 'an idea whose time has come'. The need for global economic development is long overdue, and yet it continues to be an objective that is either underachieved or unattained in most parts of the world.

Extracting insights from empirical evidence pertinent to global trends in growth and economic development represents one facet of the elucidation; the other pertains to using the observations made to build a development paradigm; I will proceed to do this on the basis of observations and inferences arrived at so far.

Having provided a description of the basis on which economic growth may be classified, coupled with an outline of the production function of development, which can be a tool of effective a priori assessment of growth outcomes, the next step is to work towards the evolution of a new development paradigm.

## Evolution of the development paradigm

The lessons drawn from economic experience will make a valuable contribution towards attaining an extremely important objective; that of evolving a paradigm that will be an effective guiding principle. The realization that growth is a necessary but not sufficient condition for development should be reflected much more than it presently is in general economic analysis. The most important step in this direction would be to accept that growth is an input in the process where the final composite output is development. This will be the fundamental principle that will guide the evolution of the development paradigm.

The development paradigm would consist of three constituents or fundamentals. These are:

1. Growth rate of GDP that has a moderate to high development quotient.
2. Effective economic management (EEM).
3. Reform (economic and non-economic).

### An enunciation of the P-EPP principle

The first constituent of this paradigm would be a multipronged growth strategy, which may be defined as one that is rooted in what I describe as a P-EPP principle. This means the pursuit of a growth-oriented strategy that is pro-environment, people and prosperity. The fact that measures pursued so far have hardly ever been in consonance with this rule of thumb is not a revelation. The baffling fact is that, despite enduring the irreversibly damaging consequences of environmental damage and the ubiquitous deprivation that exists in large parts of the developing world, the thrust of economic progress is starkly single-pronged.

Notably, those nations that maybe ranked as the most promising in the world have partially adopted P-EPP. Thus, the United States, India, China and East Asia (which are fairly divergent systemically and structurally) have in common the fact that they pursued measures that embody some tenets of P-EPP but each also has a distinct component that is non-P-EPP.

The production function for development would enable us to ascertain with a higher degree of precision the extent by which a particular growth strategy diverges from the P-EPP principle. However, until we have such a tool, an analysis of the empirics of growth in a particular region indicates whether economic progress is P-EPP, partly P-EPP or non-P-EPP. The immediate implication of this would be that a 10 per cent annual growth rate (for instance) that is based on the P-EPP axiom would bring in its wake a set of outcomes entirely different from 10 per cent non-P-EPP growth rate of GDP.

Countries that have experienced high growth rates for a certain period of time but have not witnessed significant improvements in employment, poverty reduction and other human development indicators are obviously those that have not pursued a path to economic progress that is oriented towards the P-EPP principle.

The global economy has unravelled before us numerous instances of economic prosperity that stems from measures that are not consonant with the P-EPP principle, at least not entirely. Perhaps it is this fact that has obscured the need for broadening the basis on which growth rates increase. It is not surprising that inclusive development is a term used rather frequently and seldom achieved. It maybe defined as a process of economic progress that will ensure the percolation of the benefits of growth to those who find themselves mired in abject poverty and deprivation.

Over 1985–2000 only 16 developing countries had a per capita income growth that was more than 3 per cent per annum. Fifty-five per cent had a per capita income increase that was less than 2 per cent and 23 per cent had negative growth (International Labour Organization Report on Globalization, 2004).

Transforming the nature of growth is an impending challenge that confronts most nations in this world; these include those who have successful and vibrant economies, those that are struggling to step up progress and those who can barely manage to keep their financial systems afloat. The reason for this is a globalized imperative – the objective of sustainable development. Considerations that have been relegated to the periphery of decision-making need to be accorded overarching importance, not just to ensure the attainment of some long-term goal, as some would say, but to sustain present levels of progress and to ensure that this does not taper off for a very long time. This is not intonation of pessimism but realism.

Cutting across all the reasons just implied, consider a single fundamental. In the global economy there are hardly any initiatives that can be as tactical and essential as the pursuance of the P-EPP principle. Market expansion is at the core of attractive financial bottom lines and it is the pursuance of the P-EPP principle that is becoming the pivot of increasing demand and the expanding markets.

When the benefits of economic progress are enclaved it shuts out huge potential markets because those who are bereft of the means of sustenance or who lack the basic amenities required for a minimally decent standard of living represent a large chunk of latent demand that is not tapped. When a sizable proportion of the world's population can barely eke out a livelihood it imposes severe constraints on their affordability and the net outcome of this is a slower pace of opportunity creation. Crass as this may sound, the fact is that, when viewed over a longer time horizon, the persistence of this feature does not reflect much commercial logic. If the extent of poverty and levels of unemployment had been much less this would have meant a higher aggregate global income and obviously bigger markets and a quickened pace and increased extent of opportunity creation.

Those who live on the margins of existence are not a minority, they account for over 1.5 billion of the world's population. Tremendous wealth did not do much to alter the stubborn persistence of underdevelopment. We are faced with a rather peculiar situation in the global economy. On the one hand, phenomenal economic progress has occurred, despite measures that were not poverty reducing or environment friendly. On the other hand, its biggest beneficiaries were the more developed or among the relatively prosperous in the developing world. Their diverse systems apart, countries that gained from globalization had a similarity in that they had moderate to high levels of EEM and patterns of economic progress were at least partly consistent with the P-EPP principle.

Ensuring that growth strategies adopted are based on the P-EPP principle entails two other constituents: effective economic management and economic reform. These elements can be discussed in extensive detail, enough to provide subject matter for another book. However, in the current context, it is the link that both these integral dimensions have with sustainable development that will be focused upon.

### Effective economic management

A country is endowed with resources that are both tangible and intangible and this gives it potential to have certain core competences. Perhaps even more important than a country's inherent resource endowments is the manner in which these inputs are mobilized and harnessed. EEM refers to the continuous endeavour to improve and optimize the management of a country's resources and create new sources of growth and opportunity creation. Innovation and human resource capital formation are important instruments in this process and, although policy-making sets the ground for measures that will provide a stimulus in this direction, much more needs to be done to ensure that the marginalized segments of society are participants in this process of opportunity creation. An alternative definition for EEM is the ability (or lack of ability) that a country's governance, business corporations, civil society and institutions have in the management of its inputs, and this includes economic growth.

A multidimensional growth strategy presupposes a broader and more inclusive definition of capital accumulation. It is important to think of capital not merely as a financial parameter but to extend its definition to all those processes, inputs and facilitators, such as managerial, organizational and technical capabilities, that enhance the effectiveness of a given quantity of resources.

Equally important at this point in time is the need to explicitly account for all those parameters and structures that help not just in the attainment of growth but also in the management and optimization of economic progress once this is achieved. If one were to use a simple analogy to underscore the point made: compare a business enterprise with a nation. It is true that the vast difference between the scale of operation involved in a single company and the relatively gigantic and multivariate task of managing a country render this a highly inappropriate example in some ways but a modest-sized company cannot disassociate its profitability benchmarks from an entire range of functions that include marketing, human resource development, corporate governance, business development and inventory management.

Acquiring the resources required represents one aspect of enterprise management; the other equally crucial one relates to organizing the tangible and intangible inputs that a firm, company or corporation has in order to create a structure or structures that will enable it to optimize its financial outlays. This may seem a rather simplified interpretation of management practice but it makes an important point: evidently, a business entity cannot adopt a narrow-based view of its operation, functional and viability norms. Scale this fact up to a larger context and we see that a growth strategy cannot be effective if it does not account for the less visible or intangible inputs that it needs to harness to maximize the growth-enhancing impact of any measure. Knowledge capital, governance and unexplored technical and innovative capabilities are factors that are critical to economic progress; this has been widely acknowledged but somehow policy practice and current growth prescriptions do not accord enough importance to the creation of structures that enable harnessing and productive utilization of these factors.

It is worth noting that one of the preoccupations of economic analysis has been to evaluate the reason underlying the differential impact that identical levels of investment have on apparently similar countries. What has made or will make the difference?

The answer to this could be a vague one that attributes the differential to the random variable (for all practical purposes one might as well call it the X factor). Alternately, we could attempt to demystify whether the better performance of certain countries could be the result of parameters or structures that that were more conducive to economic progress relative to those that prevailed (or didn't) in others. Given a certain quantity of resources, the profound effect that effective economic management (EEM) has in the determination of sustainable progress is repeatedly demonstrated by the stories of economic success and the sad tribulations of failure. Effective economic management is, thus, as integral to the effectiveness of economic progress as is the quantitative increase in national income growth rates. It is an equally pivotal input/prerequisite if a country is to have a process of growth that brings with it development. Alternately expressed, the achievement of growth that is consistent with the P-EPP principle requires EEM.

Inevitably the question that arises: what indicates EEM? The perpetuity of underdevelopment mirrors the lack of EEM, as do the present outcomes of globalization. There are a number of indicators that can be used to assess the extent of EEM; however, the most holistic of these would be the effectiveness and scope with which institutions in any country function. Added to this would also be the expeditiousness and efficiency with which the spheres or areas of institutional reform are addressed.

Defining institutions is not an easy task because the term is a fairly collective and wide-ranging one that encompasses the role of political, governmental and social variables in determining the gap between potential economic achievement and its actual realization. Having said it is relevant to cite Douglass North's well-known definition of institution. According to North, institutions are constraints that structure political, economic and social interactions and consist of formal regulation such as constitutions, laws and property rights and informal measures, such as sanctions, taboos, customs, traditions, codes of conduct, conventions and norms of behaviour.

Institutions that operate at the macroeconomic and microeconomic level include those that are controlled by the government and those that lie outside its purview. These exert a considerable and sometimes predominant influence on the transmission mechanisms or channels through which the benefits of growth will percolate. Thus, the magnitude of poverty reduction, the performance of human development indicators and the improvements in the distribution of income are linked to the efficacy with which institutional mechanisms work. Douglass North, in his Nobel Prize Lecture (1933), stated, 'It is the interaction between institutions and organization that shapes the institutional evolution of an economy. If institutions are rules of the game organizations and their entrepreneurs are their players.'

Thus, the principles underlying policy formulation represent one determinant of its impact; another equally vital aspect pertains to the efficiency with which measures enacted are implemented. If those institutions that can transmit benefits of an increase in GDP growth rates to the lower income groups are strong, resilient and well functioning it is very likely that rising levels of development will be the accompaniment to an increase in economic growth. Such a scenario will also embody an instance of effective economic management.

Besides the prevalent structure of a country's institutional framework and the efficiency with which it functions, the investment climate that exists in a particular economy also provides us with another indicator of EEM. The World Bank studied the impact that the investment climate has on growth and productivity. One of its findings, as mentioned in the World Development Report of 2005, was:

> A good investment climate is not just about generating profits for firms – if that were the goal the focus could be narrowed to minimizing costs and risks . . . A good investment climate is one that benefits everyone in two dimensions. First it serves society as a whole, rather than just firms, through its impact on job creation, lower prices and broadening the tax base. Second it embraces all firms not just larger or influential firms.

One of the most distinct manifestations of a good governance is the investment climate and the far-reaching significance of its economic role on the costs of production, competitiveness of industry and other sectors and the extent and pace of opportunity creation is undeniable.

India and China demonstrated that it is the discernible change in the investment climate facilitated by initiation of certain policies collectively termed as liberalization that led to an expansion of investment and an increase in productivity. As a matter of fact, if liberalization is viewed as an initiative that is directed towards facilitating continuous improvements in the investment climate, economic liberalism may have had a more positive impact in developing countries. It is through a better, sounder and more reliable investment climate that governance can ease out constraints on economic growth, and it is the existence of a strongly entrenched political economy of underdevelopment that impedes a faster improvement in the investment climate. For instance, India, has a fairly good investment climate as a result of taking certain steps that gave it a more effective regulatory and institutional framework. As elucidated in Part I of this book, however harnessing the tremendous economic potential of the Indian economy entails further improvements in its investment climate if opportunity creation is to be stepped up. China, too, needs to initiate certain changes in its institutional environment.

Thus, investment climate is the transmission mechanism through which EEM will impact the costs and profitability of not just the commercial establishment but the duration of economic progress. In the context of any national economy it is probable that the coexistence of economic progress with low levels of EEM will result an investment climate that is not very satisfactory and in certain instances even unsatisfactory.

Governance is an important input; more often not it can decide the duration of economic progress. The imminent question is how much sustained economic progress would be affected by the quality of governance and this includes an entire spectrum of variables – some would say the 'intangible inputs' – such as the institutional and regulatory framework, the investment climate and the appropriateness of the policies implemented insofar as the indigenous context of a country is concerned. Plausibly, the answer is: *considerably!*

It is not as if those nations that have economic and political systems that are underpinned by EEM do not have their problems of inefficiencies in the allocation of investment, implementation of core-sector projects or, for that matter, in the way their financial and banking spheres function. EEM is not an idiom of perfection, it does not preclude instances of corruption or inefficiency in the allocation of resources. Countries with a high level of EEM do not have perfectly functioning economies; however, they do have systems that are characterized, by and large, by the productive and efficient allocation and utilization of a bulk of their resources.

Transient irregularities in an environment that is predominated by effective management, not only of the financial resources mobilized and deployed but also of an entire structure of pro-development institutions, policies and non- policy mechanisms, such as civil society, is at stark variance with a scenario where the lead story is one of a consistent underdevelopment or a prolonged imbalance between growth and development.

Although India and China are the frontrunners as far as promising growth prospects are concerned, the constraints and challenges that confront these nations evidence the scope for improving their performance in economic management. The Indian and Chinese economies can be described as having moderate levels of EEM and this is quite unlike most other countries in the subcontinent, which score fairly low insofar as EEM is concerned. As a matter of fact, regions in South Asia represent instances of economic growth against a backdrop where corruption runs rife, institutional weaknesses are hardly unusual and levels of infrastructure and human capital are much lower than they should be. A note about the present situation of some nations in South Asia is provided in the appendix.

From an academic perspective this is an interesting phenomenon because it demonstrates that an array of serious setbacks did not hinder growth prospects. Furthermore, it also reveals the immense potential of South Asia, where moderate levels of economic progress occur despite the present constraints. South Asia must improve its EEM, even as it finds itself at the centre of what may be termed as the Asian economic renaissance. Herein, it is obvious that improved delivery systems, a faster pace of infrastructural provision and narrowing the scope of crony capitalism would foster much higher levels of growth and development in the region.

The coexistence of moderate to high levels of economic growth with an unsatisfactory performance with regard to economic management will most certainly not translate into higher levels of development. Moreover, if the benefits of growth do not percolate beyond a small proportion of the population rather low or negligible levels of EEM are indicated.

The fall-out of having low levels of EEM despite increasing levels of economic progress is the existence of alarming inadequacies in social infrastructure provision and an extent of poverty that can be mitigated with an improvement of resource allocation. This is the situation that characterizes India and South Asia. Poverty and pervasive malnourishment in the lower income groups in a nation that is underdeveloped and poor is inevitable; however, the existence of these ills in a nation that is among the fastest-growing denotes a pressing need to increase the EEM quotient. Notably, the inability to mobilize resources is a matter of concern; perhaps it is even more disturbing to witness the coexistence of sizable resources with a tardy record of improvements in human development indicators.

Thus, the take-off to higher levels of development entails much more than higher levels of growth. Even if a country experiences an increase in its GDP or GNP growth rates over a few years it does not always fructify into rising levels of development.

Generally speaking, a country's trajectory of development can be divided into four distinct phases. The first phase is the take-off to growth. If this is in a context that has moderate to high levels of EEM there will be developmental gain and the lag between the first and the second phase would be a shorter one. The second phase would encompass a take-off to higher levels of EEM and economic reform. Understandably this would occur more expeditiously in better-managed countries than those nations with a low quotient of EEM. The third phase would represent the take-off to development. The fourth phase would be the take-off to sustainable development.

Having described the trajectory of development as four distinct stages a mention must be made of some important points: These are:

1. It must be noted that the interval of time between each phase may vary from being rather short to extremely long.
2. Empirical evidence is replete with instances of countries where the take-off to growth does not always result in an increase in EEM and reform.
3. A quickened pace of development involves stepping up EEM and economic reform; at which point, after its take-off, development will accelerate depends upon the pace at which economic management is improving and reform is occurring. Thus, once the take-off to growth has occurred, if the lack of EEM and economic reform persists it is improbable that the take-off to development will happen.

In terms of the development paradigm India for instance is decidedly at stage 3 where the take off to development has happened, but the fructification of socio-economic goals has to occur at a much faster pace if it is to achieve sustainable development (stage 4). See Figure 20.1.

The Economic Survey of India (2006–7) says: 'The economy appears to have decidedly taken of and moved from a phase of moderate growth into a new phase of high growth. Achieving the necessary escape velocity to move from tepid growth into sustained high- growth trajectory requires careful consideration of two issues and three priorities. The two issues are: the sustainability of high growth with moderate inflation and the inclusive nature of such high growth.'

Development does not represent a static point of irreversible prosperity; it is certainly a situation that one cannot be complacent about; it is not a situation that is devoid of any asymmetries, inequalities and disparities. In the contemporary world, development can be described as the prevalence of high levels of per capita affluence and the absence of absolute poverty. It is, thus, about having every individual obtaining an entitlement to have a certain standard of well being; this does not presuppose equity but it requires bridging the glaring imbalances between economic progress, EEM and reform.

In the context of the development paradigm, the concept of inclusiveness denotes the formulation and implementation of strategy that encompasses an increase in the three constituents of the development paradigm. The deterrent that preempts the forces of development from working expediently and effectively is a prolonged imbalance between the constituents of the development paradigm – the rising levels of economic growth and progress are not accompanied by an increasing quotient of EEM and reform. It is this that forms the crucible of instability, unrest and upheaval in the contemporary global economy. It is minimizing this imbalance, which deters and preempts a faster pace of development, that should be placed on the centre-stage of all economic agendas.

Once achieved, economic development needs to be sustained and it is this that entails a continued improvement in the process of economic

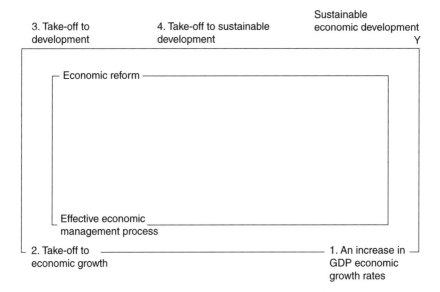

*Figure 20.1* The development paradigm

management and reform. Importantly, at any point on the trajectory of development a country can lapse into a scenario of reduced levels of economic progress, declining standards of living and rising levels of poverty if there is a persistent deterioration in its EEM quotient or economic reform comes to a standstill.

As shown in Figure 20.1 at any point between 1 and 4 a slackened pace of EEM and reform can bring in its wake problems such as an increase in the inequalities of income, a lack of opportunity creation, socio-economic polarization and other features that weaken the sustainability of development. In terms of Figure 20.1, it is, thus, the proximity to point Y or the distance from Y that indicates the degree of development or underdevelopment in any nation.

When viewed within the construct of the development paradigm, the extremely elusive ideal scenario would be characterized by high levels of economic progress and EEM along with an expeditious pace of reform. Given that the ideal hardly ever exists, the more realistic combination would consist of increasing levels of economic progress with a rising quotient of EEM and reform; in this instance, the extent by which resource management improves or the pace at which reform occurs may be slower than the increase in economic growth. This is the situation that exists in those developing countries that are taking strides towards economic progress, such as India and China. Sadly, this a combination that does not exist in most parts of the developing world. Instead, the precarious coexistence of some or no economic progress with negligible levels of EEM and reform that perpetuates itself from one decade to another is an acutely unfavourable feature.

As a matter of fact, a prolonged delay between increasing levels of economic growth and a faster pace of development reflects a clear and sizable inadequacy of opportunity creation, particularly among the lower income groups. Improving economic management is a tough call, particularly if economic progress occurs amid rampant corruption and political cronyism and despite low standards of EEM. It is not uncommon to find that measures that underlie temporary spurts of prosperity are not conducive to increasing EEM. For instance, trade liberalization that adversely corrodes the interests of small farmers or cutbacks in fiscal deficits made by a reduction in the allocations towards health care and education are instances of initiatives that may be growth enhancing over the short term but are certainly indicative of poor economic management. Raising national income growth rates through policies that impede other measures directed towards tackling the fundamental constraints and systemic inefficiencies that cause underdevelopment would definitely crowd out EEM.

Thus, whether or not high economic growth would result in a faster pace of employment provision or opportunity creation is determined largely by the ability of policy and non-policy measures to direct resources towards strengthening transmission mechanisms of growth. The existence of weakened transmission mechanisms, or their inadequacy, is an unmistakable indicator of poor economic management. This takes us on to a concise description of the features that preempt, discourage or enfeeble the systems and structures that are required for a high degree or extent of EEM.

Underlying the rather frequently occurring trade-off between growth and development is this conflict of objectives that arises between two realms that may not have always seem distinctly opposed to each other but certainly have a set of priorities that are fairly divergent. Vested interests of certain powerful social and political lobbies may have considerations that run counter to those that are rooted in developmental imperatives. Such special-interest agendas work through institutions that fall within the domain of the state and outside of it to undermine either subtly or overtly all those mechanisms that are required to initiate and propel development.

Across a number of countries in the developing and underdeveloped world it is development that becomes the casualty of an implicit and sometimes explicit tussle between those who support, perpetuate and advocate growth-inducing measures that are disembodied from developmental concerns and those who pursue and uphold measures that are consistent with the attainment of development.

The political economy of underdevelopment is pitted, thus, against that of development but this regressive feature cannot be ascribed merely to a clash of interests between the haves and have-nots. The problem is more complex. It is not as if the political economy of development comprises merely individuals from the lower rungs of the socio-economic hierarchy; as a matter of fact, it is a heterogeneous mix of powerful business interests, development agencies and intermediaries such as civil society and citizen pressure groups. However, on the overall the status quo in most developing countries is one where the collective strength wielded by the political economy of underdevelopment outweighs the clout exercised by those that uphold developmental considerations. Undeniably, it is the poorer sections that bear the worst brunt of the consequences that arise from this feature. Those with a sizable proportion of poor individuals, who lack bargaining position, are likely to have a situation where the forces of development are overridden by underdevelopment.

The underpinnings of strategy formulation in countries that have a large expanse of poverty and stark disparities in income are more likely to be tilted in favour of those groups and vested interests that align themselves with structures that perpetuate underdevelopment. The adage 'poverty stokes itself' certainly applies. Underdevelopment persists not because of resource inadequacies but as a result of a political economy that impedes mobilized resources from being efficiently allocated in sufficient measure and utilized in accordance with developmental priorities. Perhaps at this point a clarification needs to be made with regard to the impact that the political economy of underdevelopment has had on growth. As we have seen, there are numerous instances of rising economic growth rates against a backdrop where forces that perpetuate the ills of underdevelopment are distinctly stronger and more entrenched than those that foster development. If this had not been the case, it is possible that the political economy of underdevelopment would have perished or shrunk to so minuscule a size that it hardly mattered.

At this point it would be useful to cite the instance of one of the most underdeveloped regions of the world – Sub-Saharan Africa (SSA). It is not as if SSA did not pass through phases of increasing economic growth rates. It did; and yet development has been a rather elusive feature in this part of the globe.

The phrase 'poverty trap' has been used rather frequently in the context of SSA; however, it can convey a rather misleading concept. Somehow, the 'poverty trap' has come to be understood as a phenomenon that arises from the stubborn persistence of low income, which in turn perpetuates low savings and investment. This is a correct description but it represents only one aspect of seemingly unrelenting underdevelopment. Empirical evidence tells us that there is no such thing as irreversible economic progress. India and China's economic experience itself bears indisputable testimony to this fact. Insofar as the concept of poverty trap conveys that it is extremely difficult to attain economic development in many regions of the continent it is useful.

However, by no means should it continue to underscore the rather erroneous presumptions about the irrevocable nature of poverty in the underdeveloped nations of Africa, as anywhere else. As a result of policy improvements initiated in the mid-1990s, some of the nations in SSA have had lower levels of inflation and smaller fiscal deficits despite minimal cutbacks in public spending. Since the last decade middle income SSA countries have had an average annual per capita growth rate of nearly 4.5 per cent and their fiscal positions are improving. As far as the low income SSA countries are concerned, although there has been some economic progress, the challenge is to improve their fiscal and balance of payments situation. Over the last few decades on the aggregate the problem in SSA as a whole has not been the absence of growth but the inability of countries to sustain economic progress. This gives to improvements in their growth performance a fragile basis and it is strengthening the fiscal fundamentals and increasing the productivity of both public and private investment that will is a requisite for consistent economic growth. It is the macroeconomic environment that will be the most important determinant of financial and fiscal stability and the sustainability of savings and investments.

The dramatic reversals of economic progress in the Congo provides us with a rather sad account of weak governance and institutions, which finally led to a precipitous decline in per capita incomes from almost $1000 during the mid 1980s to less than $900 by 2000. The rising oil prices over 1979–86 led to an acceleration of economic growth in the region. There was an increase in public investment, not surprisingly given the expansion of government revenues. However, this spurt of economic progress could not be sustained due to inappropriate policies, such as an overvalued exchange rate and incipient institutions, both of which were symptomatic of a lack of EEM.

The economic experience of a number of African countries elucidates that what exists is a vicious circle between low levels of economic progress, a negligible quotient of EEM and the absence or blatant inadequacy of reform that perpetrates poverty, resource mobilization and the inadequacy of capital accumulation. Undoubtedly, a better quality of governance could have prevented the adverse setbacks.

Poverty is the outcome of mechanisms that constrict resource accessibility and, therefore, it is important to differentiate between attributing underdevelopment to a lack of resources and viewing poverty as an outcome of a much wider vicious circle that involves governance, politics and polarization.

It is striking at the root of what I term as a 'rut', which exists because of the political economy of underdevelopment and negligible EEM, that would unshackle a country from the trappings of poverty and deprivation. It is this that needs to be the overriding focus of government. The endeavour to garner financial resources in the absence of simultaneous initiatives to improve the quality of governance and economic management would mean that economic growth would be a temporary phenomenon.

Evidently, if economic growth is nurtured by those considerations that derive large gains from the existence of rampant deprivation and poverty, economic progress would be a short-term phenomenon. Herein, sporadic spurts of economic prosperity, usually fuelled by unsustainable measures such as external borrowings in a number of underdeveloped and developing nations, don't make much of a dent in the prevalent extent of underdevelopment. More often than not, one ramification of not having EEM or having a 'vibrant' political economy of underdevelopment is external indebtedness. It must be noted that countries that are unduly reliant on foreign aid, borrowings and other financial arrangements with international financial institutions find themselves almost bereft of a bargaining position that enables them to have an appropriate growth strategy. A situation wherein strategy formulation is conditioned by the priorities of structural adjustment programmes rather than the exigent developmental priorities of a country reflects most undoubtedly an erosion of economic democracy. This is among the most damaging consequences that can arise when the political economy of underdevelopment outweighs the political economy of development.

Thus, it would be unrealistic to expect the practice of EEM in a nation where policy choices are steered by the political economy of underdevelopment. Recurrent reminders corroborate that the disbursement of financial assistance, which is linked to structural adjustment programmes of the type that certain Latin American countries received during the 1980s and some African countries obtained over the 1990s, decreed adverse consequences and runs counter to the principle of EEM.

## The curative: a transition from resource mobilization to resource management

As far as most developing nations are concerned, fostering a higher extent of EEM does not require a dramatic interlude of upheaval because there exists a political economy of development, however narrow based this may be, in most underdeveloped and developing countries and strengthening and expanding this needs to be at the core of growth strategies. At the household and village levels, measures to improve poverty reduction, human capital formation and employment (including self-employment) do not require much pecuniary resource. The use of micro-finance and its encouraging outcomes in villages that have had extreme poverty in Bangladesh, as also the case (to a lesser extent) in India, underscore that it is not merely the quantity of finance available but that the qualitative aspect of its disbursement also determines the outcomes of poverty alleviation and human development. Even in situations of extreme deprivation, improvements in resource management combined with marginal increments of investment at the village and provincial level can result in discernible levels of progress. Moreover, an improvement in the plight of the lower income groups would also give them a bargaining position or a 'voice', as it were, and this will reinforce the dynamics of development.

In a scenario of extreme underdevelopment, ridden with civil unrest and political uncertainty, it is possible that increasing the extent of EEM would be preceded by tumult and upheaval. However, even in an environment of this kind, the attempts made to optimize the allocation and productivity of resources at the grassroots can have encouraging results. Understandably, the most difficult aspect of facilitating EEM arises in contexts that are completely devoid of it. It is in this realm that development agencies can play an important role in enabling the poorest countries to create the mechanisms and an environment that will foster EEM. Notably, the term 'role' here does not refer merely to financial assistance but to a package of measures that would enable the least developed nations to strengthen the political economy of development.

The persistence of poverty, deprivation and an untapped potential of opportunity creation represent some of the monumental costs of detracting from development considerations. However, even if development-linked considerations are obscured during the initial phase of economic progress, there are quite a number of instances wherein improvements in economic management occur once economic progress takes off in a country. Subsequent to an increase in economic growth rates, the implementation of poverty reduction policies, a higher degree of transparency and more expedient infrastructure provision indicate a rising level of EEM. On the whole, this has been the case in South Asia; however, the pace at which the extent of EEM rises needs to be stepped up. It is interesting to note that the impetus that EEM provides to a nation's economy is considerable. A huge amount of resources can be mobilized by significant improvements in the economic management of a country but, however resource abundant a nation may be, the lacunae of EEM results in an extremely suboptimal allocation of resources.

Empirical evidence has revealed repeatedly that it is not so much the availability or absence of resources (natural or financial) that defines the resource constraint but the presence or absence of the ability to harness resources that are available and to build on strengths or endowments that a country has that will determine how resource-abundant country is or how constrained it is.

It is unfortunate to encounter a scarcity of resources; it's even worse to have resources and not utilize them. Thus, among the most alarming resource constraints that a nation can be confronted with is an inadequacy or an absence of EEM.

Amid binding resource constraints the ability to step up economic progress seems an untenable objective. However the inadequacy of savings and investment is a challenge that can be surmounted by EEM. The East Asian economic experience provides an endorsement of this fact. In contrast, countries experience capital flight when resources are mismanaged in a manner that creates a dearth of productive investment opportunities. As such, by some means such as an infusion of foreign investment, if growth rates increase without an improvement in economic management they will perpetuate the poverty trap.

In a world where wealth abounds and there exists a huge amount of capital that needs to be ploughed into spheres that have productive, profitable and safe investment opportunities, mobility of capital and the success of resource mobilization efforts is decisively determined by EEM. An illustrative instance that corroborates this is the economic experience of Singapore.

## Singapore: exemplifying EEM

Singapore exemplifies one of the most illustrative manifestations of the stupendous impact that EEM can have in resource generation. Singapore was not a resource-abundant country during the early 1960s; its economic experience chronicles an ascent that was propelled by efficient governance systems and a rapid increase in human capital formation and productivity. By the early 1980s it was among East Asia's most promising nations and it is unequivocally among the most advanced nations of the contemporary global economy. Through high levels of foreign investment and technological advancement Singapore's economic growth rates rose and with it the nation developed at a pace that was unprecedented. Over three decades, beginning in the late 1960s, the city state's transformation into a developed nation was achieved over a much shorter time span than that in other advanced countries. The economic prescription that Singapore pursued was not a complicated one and the success that it brought in its wake was largely attributable to the creation of a system that was underpinned by EEM, a pragmatic government and an honest and productive civil service.

There are valuable insights that Asian developing nations can draw from the economic experience of Singapore. There has been some discussion about this aspect and, although there are economists who contend that we should not draw comparisons between Singapore and, for instance, India, as both these nations have vast differences in logistics and size, I uphold another view. Irrespective of the differences (every nation is a unique entity), there are certain elements of Singapore's economic experience that may be be applied to most developing nations.

Singapore demonstrated that the most important resource for any country is the ability to elicit extremely high levels of efficiency and productivity from endowments and inputs that it has and can acquire. It is not high levels of investment or technical advancement alone that explain the island's transformation but the strategic framework in which these have been utilized as instrumentalities of economic progress.

If massive infusions of investment and technical excellence were sufficient conditions for development then there would have been many more developed countries. The capability to utilize effectively, efficiently, productively and strategically the resources and strengths that a country has is the most important input. In the absence of this, the gains from an abundance of natural resources and technical expertise will be confined to an enclave. This fact is substantiated by a number of countries, such as those of Latin America and Russia.

Growth accounting, thus, has to account for the levels of EEM that exist in a particular region or country because the outcomes of resource mobilization and its deployment in a scenario where even moderate levels EEM exist will be different if not divergent from a context where this is absent. Whether EEM is categorized as a tangible constituent of development or an intangible one, its role in determining the course of economic progress and setting the pace of development is a profound one. Moreover, the levels of EEM among the most crucial determinants (if not the most important) of both the impact and also the nature of economic growth.

Amartya Sen's incisive research about poverty and issues related therein elucidated that the poor are poor because their set of capabilities is small, not because of what they do not have but because of what they cannot do. Poverty describes a situation of compressed opportunity creation and not a lack of opportunity. The accessibility that individuals do not have to a wide range of infrastructural goods makes it extremely difficult for them to use their own talent and skills to carve out even a basic livelihood. Thus, the remedy to constrained access is not merely enhanced mobilization but better allocation and management of resources.

## Reform: it cannot cease

Economic reform is the third constituent of the development paradigm. It must be mentioned that theoretically, although reform has been presented as a distinctly separate element, it cannot be disassociated from the EEM. Importantly, economic reform includes the process that facilitates an improvement in economic management and it also encompasses the measures that would encourage or even enable the adjustments that are required for sustaining economic progress and with it EEM. Thus, even if economic growth rates are increasing and a country has a reasonably good quotient of EEM, reform cannot be dispensed with if development is to be sustained.

Compare the process of reform in any country to the process of human evolution. The commonality is that both do not cease. At various levels of development a country has to adapt and reorient its systems to newer sources of economic progress. The distinguishing feature is the kind of reforms that a country needs to undertake. The US, Japan and India are not exempt from the process of reform but the composition of reform would differ in each instance.

For example, as the United States finds itself having to tackle its sizable trade deficit, rising costs, slackened social sector spending, increasing inequalities and a deterioration of standards of living in certain socio-economic categories, it provides the world with an endorsement of a fundamental fact that has been overlooked.

From the perspective of most manufacturers the efforts to maintain America's leadership in innovation and technology must begin with improvements in the basic education delivered by the US public schools . . .

In general there is a need for a more aggressive look at how existing economic development programmes could best reinforce a community development of a sound approach to building a more diversified and strengthened local economy. Reinforcing the focus of communities on building more diversified economic bases is one of means of attractive and retaining manufacturing companies. (Manufacturing in America: A Comprehensive Strategy to Address the Challenges of US Manufacturers (January 2004), *US Department of Commerce Report*)

It would thus be a mistake to assume that even a high degree of economic advancement takes away the imperatives of improving the quotient of EEM and reform.

Yet another corroboration of this fact is given to us by Japan, which was reeling under an economic slowdown for the five years leading up to 2004. The negligible growth phase that the country passed through was the result of a number of factors, a crucial one being the compelling need for reform in the country's financial sector. As the country exhibits signs of an economic recovery, with its growth rates inching up, it is evident that reform will be a vital constituent of Japan's economic agenda for some time to come: 'And Japan thrived. Indeed in the four decades after the Second World War it was the world's greatest success story. But the success was not everlasting.' (*The Economist*, 16 September 2006).

When Junichoro Koizumi took over the reins of government in Japan in 2001 the country's financial system was plagued with corruption, a lack of accountability and of course political patronage had played its definite role in eroding the effectiveness of government functioning. Increasing public spending by successive governments averted a worse deflation but the outcome of rising expenditures was an internal public debt situation that became worrisome. Finally it was obvious that reform was a task that Japan was not exempt from even though it was among the world's most advanced economies. Japan Post, a financial monolith which is among the world's largest banks with US$ 2.8 trillion in savings and life insurance accounts is characterized by the nexus between political lobbies and the investments that is made in certain public works projects.

Setting into motion the measures towards the privatization of Japan Post proved to be among Koizumi's toughest challenges, this was inevitable and he faced stiff resistance from the old-guard LDP (Liberal Democatic Party members). However despite the deterrents that came his way, Koizumi seemed to determined to privatize the country's postal saving system. Even, if the post office is not yet privatized, according to Yasuhisa Shiozaki, a deputy foreign minister, Koizumi destroyed the country's most powerful political machine and put an end to pork barrel politics (*The Economist*, 16 September 2006). Japan's economic recovery began in 2002 and the country is showing signs of strong resurgence at this point.

Shinzo Abe became the new leader of Japan in September 2006 and is, undeniably, steering the country onto the path of consistent economic recovery and buoyancy, which is the most important task he paces.

The imminent question is: is there a general model or package of economic reform? Empirical evidence tells us that the instruments (policy and non policy) of reform in each country vary in accordance to their respective socio-economic and political structures. However, cutting through these differences, there is a striking commonality. The fundamental function of economic reform in every country is similar: to create or transform systems and sustain structures that will support higher levels of growth and development.

Growth that is based on or propelled by EEM and economic reform will translate into higher levels of development. At the other extreme is a scenario where economic progress continues to be disembodied from improvements in the overall resource management of the country and economic reform.

In terms of the analysis presented there are some nations, such as India and China, that find themselves with significant levels of growth rates and a moderate quotient of EEM and economic reform. The crux of sustaining increasing levels of prosperity for these two is to step up the pace and extent of EEM and economic reform. Interestingly, even if one were to view some of the most advanced nations of the world, which are characterized by the prevalence of a high degree of EEM and economic reform, the compulsions of sustainable development spell out the need for a continuous process of upgrading resource management and systemic improvements.

Plausibly, the nature and extent of reform that developed nations require would be quantitatively minimal relative to the imperatives of EEM and reform in the developing world. Having said this, even in an environment of economic advancement, the improvements in these two constituents of the development paradigm comprises a vital dimension of sustainable development. Development is not a constant; its achievement represents one aspect of a nation's success and the other pertains irrevocably to the endeavour to sustain it.

Globalization has been a wondrously successful instrument of wealth creation; overall, however, so far globalism can at last be described as development neutral. Palpably, the inadequacies and weaknesses of economic reform across a wide spectrum of countries in the developing world cannot be isolated from the larger macrocosm of a process of globalization that could have been managed more effectively. This was not the case; instead a rather rapid pace of globalization occurred in conjunction with weakening transmission mechanisms. A desultory approach to financial liberalization, patterns of skewed trade liberalization and the narrowed scope for development agencies such as the United Nations stripped globalization of its transformative potential.

The resurgence of the neo-classical growth model did not have to relegate poverty and distributional considerations to the periphery of economic policy, but this is exactly what happened. The arbiter of this school of thinking was the generalized prescription of neo-liberalism, which guided the policies implemented for the preceding two decades. As has been elucidated in this book, empirical evidence reveals that that this was not the appropriate strategy for underdeveloped nations to pursue in the absence of measures to strengthen and build transmission mechanisms from growth to development.

Expectedly, hardly any of the least developed nations were among those that gained from globalism. Globalization could have played an important role as a facilitator of significant improvements in EEM in countries that were lacking in it but it did not.

Vast tracts of underdevelopment indicate the prevalence of low or negligible levels of EEM. The interplay between the political economy of underdevelopment that existed within least developed and developing countries and the larger reality of an ineffectively managed process of globalization would, inevitably, obviate development. Thus, the macrocosm of reform in the global economy requires that it becomes pro-development and this spells out a role for globalization that is much more inclusive and one that is that is based on structures that are much more consonant with the P-EPP principle of growth. Fundamentally this would entail the following.

(i) Competitiveness that is based on low wage costs should be driven by knowledge-driven core competences. Related to this key proposition, is the need to differentiate between marginal exploitative efficiency and marginal productivity. The former refers to efficiency-enhancing measures that aggravate unemployment, poverty and inequalities and the latter to those that are consistent with developmental considerations.

(ii) The fervent globalized advocacy and expeditious pursuit of strategies that are energy conserving, employment providing and poverty reducing.

(iii) As is the case with growth so also with liberalization; it is necessary that its goal extends beyond the purpose of unshackling market forces towards becoming a medium that will reinforce and spur the expansion of the political economy of development. The next phase of liberalism should avowedly focus on freeing countries from the stranglehold of a political economy of underdevelopment that constrains capital accumulation, EEM and reform.

(iv) In the same way that economic liberalization did not do much for development in a number of poorer countries, financial liberalization too became delinked from the larger objective of financial reform. Easing constraints on capital mobility and availability, freer exchange rates and an expansion of stock exchanges represents one aspect of financial reform. Another feature of financial development in an economy is its untapped potential for the expansion of products and services that would increase capital accumulation among the lower income groups and, in doing so, bridge the severe resource constraints that the underprivileged sections are confronted with. Even in instances where this is occurring its pace and extent needs to be stepped up. Plausibly, if the proliferation of financial products and services suited to the requirements of the poor occurs at a rate that is a fraction of those introduced for the relatively affluent the process of financial development would be greatly expedited.

(v) The narrowed scope of global governance functions undertaken mainly by the United Nations and the International Labor Organization did not augur well insofar as strengthening global development mechanisms was concerned. Concurrent with the shrinking role that these important institutions had in geopolitics was the ground that the Bretton Woods institutions such as the World Bank and International Monetary Fund continued to gain and the influence that these mustered over policy agendas during the last three decades. Reform in the context of the globalization requires an enhanced role and an expanded scope for the institutions of global governance. Revitalizing these does not mean a diminution of the clout that is wielded by Bretton Woods, it represents the restoration of vital initiatives and the revitalization of agencies that can have a crucial role in strengthening the mechanisms of global development.

## Appendix

Other countries in South Asia, such as Bangladesh, Bhutan, Sri Lanka, Maldives and Pakistan, have had average growth rates of about 5 per cent over the last five years. There have been some gains in poverty reduction; however, on aggregate, much more needs to be done in terms of increasing public investment and human capital formation if a greater magnitude of development is to occur. When compared to human development indicators that prevailed in East Asia about a decade ago, South Asia lags behind in terms of the investment – GDP ratios, poverty reduction, infrastructure provision and technology intensity of manufacturing employment creation. The take-off to development in this region has begun; however, the process is not a stable or consistent one. The reason for this varies from nation to nation; for instance, Sri Lanka and Nepal find themselves embroiled in civil conflicts that have inflicted a heavy toll on their treasuries and impeded a faster pace of progress. This apart, rampant corruption, high fiscal deficits and governance systems that should function with a much higher degree of efficiency are some of the manifestations of a low quotient of EEM, which is holding back a faster pace of development.

# Bibliography

## 1 The New Age Paradox

Bell, Stephanie and Wray, Randall (2004) *The War on Poverty after 40 years: A Minskyan Assessment*, Working Paper 404, Levy Economics Institute, Bard College.

Cornia, Giovanni André, Jolly, Richard and Stewart, Frances (eds) (1987) *Adjustment with a Human Face, Volume 1*, UNICEF, Clarendon Press, Oxford.

Emerrij, Louis, Jolly, Richard and Thomas Weiss S. (2001) *Ahead of the Curve: United Nations Ideas and Global Challenges*, United Nations Intellectual History Project,[1] Volume 1.

Purushothaman, Roopa and Wilson, Dominic (2003) *Dreaming with the BRICS*, Goldman Sachs, 1 October.

United Nations (1949) *World Economic Report*.

United Nations (1951) *Measures for the Economic Development of the Underdeveloped Countries*, Report submitted by an Expert Panel.

UNDP (2003) *Human Development Report*, New York, UNDP.

UNDP (2004) 'Cultural Liberty in Today's Diverse World', *Human Development Report 2004*, New York, UNDP.

UNCTAD (1999) 'Trade, External Financing and Economic Growth in Developing Countries', *Trade and Development Report*.

UNCTAD Secretariat (2004) *The Least Developed Countries Report Linking International Trade with Poverty Reduction*, New York and Geneva.

UN Secretary General (2005) Report, *Investing in Development: A Practical Plan to achieve the Millennium Development Goals*.

World Bank (2004) 'Policies and Actions for achieving the Millennium Development Goals and Related Outcomes', *Global Monitoring Report*, Washington, DC.

## Part I The Rising Superpowers: Issues, Implications and the Future

Boston Consulting Group (2006) *The New Global Challengers, How 100 Top Companies From Rapidly Developing Economies are Changing the World*, May.

## 3 India: Her Tryst With Globalization

Asian Development Bank (2004) *Asian Development Outlook*, Manila, Philippines.

Asian Development Bank (2005) India Economic Bulletin, January, Manila, Philippines.

AT Kearney (2005) News release, 7 December, Washington, DC.

---

1 In 1999 the United Nations commenced the intellectual history project with the objective of educating the public and encouraging global scholarly discourse about the UN. *Ahead of the Curve* is the first in the series of seven books that were planned under the auspices of the United Nations Intellectual history project.

Fischer, Stanley (2002) *Breaking out of the Third World: India's Economic Imperative*, International Monetary Fund, Washington, DC.

Government of India (2002) *Report of the Steering Group on Foreign Direct Investment*, Planning Commission, New Delhi, August.

Kelkar, Vijay (2004) 'India on the Growth Turnpike', Australian National University.

Kohli, Atul (2006) 'Politics of Economic Growth in India: Part 1 The Eighties', *Economic and Political Weekly*, Mumbai.

Kohli, Atul (2006) 'Politics of Economic Growth in India: 1980–2005 Part 2 The Nineties and Beyond', *Economic and Political Weekly*, 8 April, Mumbai.

Nayyar, Deepak (2006) 'Economic Growth in Independent India', *Economic and Political Weekly*, 15 April, Mumbai.

Mohan, Rakesh (Deputy Governor of the Reserve Bank of India) (2005) 'The Indian Economy in the Global Setting', Address at the Indian Merchants' Chamber, 17 October Mumbai.

Rodrik, Dani and Subramanian, Arvind (2004) *From Hindu Growth to Productivity Surge: The Mystery of the Indian Growth Transition*, International Monetary Fund, Washington, DC, May.

UNCTAD (2004) 'The Shift Towards Services', *World Investment Report*, New York and Geneva.

## 4   Economic Reform: Moving Beyond Liberalization

Devarajan, Shatayanam and Wabi, Ijaz (2006) 'Economic Growth in South Asia', *Economic and Political Weekly*, Mumbai, 19 August.

Government of India (2004), National Common Minimum Programme, New Delhi, May.

Government of India (2004–05) *Poverty Studies and Estimates*, National Sample Survey Organization (NSSO).[2]

Government of India (2005) 'Millennium Development Goals', *India Country Report*, Ministry of Statistics and Programme Implementation, New Delhi.

Government of India (2006) 'Approach Paper of the Eleventh Five-Year Plan of India'.

Government of India (2006–07) *Economic Survey of India*, New Delhi.

Government of India (2006) *Interim Report of the Oversight Committee on the Implementation of the New Reservation Policy in Higher Educational Institutions*.

International Labour Organization (ILO) (2000) *Privatisation in South Asia*, South Asia Multidisciplinary Advisory Team, Geneva.

Kessides, Ioannis N. (2004) 'Privatisation, Regulation and Competition', *World Bank Policy Research Report*, Washington, DC, World Bank and Oxford University Press.

Khosla, Vinod and Wadhwani, Romesh (2005) 'Accelerating Investment in India', *Economic Times*, 1 September.

Shashank, Luthra, Ramesh, Mangaleswaran and Asutosh Padhi, (2005) *When to Make India a Manufacturing Base*, McKinsey Global Institute.

Mutatkar, Rohit (2005) *Social Group Disparities and Poverty In India*, Working Paper WP-2005-004, Indira Gandhi Institute of Development, Mumbai.

Nagaraj, R. (June 24, 2006) 'Public Sector Performance since 1950: A Fresh Look', *Economic and Political Weekly*, Mumbai.

---

2  The National Sample Survey Organisation is the primary data collection wing of the Ministry of Statistics and Programme Implementation.

Nasscom (2006) 'The Information Technology Industry in India', *Strategic Review*.

Nilekani[3] Nandan (2004) 'The Measurement Problem', *Economic Times*, 1 November.

National Association of Software and Service Companies (Nasscom) and the Mckinsey Study (2005) *An Executive Summary*, December.

Panagriya, Arvind (2004) 'India in the Eighties and Nineties, A Triumph of Reforms', January.

Patodia, D.N. (2006) 'Catch an Elephant by its Ears', *Hindustan Times*, 1 February.

Srinivisan, T.N. (2003) *India's Economic Reforms: A Stock-Taking*, Working Paper 190, Stanford Center for International Development, Stanford University, Stanford, October.

Virmani, Arvind (2005) *Policy Regimes, Growth and Poverty in India: Lessons of Government Failure and Entrepreneurial Success*, Working Paper 170, Indian Council for Research on International Economic Relations (ICRIER), India, New Delhi.

# 5   India: Unleashing Opportunity Creation

Banga, Rashmi (2005) *Role of Services in the Growth Process, A Survey*, ICRIER, New Delhi.

Banga, Rashmi (2005) 'Foreign Direct Investment in Services, Implications for Developing Countries', *Asia Pacific Trade Investment Review*, vol. 1, no. 2.

Government of India (2005–2006) *Economic Survey of India*, New Delhi.

Government of India (2006–07) Mid-term Appraisal of the Tenth Five-Year Plan, New Delhi.

Hansda, Sanjay K. (2002) *Sustainability of Services Led Growth, An Input-Output Analysis of the Indian Economy*.

Kapur, Devesh and Ramamurthi, Ravi (2001) *India's Emerging Competitiveness in Tradable Services*, Academy of Management in India, May.

Kijima, Yoko and Lanjouw, Peter (2003) *Poverty in India during the Nineties*, Development Research Group World Bank Team, Washington, DC.

O'Connor, David (2003) *Of Flying Geeks and O Rings*, Organization for Economic Co-operation and Development (OECD), Paris, December.

Poddar, Tushar and Yi, Eva (2007) *India's Rising Growth Potential*, Global Economics Paper 152, Goldman Sachs.

Rodrik, D. and Subramanian (2004) *Why India Can Grow at 7 per cent a year or more – Projections and Reflections*, Working Paper WP/04/18, International Monetary Fund, Washington, DC.

Tendulkar, Suresh D. and Sundaram, K. (2002) *Issues in Employment and Poverty*, Discussion paper.

# 6   A Multisectoral Pattern of Economic Growth: Important Issues

Das, Deb Kusum (2003) *Manufacturing Productivity Under Varying Trade Regimes: India in the 80's and the 90's*, ICRIER, New Delhi, July.

Goldar, Biswanath (2004) Indian Manufacturing: 'Productivity Trends in Pre- and Post-Reform Periods', *Economic and Political Weekly*, Mumbai, 20 November.

Government of India, (2002–2003) *Annual Survey of Industries*, New Delhi.

Government of India (2003–2004) *Annual Survey of Industries*, New Delhi.

---

3  Nandan Nilekani is the CEO of Infosys one of India's leading corporate houses and among the most important companies in the ambit of Information Technology.

Government of India (2005–2006) *Economic Survey of India*, New Delhi.

Surender, Kumar (2004) *A Decomposition of Total Factor Productivity Growth: A Regional Analysis of Indian Industrial Manufacturing Growth*, National Institute of Public Finance as Policy, New Delhi.

Reddy, Dr Y.V., Governor Reserve Bank of India (2005) Inaugural Address at the Annual Conference of the Indian Economic Association, 27 December.

Singh, Nirvikar (2006) *Services-led Industrialisation in India, Prospects and Challenges*, Stanford Center for International Development, Stanford, August.

Unel, Bulent (2003) *Productivity Trends in Indian Manufacturing in the Last Two Decades*, IMF Working Paper WP/03/22, Washington, DC.

Yi, Eva and Poddar, Tushar (2007) *India's Rising Growth Potential*, Goldman Sachs Report, Global Economics Paper 152, 22 January.

# 7   India's Economic Ascent: Insights and Issues

Chelliah, Raja J. (1996) *Towards Sustainable Growth: Essays in Fiscal and Financial Sector Reforms in India*, Oxford University Press.

Dreze, Jean and Sen, Amartya (eds) (1996) *Selected Regional Perspectives*, Oxford University Press, New Delhi.

Jalan, Bimal (ed.) (1992) *The Indian Economy: Problems and Prospects*, Penguin Books.

Palkivala, N.A. (1987) *We the People*, Strand Book Stall, Mumbai.

Panchamuki, V.R. (2001) 'Lessons from the National Experience of India in Mobilizing Domestic and External Resources for Economic Development', *Asia Pacific Development Journal*, June.

Tharoor, Shashi (1997) *India From Midnight to Millennium*, Viking (Penguin Books).

# 9   China: Its Ascent as an Economic Powerhouse

Burstein, Daniel and De Keijzer, Arne (1998) *Big Dragon: China's Future*, Simon Schuster, New York.

Chow, Gregory (2005) *Globalisation and China's Economic and Financial Development*, Princeton University, September.

Government of China (1984) 'Document 1, Circular of the Central Committee of the Chinese Communist Party on Rural Work', 1 January.

Government of China (2005) 'Report on the Work of the Government', delivered by Premier Wen Jiabao, at the Third Session of the Tenth National People's Congress, 5 March.

Government of China (2006) 'Report on the Implementation of the 2005 Plan for National Economic and Social Development and on the 2006 Draft Plan for National Economic and Social Development', at the Fourth Session of the Tenth National People's Congress, 5 March.

Kemenade, Willem Van (1998) *China, Hong Kong and Taiwan Inc.*, Vintage Books, New York.

Murray, Bruce (2004) 'China's Economic Performance and its impact on Asia', Presentation, Asian Development Bank, June.

Quian, Ying Yi (1999) 'The Process of China's Market Transition (1978–99), The Evolutionary, Historical and Comparitive Perspective', Stanford University, Stanford, April.

Sachs, Jeffrey D. and Woo, Wing Thye (1997) *Understanding China's Economic Performance*, Development Discussion Working Paper 575, Harvard Institute for International Development, Harvard University, March.

Shankar, Oded (2005) *The Chinese Century*, Wharton School Publishing,

Shane, Mathew and Gale, Fred (2004) *China: A Study of Dynamic Growth*, United States Department of Agriculture, WRS-04-08, October.
Woo, Wing Thye (1999) The reasons for China's Growth, January.

# 10   State-owned Enterprise Restructuring in China: Issues and Challenges

Diehl, Markus and Schwickert, Rainer (2005) *Monetary Management of Transition in China, Balancing Short-Run Risks and Long-Run Optimality*, Kiel Germany Institute for World Economics, June.
Farell, Diane, Lund, Susan and Morin, Fabrica (2006) 'How Financial System Reform Could Benefit China', *McKinsey Quarterly*, McKinsey Global Institute.
Guo, Sujian (2003) The Ownership Reform in China: What Direction and How Far, *Journal of Contemporary China*.
Hongbin, Qu (2005) 'Reducing the Savings Glut', *China Economic Insight*, Hong Kong Hong Shanghai Banking Corporation Global Research, June.
Jefferson, Gary H., Jian, Su, Yuan, Jiang and Yu, Xinhua, (2003) 'The Impact of Share-holding Reform and Chinese Enterprise 1995–2001', William Davidson University, University of Michigan Business School, June.
Leung, Erika, Liu, Lily, Shen, Liu, Taback, Kevin, Wang, Leo and Myers, C. Stewart (Advisor) (June 2002) *Financial Reform and Corporate Governance in China*, MIIT Sloan School of Management, Fiftieth Anniversary Proceedings.
Ma, Guonan (2006) *Who Pays China's Bank Restructuring Bill?* CEPII, Working Paper 2006-04, February.
Pei, Minxin (2006) *The Dark Side of China's Rise*, Carnegie Endowment for International Peace Report, March.
Ping, Luo (2003) 'Challenges For China's Banking Sector and Policy Responses', China Banking Regulatory Commission, Speech delivered by Luo Ping at a Seminar in New Delhi, 14 November.
Pingyao, Lai (2003) *China's Economic Growth, New Trends and Implications*, Chinese Academy of Social Sciences, November.
Podpiera, Richard (2006) *Progress in China's Banking Sector Reform. Has Bank Behaviour Changed the International Monetary Fund*, Washington, DC, March.
Shirai, Sayuri (2002) Banking Sector Reforms in the People's Republic of China, Progress and Constraints, Tokyo Asian Development Bank Institute.
Takeshi, Jingu (2002) *Moving Forward in Reforming China's Capital Market*, Nomura Research Institute, Japan.
Xu, Lixin Colin, Zhu, Tian and Lin, Yi Min (2002) *Politician Control, Agency Problems and Ownership Reform: Evidence From China*, World Bank Development Research Group and Hong Kong University, June.
Yasheng, Huang, Sarch, Tony and Stenfeld, Edward (eds) (2005) *Financial Sector Reform in China*, Asia Public Policy Series, Harvard University Asia Center.
Yusuf, Shahid and Kaoru, Nabeshima (2006) *Two Decades of Reform: The Changing Organisation and Dynamics of Chinese Industrial Firms*, Development Economics Research Group, World Bank, Washington, DC, January.

# 11   Economic Reform in China: The Ensuing Phase

Asian Development Bank (2001) *Preparing a Methodology for Development Planning in Poverty Alleviation Under the Poverty Strategy of the People's Republic of China*, Manila, November.

Bremner, Brian, Dexter, Robert and Balfour, Frederick (2004) 'Headed For a Crisis', *Business Week*, 3 May.

Hongbin, Qu (2006) 'Exports the Solution to Rural Problem', *China Economic Insight*, Hong Shanghai Banking Corporation Global Research, Hong Kong, April.

Islam, Nazrul and Dai, Erbiao (2004) *Alternative Estimates of TFP Growth in Mainland China: An Investigation Using the Dual Approach*, International Center for the Study of East Asian Development.

Li, Bingquin and Piachaud, David (2004) *Poverty and Inequality and Social Policy in China*, Centre for Analysis of Social Exclusion, Lava School of Economics.

Liang, Hong and Yi, Eva (2005) *China's Ascent: Can The Middle Kingdom Meet Its Dreams*, Goldman Sachs, Global Economics Paper 133, November.

People's Bank of China (2004) *Report on the Implementation of Monetary Policy*, 2004Q1.

Qian, Yingyi (1999) 'The Process of China's Market Transition (1978–98): The Evolutionary, Historical and Comparative Perspective', Stanford University.

Statistical Yearbook of China (2001) Central Bank of China.

UNDP (2005) *China Human Development Report*, New York, UNDP.

Wang, Xialu (1999) *Sustainability of China's Economic Growth: China Update*, National Center for Development Studies.

Woo, Wing Thye (2004) 'The Structural Obstacles to Macroeconomic Control in China', Economic Department University of California.

World Bank (2003) *Report on China's Economic Performance*, April.

Yifu Lin, Justin (2004) 'Is China's Growth Real and Sustainable?', China Center for Economic Research, Peking University, February.

Yifu Lin, Justin and Liu, MingXing (2004) 'Development Strategy, Transition and Challenges of Development in Lagging Regions', China Center for Economic Research, Peking University, February.

Zhang, Amei (1993) *Poverty Alleviation in China: Commitment, Policies and Expenditures*, New York, UNDP.

Zhang, Xiabo and Fan, Shenggen (2000) 'Public Investment and Regional Inequality in Rural China', International and Food Policy Research Institute, Environment and Production Technology Division, December.

## 12  Human Capital Formation: Trends, Implications and Future Prospects in China

Blumenthal, David and Hsiao, William (2005) 'Privatization and its Discontents: The Evolving Chinese Healthcare System', *New England Journal of Medicine*, September.

*China Daily* (2005) 'Health Minister of China Gao Qiang cites Poor state of Health System', 8 August.

Government of China (1985) 'Communist Party Central Committee Decision on Reform of Science and Technology Management System' [the objective of this was to reform operational and organizational structures, and the personnel system in the scientific and technological sector].

Government of China (1991) 'State Council Document No. 4 issued by the Standing Committee of the National People's Congress on the Strict Prohibition Against Prostitution', 4 September.

Kuijs, Louis and Wang, Tao (2005) *China's Pattern of Growth: Moving to Sustainability and Reducing Equity*, Research Paper 2, World Bank China Office, October.

US Embassy, Beijing, China (2002) *A Special Report for the Environment, Science and Technology Section*, 'An Evaluation of China's Science and Technology System and its Impact on the Research Community'.

Wang, Dr Jian, Wen, Dr Hai and Yonghua, Dr Hu (n.d.) 'China Healthcare and Health Insurance Reform', China Center for Economic Research.

Wang, Yan and Yao, Yudong (2001) *Sources of China's Economic Growth 1952–99: Incorporation of Human Capital Accumulation*, World Bank, Economic and Poverty Reduction Institute, Washington, DC, July.

World Bank (2003) *Country Economic Memorandum*, 'Promoting Economic Growth with Inequity', Washington, DC.

## 13   China's Foreign Direct Investment Story: An Evaluation

Bhalla, A.S. and Qiu, S. (2002) *China's Accession to the WTO: Its Impact on Chinese Employment*, New York and Geneva UNCTAD, November.

Government of China (1996) *Outline of the Report of the Ninth Five-Year Plan (1996–2000)*.

Graham, Edward M. and Wada, Erika (2001) *Achieving High Growth Experience of Transitional Economies in East Asia*,

Hayes, Keith, Warburton, Max, Lapidus, Gary, Shiohara, Kunihiko, McKenna, Shane and Chang, Young (2003) *The Chinese Auto Industry*, Goldman Sachs, Global Equity Research, 21 February.

Morrison, Wayne (2001) *China–US Trade Issues*, CRS Issue Brief for Congress, Foreign Affairs and Defense Division, Government of United States of America.

Morrison, Wayne (2005) *China–US Trade Issues*, CRS Issue Brief for Congress, Foreign Affairs and Defense Division, Government of United States of America.

Lardy, Nicholas (2003) *Trade Liberalization and Its Role in Chinese Economic Growth*, Institute For International Economics, Washington, DC, November.

Li, Yuefen (2001) 'China's Accession to World Trading Organization (WTO)', United Nations Conference on Trade and Development, November.

Nolan, Peter and Jin, Zhang (2002), *The Challenge of Globalisation For large Chinese Firms*, UNCTAD Discussion paper, Geneva, July.

Rodrik, Dani (2006) 'What's So Special about China's Exports', Harvard University, January.

*Shenzen Daily* (2006) 'A news report about the restrictions on high technology exports to China', 29 June.

Thorpe, Michael (2002) *Inward Foreign Investment and the Chinese Economy*, Paper Presented at the New Zealand Annual Economists Conference, June.

Tseng, Wanda and Zebregs, Harm (2002) *Foreign Direct Investment in China: Some Lessons For Other Countries*, International Monetary Fund, Washington, DC.

United States Economic and Security Review Commission (2005) *Report to Congress* (109th Congress), Washington, DC, November.

Unites States Trade Representative (2004) *Report to Congress in China's WTO Compliance*, 11 December.

Xiaohui, Liu and Chang, Shu (2001) *Determinants of Export Performance, Evidence From Chinese Industries*, September.

## 14   China's Economic Experience: Insights, Lessons and a Perspective

Fukasaku, Kiichiro and Lecomte, Henri (1996), *Economic Transition and Trade Policy Reform: Lessons From China.*

Li, Minqui (2003) *The Rise of China and the Demise of the Capitalist World Economy. Exploring the Historical Possibilities in the 21st Century*, November.

Organisation for Economic Co-operation and Development (2002) 'China in the World Economy', *Synthesis Report*, Paris.

Virmani, Arvind (2005) *China's Socialist Market Economy: Lessons of Success*, Indian Council For Research on International Economic Relations, New Delhi, December.

Hongkong Shanghai Bank (2006) Global Research, *China Economic Insight*, April, The quote by the Governor of the People's Bank of China is an excerpt from a summary of his speech about China's trade balance and exchange rate on 20 March 2006.

## 15  When Elephants Walk and Dragons Dance: A Comparison between the Indian and Chinese Economies

Bagchi, Amiya (2006) 'China and India: From Where to Whereto – a Preliminary Investigation' (Paper presented to International Development Economic Associates and UNDP conference on Post Liberalisation Constraints on Macroeconomic Policies), January.

Boston Consulting Group (2006) *The New Global Challengers: How 100 Top Companies from Rapidly Developing Economies are Changing the World*, May.

Chaudhuri, Shubham and Ravallion (2006) *Partially Awakened Giants: Uneven Growth in China and India*, World Bank Policy Research Working Paper, Washington, DC, November.

Desai, Meghnad (2003) *India and China in the Comparitive Political Economy.*

Khanna, Tarun and Huang, Yasheng (2003) 'Can India Overtake China?' *Foreign Policy Journal*, December.

Lane, Philip and Sergio, L. Schmukler (2006), *International Financial Integration: China and India*, May.

National Intelligence Council[4] (2004) 'Mapping the Global Future 2020 Project', *Council Report.*

Srinivasan, T.N. (2003) 'China and India, Growth and Poverty 1980–2000', Stanford Center For International Development, Stanford University, September.

Tilman, Altenburg, Schmitz H. and Stamm, Andreas (2006) *Building Knowledge Based Competitive Advantages in China and India: Lessons and Consequences for Other Developing Countries.*

UNCTAD (2005) *Trade and Development Report*, New York and Geneva.

Xie, Andy and Ahya, Chetan (2004) *India and China: A Special Economic Analysis*, Morgan Stanley, July.

## Part II  Globalization: A Process of Incomplete Economic Integration

## 16  Globalization: Vision and Reality

Berg, Andrew and Kreuger, Anne (2003) *Trade, Growth and Poverty: A Selective Survey*, International Monetary Fund, Washington, DC.

---

4 The National Intelligence Council is a center of strategic thinking with the US government and reports to the director of National Intelligence. Furthermore, the Council provides the President and senior policy makers with analyses of foreign policy issues.

Bosworth, Barry P. and Collins, Susan M. (1999) 'Capital Flows to Developing Economies Implications for Saving and Investment', Brooking Papers of Economic Activity.

Center for Global Development when? Rich World, Poor World: A Guide to Global Development, Global Trade, the US and Developing Countries, Washington, DC.

Cline, William (2003) 'Trading Up, Trade Policy and Global Poverty' (Brief), Center For Global Development, Washington, DC, September.

Global Economic Prospects (2005) *Trade, Regionalism and Development*, World Bank, Washington, DC.

Dollar, David and Kraay, Aaart (2000) *Growth is Good for the Poor*, Development Research Group, World Bank, Washington, DC, March.

Douglas, A. Irwin and Marko, Tervico (2000) *Does Trade Raise Income, Evidence* from the 20th Century, National Bureau of Economic Research (NBER), Working Paper 7745, June.

Fischer, Stanley (2002) 'Liberalization of Global Financial Services', Address at the Conference on Further Liberalization of Global Financial Services, Institute for International Economics, Washington, DC.

Khan, A. Haider, (2003) 'Globalization and its Challenges', University of Denver, November/December.

Rodrik, Dani (2001), 'The Governance of Trade as if Development Really Mattered', Harvard University, April.

Rousseau, Peter L. (2002) *Historical perspectives on Financial Development and Economic Growth.*

Sachs, Jeffrey and Warner, Andrew (1995) 'Economic Reform and the Process of Global Integration', Brooking Papers on Economic Activity.

Stiglitz, Joseph (2002) *Globalization and Its Discontents*, Penguin Books (London) and W.W Norton and Company (USA).

Stiglitz, Joseph E. and Charlton, Andrew (2004) *A Development Round Of Trade Negotiations.*

UNCTAD (2004) *The Least Developed Countries Report Linking International Trade With Poverty Reduction*, New York and Geneva.

UNDP (2003) 'Millennium Development Goals: A Compact among Nations to End Poverty', *Human Development Report*, New York, UNDP.

Wolf, Martin (2005) 'Will Globalization Survive', Institute of International Economics, Third Whitman Lecture, April.

World Bank (2001) 'Building Coalitions For Effective Development Finance', *Global Development Finance Report*, Washington, DC.

World Bank (2002) *Policy Research Report*, 'Globalization, Growth and Poverty', Washington, DC, January.

World Bank (2004) 'Policies and Actions for Achieving the Millenium Development Goals and Related Outcomes', *Global Monitoring Report*, Washington, DC.

World Bank (2005) 'Trade, Regionalism and Development', *Global Economic Prospects Report*, Washington, DC.

World Trade Organisation (2004) 'Agreement on Agriculture', *Doha Ministerial Declaration.*

## 17   Revisiting the East Asian Miracle

Birdsall, Nancy (2005) *Reflections on Our Common Interest*, Testimony for the Senate Committee, President, Center for Global Development, Washington, DC, 17 May.

Booth, Anne (1998) 'Initial Conditions and Miraculous Growth: Why is South-East Asia different from Taiwan and Korea', School of Oriental and African Studies, University of London.

Crafts, Nicholas (1999) *East Asian Growth before and after the Crisis*, International Monetary Fund Staff Papers, vol. 46, no. 2, Washington, DC.

Department of Foreign Affairs and Trade (Australia) (1995), *Growth Triangles of South-East Asia*.

Goh, Keng Swee (1995) *The Economics of Modernization*, Federal Government (Singapore).

Hammouda, Hakim Ben (2004) 'Trade Liberalisation and Development, Lessons for Africa', Economic Commission of Africa.

Jomo, K.S., *Growth After the Asian Crisis: What remains of the East Asian Model?*, G-24 Discussion Paper series.

Quibria, M.G. (2002) *Lessons from the East Asian Miracle Revisited*, ADB Institute Research Paper 33, Tokyo, Japan, February.

Shantayanan, Devarajan, Easterly, William R. and Low, Howard Pack (2002) 'Investment is not the Constraint on African Development', Center for Global Development, October.

Stiglitz, Joseph and Shahid, Yusuf (eds) (2001) *Rethinking the East Asian Miracle*, World Bank, Washington, DC.

UNCTAD (2001) *Economic Development in Africa, Performance, Prospects, Policy Issues*, New York and Geneva.

UNCTAD (2003) 'Capital Accumulation Growth and Structural Change', *Trade and Development Report*, New York and Geneva.

UNCTAD (2005) *Economic Development in Africa: Rethinking the Role of FDI*, September.

United Nations Economic Commission on Africa (2004) 'Unlocking Africa's Trade', *Economic Report on African Potential*.

United Nations Economic Commission on Africa (2007) 'Accelerating Africa's Development through Diversification', *Economic Report on Africa*, Addis Ababa, Ethopia.

Weiss, John (2005) *Export Growth and Industrial Policy: Lessons from the East Asian Miracle*, Asian Development Bank Institute Discussion Paper, Tokyo, Japan, February.

World Bank (1993) 'The East Asian Miracle: Economic Growth and Public Policy', *World Bank Policy Research Reports*, Washington, DC.

World Bank (2005) 'A Better Investment Climate for Everyone', *World Development Report*, International Bank for Reconstruction and Development and World Bank, Washington, DC.

# 18   The Stilettoization of Economic Progress

Birdsall, Nancy (2005) *The World is Not Flat in Our Global Economy: Inequality and Justice*, United Nations World Institute of Development Research.

International Labor Organization (2007) 'Global Employment Trends', (Brief), Geneva, January.

Kirkpatrick, Colin and Barrientos, Armando (2004) *The Lewis Model After 50 Years*, Manchester School, vol. 72, no. 6.

UNCTAD (2002) 'Escaping the Poverty Trap', *Least Developed Countries Report*, New York and Geneva.

UNCTAD (2006) 'Developing Productive Capacities', *Least Developed Countries Report*.

UNDP (2004) 'Cultural Liberty in Today's Diverse World', *Human Development Report*, New York.

UNDP (2005) 'International Co-operation At the Crossroads, Aid Trade and Security In An Unequal World', *Human Development Report*, New York.

UNDP (2005) 'Investing in Development: A Practical Plan to Achieve the Millennium Development Goals', *Report to the United Nations Secretary General*, United Nations Millennium Project, New York.

United Nations Children's Fund (UNICEF) (2004) *The State of the World's Children*, New York.

World Bank (2006) 'Equity and Development', *World Development Report*, Washington, DC.

## Part III Bridging the Gap between Growth and Development: Evolving A Paradigm

Anderson, James E. (1999) 'Why do Nations Trade (So Little)?', 15 August.

Brett, Dr F.A. (2000) *Development Theory: Universal Values and Competing Paradigms*, London School of Economics and Politics.

Easterly, William R. (2004) *Globalisation, Inequality and Development*, December.

*Economist, The* (2006) 'The Man Who Remade Japan', 16 September.

*Economist, The* (2006) 'Assertive Abe', 30 September.

Edison, Hali (2003) *Testing the Link between Institutional Quality and Economic Performance*, International Monetary Fund, Washington, DC.

International Labor Organization (2004) *A Fair Globalisation: Creating Opportunities For All*, World Commission on the Social Dimension of Globalisation, Geneva.

Heshmati, Almas (2005), *The Relationship Between Income Inequality*, Poverty and Globalisation, World Institute For Developing Economics Research, United Nations, June.

Mardick, Jeff (2002) *Why Economies Grow, The Forces That Shape Prosperity and How to Get Them Working Again*, USA Century Foundation Books.

McKinley, Terry (2003) *The Macroeconomics of Poverty Reduction: Initial Findings of the United Nations Development Programme*, Asia Pacific Regional Program (Bureau for Development Policy), August.

North, Douglas C. (1933) Nobel Prize Lecture, 9 December.

North, Douglas, (1996) *Institutions, Institutional Change and Economic Performance*, England, Cambridge University Press.

Palma, Jose G. (2006) *Growth After Globalisation: A Structuralist–Kaldorian Game of Musical Chairs*, Faculty Of Economics, University of Cambridge, April.

Rajan, Raghuram and Zingales, Luigi (2003) *Saving Capitalists From the Capitalists*, New York, Crown Business.

Ravallion, Martin (2004) *Pro-Poor Growth: A Primer*, Development Research Group, World Bank, Washington, DC.

UNCTAD (2002) 'Transnational Corporations and Export Competitiveness', *World Investment Report*, New York and Geneva.

UNCTAD (2003) '*Capital Accumulation, Growth and Structural Change*', Trade and Development Report, New York and Geneva.

UNDP (2005) World Resources Report, New York.

United Nations (2006) 'Diverging Growth and Development', World Economic and Social Survey.

US Department of Commerce (2004) *Manufacturing in America: A Comprehensive Strategy to Address the Challenges to US Manufacturers*, Washington, DC, January.

Vandemoortele, Jan (2002) 'Are We Really Reducing Global Poverty?', United Nations Development Progamme, New York.

Verdier, Thiery (2004), *Socially Responsible Trade Integration: A Political Economy Perspective*, April.

Wade, Robert (2000) *Governing the Market: A Decade Later*, London School of Economics and Politics, March.

World Bank (2005) 'A Better Investment Climate for Everyone', *World Development Report*, International Bank for Reconstruction and Development and World Bank, Washington, DC.

# Index